THE PRESTIGE SQUEEZE

The Prestige Squeeze

Occupational Prestige in Canada since 1965

JOHN GOYDER

McGill-Queen's University Press
Montreal & Kingston • London • Ithaca

© McGill-Queen's University Press 2009

ISBN 978-0-7735-3582-4 (cloth)
ISBN 978-0-7735-3611-1 (paper)

Legal deposit fourth quarter 2009
Bibliothèque nationale du Québec

Printed in Canada on acid-free paper that is 100% ancient forest free (100% post-consumer recycled), processed chlorine free

This book has been published with the help of a grant from the Canadian Federation for the Humanities and Social Sciences, through the Aid to Scholarly Publications Programme, using funds provided by the Social Sciences and Humanities Research Council of Canada.

McGill-Queen's University Press acknowledges the support of the Canada Council for the Arts for our publishing program. We also acknowledge the financial support of the Government of Canada through the Book Publishing Industry Development Program (BPIDP) for our publishing activities.

Library and Archives Canada Cataloguing in Publication

Goyder, John, 1946–
   The prestige squeeze : occupational prestige in Canada since 1965 / John Goyder.

Includes bibliographical references and index.
ISBN 978-0-7735-3582-4 (bnd)
ISBN 978-0-7735-3611-1 (pbk)

   1. Occupational prestige – Canada. 2. Occupations – Social aspects – Canada. I. Title.

HT675.G69 2009   305.9'00971   C2009-902731-3

Typeset by Jay Tee Graphics Ltd. in 10.5/13 Sabon

Contents

Tables

Figures

Preface

The fifteenth World Congress of Sociology, the meetings of the International Sociological Association, was held in July 2002 in Brisbane, Australia. One of the sessions by RC-28, the Research Committee on Social Stratification and Mobility, concerned the agenda for future research in inequality. The chair of the session began by listing on the blackboard the knowledge that the committee regarded as certain. Near the top was the "Treiman constant." For those who have encountered research on occupations and their relation to social inequality, this cryptic reference is full of meaning. There will be others, however, who have picked up this book because they are interested in some or another aspect of work and occupations but do not have a social stratification background. They might find it uninformative if I simply say that this is a book about the Treiman constant.

With terms such as "occupational prestige" and "Treiman constant" social scientists are referring to how occupations are evaluated by members of the public. In such research, we work not with a few hand-picked informants, useful though that might be for a study of just one occupation, but mainly with a larger cross-section, ideally a random sample of people representing all backgrounds. Some of the respondents will know a great deal about at least some occupations, and others will not. The people responding to the surveys described in the pages to follow were asked to rate occupations by their "social standing," a term often used in this research colloquially for "prestige." Whether termed social standing or prestige, the distinctions being sought are quite subtle, and yet people in surveys seem to understand what the researcher is getting at and readily offer their ratings. As later chapters describe, the prestige of an occupation does not derive just from the income earned or from the education required. High-prestige occupations command respect and even deference. A person in a high-prestige occupation is usually doing something that people feel is important, whether it is saving lives, helping the economy grow, or holding powers in trust.

The Treiman constant refers to research published over thirty years ago, in which the American sociologist Donald Treiman showed that people in different countries and living in different times rate occupations essentially in the same order. When I heard the reference to the Treiman constant at the Brisbane conference, I already had city-level data on occupational prestige from samples collected in 1975 and 2000 showing considerable change along several dimensions. The average score had moved upward, driven by rising prestige for many of the formerly low-status occupations. As a result, the hierarchy was much more squeezed than it used to be. The agreement, or correlation, between scales in my two samples from Kitchener-Waterloo was well below the norm for other across-time comparisons. It was apparent sitting in on this world stage for research on social stratification that local data from Canada, a country not very prominent on the RC-28 screen under even the best of circumstances, would be given little credence. I resolved to apply for Social Sciences and Humanities Research Council of Canada (SSHRC) money for a national-level re-study of occupational prestige in Canada, timed to take place in 2005, the fortieth anniversary of the first large study of occupational prestige in Canada, the Pineo-Porter study of 1965.

The 1965 survey was a seminal event in sociological research in Canada. Peter Pineo wrote in a 1981 *Canadian Review of Sociology and Anthropology (CRSA)* retrospective on John Porter's work that his colleague chose prestige for this first project following publication of *The Vertical Mosaic* because it was "unadventuresome" and would therefore help legitimate survey research in Canada. The proposal to compare occupational prestige in Canada and the United States was considered safe precisely because it was so likely from other research that the scales for the two neighbouring countries would be correlated in the high nineties. And they were, as revealed in a citation-classic 1967 CRSA article by Pineo and Porter, reporting main findings of the Canadian work.

The following pages report mainly on the changing patterns of occupational prestige in Canada between this foundational 1965 study and 2005. The comparison is supplemented by secondary analysis of some of the well-known data sets from the United States and from the 1975 and year 2000 samples collected in Kitchener-Waterloo, Ontario. The picture I present is of a prestige order that has shuffled itself profoundly over forty years. I chose the term "prestige squeeze" to denote this ensemble of changes. Part of the squeeze is seen in the compacted or truncated shape of today's prestige ratings, which held up in the 2005 national survey just as they had appeared in the local research from 2000. I saw a kind of squeeze also in the level of agreement between individuals as they made their ratings. In 1965, some identifiable clusters of people, the highly educated particularly, agreed relatively closely about the ratings, in contrast to other pockets of people showing little agreement. Today those groups have squeezed together, and all the usual sociological suspects in terms of demographic groups disagree among themselves when rating prestige, to about the same extent. There is squeeze in a third sense, but this is much more speculative than proven. The explanation I suggest toward the end of the book is that people in a country like Canada today are squeezed by the expectations of the culture they live in. On the one hand, people are told they live in a meritocratic society in which men and women achieve more or less than others according to how good a brain they are born with and how much use they make of that brain. On the other, we live in a me-centred culture in which all people are supposed to feel good about themselves. A hierarchy of occupational prestige in which the top positions are thought to be reached not by luck or inheritance but personal merit threatens the self-esteem of those lower down. They are squeezed by this cultural contradiction.

The writing of this book has been supported by some substantial contributions made, ultimately, by the Canadian taxpayer. I benefited from a grant from the Social Sciences and Humanities Research Council of Canada (#410–2000–0433) held between 2000 and 2002. Thanks to my two partners on that project, Neil Guppy at the University of British Columbia and Mary Thompson at the University of Waterloo, for the benefits of collaborating with two such fine scholars. The University of Waterloo assisted me in 2002 with funds from the UW/SSHRC Small Grants Program, which I used to experiment with collecting prestige ratings by means of the telephone. Thanks to Elizabeth LaVasseur who conducted some very skilful interviewing on that phase of the project. Results from this pretest study helped me in applying to the Initiative on the New Economy program within the Social Sciences and Humanities Research Council of Canada. Their support allowed the collection of the national survey that I named "Occupational Prestige in Canada: 2005" (grant #501–2002–0063 held between 2003 and 2006). The University of Waterloo assisted the completion of this project by funding their share of SSHRC Release Allowance stipends for relief from teaching both on the SSHRC grants and by granting two sabbaticals, one in 2000–1, which helped get the project underway, and another in 2007–8, which allowed me to complete the present manuscript.

A collaboration with the Government of Canada department Human Resources Development Canada (as it was then named, now Human Resources and Skills Development Canada) helped the study in several ways. HRDC, Skills Information Division, signed on to my 2003 SSHRC grant application as a Partner, enhancing the credibility of the application. Clara Hamory and Ian McRae gave me a huge amount of help when I was choosing titles to include in the 2005 survey. When I over-spent my first SSHRC grant, Clara Hamory arranged for a contract research project with HRDC that helped pay my debts. Shane Dixon, a graduate student with the Department of Sociology at Waterloo gave valuable research assistance on that project. Helpful advice from Judith Treas of the University of California at Irvine gave me a valuable link with U.S. research when I was designing the 2005 survey. Kristyn Frank, in the closing stages of her PHD program in Sociology at Waterloo at the time of writing, was an invaluable research assistant in the later phases of this research. She compiled census information about the occupations far more accurately than I would have done. Two other UW graduate students who assisted on the project were Emily Pomeroy, who showed me how the job traits codes for occupations worked, and Luc Boyer, who helped with translation of job titles into French. There are numerous colleagues with whom I have benefited from discussions about this research, either as discussants at conferences or in more informal settings. They include Rick

Helmes-Hayes, my good next-door office friend in the Department of Sociology at Waterloo, Derek Wilkinson at Laurentian, Dick Wanner at Calgary, who gave me some of his first-hand impressions of Donald Treiman's work, Doug Baer at Victoria, Neil McLaughlin at McMaster, Claire Durand at the University of Montreal, and Neil MacKinnon at Guelph. McGill-Queen's University Press arranged two anonymous reviews of the manuscript, and I appreciate the helpful suggestions from them. The reviewers allowed me to speculate well beyond the data in places, and that is what made the project the most interesting for me. Naturally the speculations, together with any other errors or problems, are my own responsibility.

I am getting a little old to have personally telephoned over two thousand Canadians and taken each through a ten-to-fifteen minute survey about the evaluation of occupations. The hard work for this study was conducted by the interviewers at Jolicoeur et associés, a Montreal-based firm specializing in high-quality survey fieldwork. I am indebted to the fieldworkers for their dedication and professionalism and to Jean-François Dion and Pierre-Alexandre Lacoste, my main contacts at Jolicoeur.

I would like to thank Jonathan Crago, editor at the Montreal office of McGill-Queen's University Press, for treating me to a coffee at the Saskatoon Congress of the Humanities and Social Sciences and for the subsequent association with MQUP, in which he assisted so much in seeing the manuscript through the various publication stages.

I am glad I was able to rope in various students at the Department of Sociology at the University of Waterloo to use parts of the prestige data for their theses. Along with Kristyn Frank, mentioned above, there was Emily Pomeroy, who wrote her master's thesis on the prestige of professions, 1965 and 2005. Mike Civak examined the phenomenon of prestige self-enhancement for his BA honours thesis, and Kristy Thacker worked on the representation of occupations in the *Globe and Mail* for her honours thesis.

Writing this book, I was reminded of what wonderous times scholars live in today in terms of access to information. I benefited from the electronic access to journals obtained simply through my library card with the Dana Porter Library at the University of Waterloo. The same card gave me access to the Inter-University Consortium for Political and Social Research at the University of

Michigan (ICPSR), and thus the 1989 NORC survey on occupational prestige. Another part of the treasure trove was the Statistics Canada information flowing into the University of Waterloo library thanks to the Data Liberation Initiative.

A final crucial debt is to Dr Peter Pineo, longtime faculty member at the Department of Sociology at McMaster University. Pineo was my dissertation supervisor in the early 1970s, and I acquired my interest in occupational prestige from my weekly meetings with him. He let me use some data from his 1965 survey with Porter for my own doctoral research. In the 2000s, as I returned to issues of occupational prestige, it was Pete Pineo who still had a copy of the 1965 data set safely in storage when it did not turn up in any library databank in the country. Without Pineo's care in keeping the data and converting them from mainframe to PC form, there would have been no book length report possible on the two surveys separated by forty years. I have attempted repayment on this part of my debt to Pineo by archiving all the data sets used herein with the University of Waterloo Library, which will make them accessible to all interested scholars.

Waterloo, November 2008

THE PRESTIGE SQUEEZE

1

Occupational Prestige:
"That Mysterious Force"

Through high employment rates and low, from the beckoning lei-sure society of the 1970s to the over-stressed workplace of the 2000s, work has remained *the* defining role identity of most people. As far back as the Middletown study of the 1920s, "the long arm of the job" has reached into people's lives (Lynd and Lynd 1929, 53). Everett Hughes (1958, 7) wrote in one of the most familiar of all sociological quotations, "a man's work is as good a clue as any to the course of his life, and to his social being and identity." By the twentieth century's end, after decades of rising labour force partici-pation among women, that comment applied equally well to both sexes. As a source of social identity, work remains the "strongest link with reality" (Breakwell 1986, 53). "[O]ccupational roles locate individuals in social space" (Treiman 1977, 1), and "[o]ccupation is still the primary way in which we identify ourselves socially" (Coxon and Davies 1986, 1). In the "Occupational Prestige in Can-ada: 2005" survey described in chapter 3, respondents were asked how important having a "trade, craft or profession" was to their identity. A full 60 percent selected the "very important" label, and another 29 percent selected "somewhat important."

For over eighty years, since George Counts's (1925) pioneering study on "the social status of occupations," sociologists have exam-ined the perceptions held by members of the public about this cen-tral component of social identity. Occupations are differentiated and unequal along many dimensions, starting with entry require-ments – whether as aptitudes, formal educational prerequisites, or informal training requirements. Occupations differ in work condi-tions, some taking place in clean, safe, and comfortable workplaces, others in surroundings of dirt, danger, and discomfort. It has never been more important than today that some occupations pay higher salaries and wages than others (see, for example, Lowe and Krahn 2000, 9–10). And, coming to the point of the study reported in the pages below, occupations differ along an intangible yet crucial dimension existing within people's minds and summative of everything just noted and more – "that mysterious force known as prestige" (Le Bon 1960 [1895], 12).

PRESTIGE

Prestige is the subjective (Grasmick 1976, 90), ideational, "in-the-head" aspect of occupations not derivable merely from counting the years of education of practitioners, from factors such as noise or smell in the workplace, or from tallying up employment income, "all relatively 'substantial' things which are not matters of opinion" (Shils 1968, 119). Indeed, as Gusfield and Schwartz (1963, 265) rightly noted many years ago, if sociologists want to know about the incomes or other such factual traits of occupations, they are better off consulting economic data from Statistics Canada or the u.s. Bureau of the Census than asking survey respondents for perceptions of what occupational incomes are. People may be only "vaguely aware" (Marshall and Gorman 1975, 43) of such details. The evaluations made by people in survey after survey of occupational prestige naturally are related to educational prerequisites and income rewards, but only approximately so: they seem to balance various factors when evaluating an occupation. The prestige scores provide "a synthesis of the total reward system" (Reiss 1961, 248). Many attempts have been made to factor the multi-dimensionality inherent in ratings of occupational prestige. That was Rossi and Inkeles's (1957) objective, along with examples such as Gusfield and Schwartz (1963), DeFleur and DeFleur (1967), Grasmick (1976), More and Suchner (1976), and Hope (1982), together with other British examples discussed in some detail below. A unifying theme here is the distinction between tangible benefits and rewards against more ethereal considerations such as value to society. Even with the more objective criteria, people are mindful in assessing occupational rewards of considerations sociological as well as economic. They may factor in educational inflation of job qualifications or the income-enhancing manipulation of supply of new practitioners by professional associations and trade unions. Education and income are largely means to ends, meaning that members of the public are not education seekers and income seekers just for intrinsic interest and basic sustenance respectively; they are "status seekers," the title of Packard's (1961) popular book from years ago. At the very high income level, money becomes so plentiful that it is no longer very interesting to those who possess it except when the financial wealth translates into prestige (Collins 2000, 21).

Prestige could begin to sound like little more than a fashion accessory when status-seeking behaviour is described in a cultural study, but several strands of scholarly thought come together in the conclusion that prestige is important to human societies. From "socioanalytic theory" within personality psychology – a perspective that "ties together strands of evolutionary biology, psychoanalysis, and sociological role theory" – the "two central motivational tendencies in human behavior are toward seeking acceptance and seeking status in social groups" (McAdams 1997, 26). Sociological work on structural-functionalist theory and the tie-in with research on occupational prestige receives attention below and again in chapter 8. Here, the argument is that prestige is part of an occupational reward system needed at the societal level. A third reason to emphasize prestige as an important object of study is its chaos-reducing qualities, of benefit both to individual and society and perhaps true even at the most basic level of brain chemistry (Freeman 1999, 193).[1] A stable prestige order creates predictability in how people will behave. For animal behaviour, that is familiar knowledge, as any manual on dog training or any Jack London novel conveys. Stable prestige gives a simplifying heuristic that makes for enhanced efficiency. Podolny (2005, 18) has argued that notion in connection with the functioning of economic markets, and few are more inclined to use prestige as a market signal than university academics, for whom the whole course of a career can rest on the prestige of the graduate school a twenty-two-year-old is accepted into: Caplow and McGee's (1958, 225) "indelible mark." The academic prestige ladder, we say, motivates and helps set standards (McLaughlin 2005, 13). So for various reasons prestige serves purposes.

Where does prestige "come from?" The answer is tied up broadly with the needs in social relations served by prestige, but the details and emphases of this account have shifted ground over time. The social-theory legacy from the 1960s and 1970s points to prestige being logical and determined from social structure, derived rather mechanically and inexorably. Wegener (1992, 256), in a careful review article on prestige research up to the 1990s, used the term "rational," as distinguished from "normative." Details will be outlined below, but briefly, in his noted book on cross-national uniformities in occupational prestige, Treiman (1977, 5) traced the causal model behind prestige ratings back to how the division of labour made for more variegated, complex power and privilege differences than had existed in the society of lords and serfs: "the division of labor gives rise to characteristic differences in power, and power begets privilege, and power and privilege beget prestige." As elaborated as early as Simpson and Simpson (1960, 135) and more fully in Marsh (1971), the intervening factors between the division of labour and occupational power differentials were, in modern societies, knowledge gained from formal education together with responsibility represented by number of subordinates. This "top-down," society-to-individual theoretical motif retained its dominance within the social-inequality literature long after its structural-functionalist social-theory pedigree lost a once-held dominance.

Another view, however, is more cultural and socially constructed. Reaching farther back into history, consider the French sociologist Gustave Le Bon of earlier mention, who had much to say about prestige in relation to collective behaviour. In reversal of the concept of power begetting prestige, Le Bon (1960[1895], 130) maintained that "prestige is the mainspring of all authority." Prestige seeps out of the culture and proceeds to exert consequences. Seeing prestige as a source of power is not, we should note, just some quaint remnant of classical sociology. Feldman and Thielbar (1972, 235) achieved some success with asking undergraduate respondents to rank ten occupations, differentiating by power, privilege, and prestige, sub-differentiating by what is, against what should be. "[P]restige justifies what degree of power should be exercised and what privileges are due," they concluded. In another example, from Sandefur (2001, 384), writing in an early-twenty-first-century issue of the *American Sociological Review*: "Prestige is a particularly potent basis for the form of power that resides in influence." The context behind this quotation was a study of prestige gradations within the legal profession. The focus on one occupation may make the reciprocal causation between power and prestige easier to see than in theorizing about the entire labour force.

Le Bon was alert to the unpredictable, conjuring-trick-like quality of prestige. "Prestige in reality is a sort of domination exercised on our mind by an individual, a work, or an idea. This domination entirely paralyzes our critical faculty, and fills our soul with astonishment and respect" (1960[1895], 130). Dictionary definitions reflect the duality being noted here. From the Oxford English Dictionary (OED), prestige implies "blinding or dazzling influence," with the connotation of "illusion," or "a conjuring trick." Webster in contrast, sees prestige more prosaically as "reputation or influence arising from success."

Veblen's (1965 [1899]) famous old classic showing how behaviours often make little sense aside from their quirky and subtle prestige implications is consistent with the conjuring theme. The more culturally rooted emphasis is more than historical curiosity, despite the structuralist preference among the mid-twentieth-century generation of occupational prestige researchers. Zhou's (2005) work, to be encountered later, draws ideas from Shils (1968) about the link between prestige and centrality within a national value system. In the concluding chapter, I shall argue that prestige ratings from 2005 need to be placed within the culture of the twenty-first-century knowledge society before they make sense.

WHY STUDY OCCUPATIONAL PRESTIGE?

A ladder of prestige for occupations placing professionals and managers at the top, clerical and skilled in the middle, and unskilled blue collar at the bottom is ubiquitous, but not universal in the twentieth-century studies. From one individual to the next, remarkable variations are seen, and some respondents on a survey are resolutely egalitarian in their ratings (e.g., Coxon and Jones 1979a, 32). A sensitive analysis of prestige rating data must attend to such diversity, along with the commonalities. At the societal level more consistency is seen (a strong theme within the literature and a point returned to below), but again variations have occurred. For example, respondents in the Iron Curtain–era study of 1966 Czechoslovakia rewrote the pecking order traditionally encountered in capitalist societies, placing "collective farmer," for instance, second out of twenty-six, with judges nineteenth (Penn 1975; and anticipated by Davis 1927). Within capitalist society, there is Haller, Holsinger, and Saraiva's (1972) research comparing isolated with urbanized areas of Brazil. The less urbanized the place, the less the prestige hierarchy resembled the norm from American industrial society. Lewis and Haller (1964) had reached the same conclusion using student samples by comparing scales for urban and rural samples in Japan. From 1950s Great Britain, Young and Willmott (1956, 342), in an unjustly neglected piece, found, after sampling carefully from within the working class, a pocket of "upside down-ers" who had a well-articulated rationale based on value to society. So, despite reasons from some sociological theory for expecting a hierarchical distribution standard across cultures, a re-study of occupational prestige is not merely the examination of the obvious. Respondents in a prestige study are not simply being graded like students on an exam for how accurately they know the facts about occupational education prerequisites or expected earnings. They are reporting on the occupational world as they know it. It is precisely that the ratings have normative and, as Collins (2000, 24) remarks, ideological components which makes them sociologically interesting.

Those close (see, for example, Kraus et al. 1978, 915–16) to the research literature on occupational prestige, a large body of knowledge engaged later in this chapter, still might wonder, "why re-analyze old prestige data, and why collect more such studies?" Students of social stratification trained during the 1960s have imprinted, virtually into their synapses, the results of the National Opinion Research Centre's (NORC) 1963 replication of the famed "North Hatt" study of 1947. The replication showed minimal change in the status ladder of occupations over this sixteen-year span and was adapted by theorists of the time in support of an argument about universal factors behind the rating of occupations in industrial society (Hodge, Siegel, and Rossi 1966, 334; Treiman 1977).

And yet it is striking what strong intuitions researchers held about historical change in prestige hierarchies, especially prior to the NORC research. Just after World War Two for example, Jacob Tuckman (1947, 71) made an observation about the Counts occupational prestige scale from 1925. At the 1946 meeting of vocational counselors in Minneapolis, Tuckman recalled, "The question was raised regarding its validity in 1946 ... It was felt that the development of vocational guidance programmes, the occurrence of a severe depression in the thirties, and the occupational redistribution of millions of workers during World War II had brought about changes in social prestige attached to various occupations."

Some ten years earlier, Nietz (1935, 454) had framed a replication of Counts' study around the issue, "has the depression had any effect on the social-status ratings?" Nietz believed that such changes would be detectable over three data sets collected in 1928, just prior to the 1929 crash, in 1932, "which was during the heart of the depression," and in 1934, which from his historical vantage point "represents the period of recovery" (455). Interpreting an increase in the prestige of policemen and soldiers, Nietz hypothesized "that the fear of riots and revolution during the depression tended to magnify the importance of these two occupations." Insurance agents gained prestige as well, possibly, he reasoned, because many families in the 1930s relied on borrowing against their life insurance policies. Barbers rose in prestige because their unemployment was less severe than for many other occupations; bookkeeping "because bookkeepers ... were utilized to help carry on investigations of various sorts attracting public attention" (458). While he also reported that, comparing his findings with those of Counts from 1925, the "extent of agreement in the rankings of the social status of the occupations in the two studies is rather remarkable" (459), it interests me that Nietz, working as he did in the early days of prestige research, *expected* social change to affect scores. Even later on, at the height of the functionalist interpretation of industrial society considered below, Paul Siegel mused over how counterintuitive was the seeming longitudinal stability of prestige scores: "This temporal stability of the prestige structure is especially striking when one considers the vast changes that have occurred in the occupational structure over the period in question – the past forty-five years" (Siegel 1971, 3).

Many researchers close to the prestige literature today might deem naive these expectations that social changes would affect the occupational prestige hierarchy of industrial society. The intuitions are, however, worth a second look, for neither Canada, the United States, Great Britain, nor any such society *is* an industrial society today, early in the new century. These societies have transformed into "post-industrial," "information," "knowledge," "third wave" (Toffler 1981), electro-chemical-technological, "technetronic" (Brzezinski 1970) societies. It is the age of "late modern society" (Giddens 1991). New "defining technologies" (Bolter 1984, 11) arrived with the micro-electronic chip, and some argued that the long run business cycle was entering a new phase in the last quarter of the twentieth century (Mensch 1979). It cannot be assumed that social change in the final quarter of the twentieth century was simply more of the same patterns seen in earlier periods.

The term "new economy" has been used for the past several years to refer to the economic side of the social changes of the latter twentieth century. The 2005 survey that this book is reporting on was funded under an "initiative on the new economy" by the Social Sciences and Humanities Research Council of Canada. New-economy rhetoric arose in the early 1990s, following the late-1980s recession and coincides with a period of economic growth with low inflation. The California Silicone Valley is the model for much theorizing about the new economy, especially ideas around the priority of a highly educated, knowledge-generating workforce. The "core values" (Carnoy 2000, 1) of the new economy – flexibility, innovation, and risk – are tied up with the economic globalization consequent to new capabilities in electronic communication, in an age where "the world is flat" (Friedman 2005). The new economy may not be as "new" as, say, the abrupt transition from communism to capitalism in the former Soviet Union. Continuity between the service sector concentration (Herzenberg et al. 1998) of the new economy and the older economy, for example, is seen with the persistent relevance of long-standing issues such as job displacement (e.g., Giedion 1948) and de-skilling (Braverman 1974). And as with the old, the benefits of the new economy have not necessarily been shared by all strata of society (Rifkin 1995; Menzies 1996). In the 1990s, there was a discernable "digital divide" (summarized in Goyder 2005a, 193–7). With reference to the low-skill service sector, economists wrote of a "productivity paradox" around computer technology (Triplett 1999). Despite these continuities with the old economy, the term "new economy" does articulate an important transition with social as well as economic consequences. Chapter 2 is devoted to recent social changes and possible implications for occupational prestige.

No equivalent social-change literature exists from the 1950s, years in which the most noted trend concerned the growth of suburban conformity, not the transformation of economies (e.g., Riesman 1953; Clark 1966). I conceived of the study reported herein as a new look at the issue of social change and the prestige of occupations, situated in a new era. More specific hypotheses about the new economy and occupational prestige appear within the next chapter. The remainder of this one examines the historical path of social theories about occupational prestige. The presuppositions about and modes of interpretations of prestige data went through marked changes over the final seventy-five years of the twentieth century. This literature will now be examined in a review leading to an analytical scheme with which to approach prestige data.

SOME EARLIER STUDIES OF OCCUPATIONAL PRESTIGE: THEMES AND THEORIES

The George Counts Study

Considering the high stakes surrounding mid-twentieth century work on occupational prestige, the modest objectives of the inaugural study are striking to the twenty-first-century reader. Counts (1925, 16) was motivated foremost by how, following the dramatic transformation of post-1914–18-war America, "much has been said and written regarding the altered condition of the teacher and the lowered prestige of those to whom society delegates the educational function." He took the two titles "elementary school teacher" and "high school teacher" and shuffled them into a pack of forty-three other occupations ranging from "banker" and "college professor" (ranked first and second respectively) down to "street clearer" and "ditch digger" (ranked forty-fourth and forty-fifth). The ratings were performed by several small samples, mainly high school students, but with one sample of college freshmen and one of Minneapolis school teachers. The key titles, "high school teacher" and "elementary school teacher," ranked tenth and thirteenth respectively.

Although lightweight by modern sampling standards, Counts's work is historically important for the way it predates the structural-functionalist period in social theory, the period gaining strength just after the Second World War and so greatly dominating much of the research on occupational prestige. We are reminded of theoretical implications around occupational prestige prior to and separate from testing the hypothesis of functional importance for occupations. Counts's objectives for social stratification theory were modest. He merely "wished to direct attention toward an important problem in vocational guidance which is seldom squarely faced." In research on occupations, Counts (1925, 16) argued, "there is a tendency to disregard the fundamental question of social status. Detailed information has been gathered with respect to the financial remuneration, security, and hazards of occupations, but the question of social rating is ordinarily dismissed with the statement that a particular calling is highly respectable."

The Counts study deserves examination for its analytical plan. For example, checking an intuition about across-group differences echoed in all later studies of prestige, he examined differences in ratings between samples from a university-oriented high school versus a trade school because "one would think that the differences in social background and vocational future between these two groups would be revealed in the occupational judgments" (1925, 19). Following another tack repeated in much later analysis, Counts, towards the end of his article, writes, "[l]et us now turn to a consideration of the extent of agreement among the individuals comprising the group" (22). Following an examination of dispersion in rankings as seen though a table of quartile ranges, Counts concludes that "while groups agree, individuals tend to disagree" (24). He discusses three possible reasons for inter-individual dissensus: "unfamiliarity" with an occupation, heterogeneity of status within occupations with highly variable earnings, and the methodological issue of "failure to follow instructions." All three themes echo down the years in later studies.

Counts bequeathed to later researchers a rich historical document on prestige studies, but it is a modern study too in some aspects, concerned then, as people are now, with how to give realistic vocational advice to youth. "If all occupations were of equal standing in the community," he concludes, "the counselor could ... think chiefly in terms of the abilities of pupils and vigorously encourage each to enter the occupation for which he (she) is best fitted." In the status-conscious world of 1925, as of 2005, prestige was a powerful "social force" (Counts 1925, 26) not to be ignored. The status-race assumptions already driving vocational guidance by the earlier twentieth century, and reflected in the Counts study, are strong. Pointing young people to the top-prestige occupations seemed to matter more than finding work congruent with their aptitudes and interests. Researchers with vocational guidance perspective have been contributing to the occupational prestige literature ever since (e.g., Plata 1975; Kanzaki 1976, 101; Fredrickson et al. 1992).[2]

The NORC Studies

Following a small development of Counts's method by Smith (1943; and see Davies 1952 for discussion of some of the other early studies), a major advance in the study of occupational prestige began with March 1947 fieldwork by NORC, using a design by North and Hatt (Reiss 1961, v). The University of Denver- (later Chicago-) based agency had recently developed capability for national-level survey research on American society. Although methodologically on a grander scale, the NORC (1953 [1947]) authors shared Counts's guidance-counseling interest. "On what basis do people choose their work?" the opening page of the NORC report began, following some sentences about the importance of occupations. The survey posed a vocational question reading, "suppose some outstanding young man asked your advice on what would be one of the best occupations to aim toward. What one occupation do you think you would advise him to aim toward?" (Reiss 1961, 259).

In this first NORC investigation appears a theme pursued in several later studies of prestige, including my own – the computing of average scores for homogeneous clusters of occupations such as "professional and semi-professional workers." As the study of occupational mobility and status attainment gathered momentum during the 1960s (e.g., Lipset and Bendix 1959; Blau and Duncan 1967), the validity of these hierarchies for sociologically meaningful groups of occupations gained importance. NORC 1947 provided one of the first such validations, and subsequent Canadian research has stressed this motif too (Pineo and Porter 1967; Pineo, Porter, and McRoberts 1977; Pineo 1981). Albert Riess (1961, 42), in his re-analysis of these first NORC data, felt that prestige "may in fact be more important in distinguishing among families of occupations than it is in discriminating among occupations within families."

The NORC researchers intuited that different categories and groups of people within U.S. society would rate occupations somewhat uniquely. This theme, taking up and expanding the line of work begun by Counts, examined mean scores for specific occupations, as well as the grand mean for all scores, the figure that later students of prestige would term "the amount of prestige in the system" (Hodge, Siegel, and Rossi 1966, 325) or in "the occupational structure" (Pineo and Porter 1967, 31). While these grand mean differences between social groups and categories seemed rather trivial for the most part, for example the means of 70.8 for rural places versus 68.8 for urban (NORC 1953 [1947], 415), the numbers became more lively for individual titles. "Musician in a symphony orchestra," for instance, scored relatively highly in urban places, while the prestige of farm ownership was granted more willingly among rural dwellers (Reiss 1961).

Reiss (1961) also looked at correlation coefficients between the scales computed for categories and groups, a concern not addressed in the 1947 report by NORC. While computing these summary statistics reducing mountains of numbers into one coefficient seemed a sensible way of grasping the meaning of the data, the correlations have led to controversy in the interpretation and social-theory meaning of prestige data. A later section of the present chapter returns to that theme.

North and Hatt with NORC had mounted a rich study with several innovations repeated in later work. They addressed the issue both of "don't know's" and apparent "do know's" founded in ignorance. Asked to define the occupation "nuclear physicist," 55 percent replied "don't know" but another 42 percent gave less than fully accurate and complete definitions. It became clear that prestige ratings are somewhat stereotypical (Coxon and Jones 1978, 3–5) around the sound of the title (Reiss 1961, 16; Pineo and Porter 1967, 30), a little "abstract" and "decontextualized," as Collins (2000, 24) says in a rather critical discussion of prestige surveying. A later chapter will show instances in Canadian data where the same work is rated differentially according to the words used to describe the job title.

NORC 1947 was alert to some of the "cognitive" issues later pursued in British research. A question in the 1947 survey asking "what makes a job 'excellent'" generated a wide spread of factors, led by pay but closely followed by service to humanity, educational preparation, and the seemingly tautological reply, "the job carries social prestige." As with title ratings themselves, evaluations of criteria showed some commonsensical patterns, such as people of lower earnings stressing job pay as a determinant of prestige (NORC 1953 [1947], 418).

At this point, the NORC report moves on to some more tangential issues, such as factors behind career choice, perceptions of schooling needed to succeed, and mobility analysis on the occupations of fathers and paternal grandfathers of respondents. The piece closes with a prescient reference to a growing problem in the industrial economy of mass production causing "individual frustration" and tending to "smother ambition" (NORC 1953 [1947], 426).

We see here how the first generation of reports on the NORC project (NORC 1953 [1947]; Reiss 1961) did not stray far from the data. As the 1960s and the decade beyond unfolded, however, increasingly bold conceptual interpretations were derived both from the same data and then from later fieldwork. Sophisticated and compelling in many respects, but also controversial, the intensity of the debate around this work did much to clarify how decisions at the data analysis stage hold repercussions for interpretation.

Interpreting the NORC Data: Structural-Functionalist Issues

The 1953 edition of the famous Bendix and Lipset reader, the authoritative anthology of the era for articles on social inequality, reprinted the "Jobs and Occupations: A Popular Evaluation" piece originating from the less widely circulated NORC house publication *Opinion News*. My own references to the NORC piece come from the Bendix and Lipset source. For the second (1966) edition of *Class, Status and Power*, Bendix and Lipset retired the 1947 article and substituted "A Comparative Study of Occupational Prestige," by Robert Hodge, Donald Treiman, and Peter Rossi, along with "Occupational Prestige in the United States: 1925–1963," by Hodge, Paul Siegel, and Rossi. The former piece was an original contribution for the 1966 edition. The latter expanded from a 1964 *American Journal of Sociology* article. The two pieces as a linked pair made an impact on the sociological community remarkable for their brief twenty-five pages cumulative length. As Blaikie (1977, 102) remarked, they became cornerstones of "a dominant absolutist paradigm."

I shall concentrate on the Hodge, Siegel, and Rossi report on longitudinal trends within the United States, while drawing in places on the cross-national paper. By now, research on occupational prestige had become widely known, with the beginnings of a cumulation of results both longitudinally and cross-nationally. As Hodge, Siegel, and Rossi (1966, 322) noted, the "prestige hierarchy of occupations is perhaps the best studied aspect of the stratification systems of modern societies."

Hodge and his co-authors on this longitudinal analysis opened with bold claims: "It appears that occupational prestige hierarchies are similar from country to country and from subgroup to subgroup within a country," they wrote. "This stability reflects the fundamental, but gross similarities among the occupational systems of modern nations. Furthermore, knowledge about occupations and relatively strong consensus on the relative positions of occupations are widely diffused throughout the populations involved" (Hodge, Siegel, and Rossi 1966, 322).

From this premise the authors could hypothesize "considerable stability over time in the prestige of particular occupations" (1966, 322). Moreover, for the whole labour force "it would be erroneous to expect any considerable change in the prestige structure" within a country, over time. As developed within this Hodge, Seigel, Rossi longitudinal paper, the derivation of the stable trends hypothesis seems largely inductive, following the numbers. From the data, prestige scores have proved invariant across cultures and differential levels of economic development, they had noted, and so invariance in prestige scores over time was implied, notwithstanding some "cogent" reasons for expecting change. The cogent reasons included "power and influence" pertaining to an occupation, "characteristics of incumbents," and "the amount of resources society places at the disposal of incumbents."

Why trust so empirical a basis for hypothesizing about longitudinal trends in prestige in the face of these persuasive counterfactuals? The cross-national article by Hodge, Treiman, and Rossi answers the question. Building their conceptual scheme from earlier work by Inkeles and Rossi (1956), Hodge and colleagues in the cross-national article took a position "stressing more heavily the many structural features which national societies of any degree of complexity share." A structural-functionalist orientation to prestige was birthing within these pages. "Specialized institutions," wrote Hodge, Trieman, and Rossi (1966, 310), "to carry out political, religious, and economic functions, and to provide for the health, education, and welfare of the population exist in one form or another in all national societies. Considering the importance of these functions to the maintenance of complex social systems, it is not surprising that occupations at the top of these institutional structures should be highly regarded." The classic Davis and Moore (1945) *American Sociological Review* article on the functional importance of occupations was not cited, but Treiman (1977, 17, note 3) did so later in his book, discussed below, and so too did Paul Siegel (1971, 2) in his frequently-cited doctoral thesis reporting on further surveys of occupational prestige collected in 1964 and 1965 by the NORC survey unit, by now relocated to the University of Chicago. High-prestige occupations, the Hodge, Treiman, Rossi passage continues, "are the very occupations which require the greatest training and skill to which the greatest material rewards accrue." Here was distinctively and avowedly structuralist, as distinguished from culturalist (Hodge, Treiman, and Rossi 1966, 310), theorizing. Interpretations referring to the cultural uniqueness of a nation were considered useful only for fleshing out occasional anomalies. "[W]e can hardly expect that cultural traditions will produce inversions of the relative positions of dominant functionaries and blue-collar workers." (1966, 312). A little oddly, the name of Talcott Parsons does not appear within the two articles just discussed, perhaps because his concept of structural-functionalism already seemed excessively speculative by the 1960s. Wegener (1992, 255) shows where Parsons fits in, noting the affinity between the finding of high consensus about prestige ratings and value integration in modern societies.

The longitudinal article capitalized on the already noted 1963 replication of the 1947 survey, an exceptionally careful re-study, even down to re-using in 1963 the out-dated quota sampling from the 1947 study. Departing a little from the emphasis in earlier work, analysis of the prestige trend data from the NORC series focused "largely on the ordering of ninety NORC occupations in two time periods and not upon changes in the prestige of particular occupations" (Hodge, Siegel, and Rossi 1966, 326). The "major result" of the replication was a Pearsonian correlation of 0.99 between the 1947 and 1963 scales showing "a striking similarity between the structure of the 1947 and the 1963 NORC scores." Blau and Duncan (1967, 120) conveyed the feeling of excitement around prestige scale correlations in their comment that "we now have a detailed study of temporal stability in occupational prestige ratings. The results are astonishing to most sociologists who have given the matter only casual thought."

In interpreting this congruency over time, Hodge, Siegel, and Rossi (1966, 327) referred to the same points stressed in the theoretical development section of the Hodge, Treiman, and Rossi cross-national analysis, that "the educational requirements, monetary rewards, and even the nebulous 'functional importance' of an occupation are not subject to rapid change in an industrial society." Any substantial amount of re-shuffling of the occupational prestige hierarchy would create problematic status inconsistencies, destabilizing to people's expectations around career and seniority.

Donald Treiman, in 1964 a graduate student member of the Hodge-Rossi team, developed the cross-national theme broached in the piece for the Bendix and Lipset reader, first in a doctoral thesis defended in 1967 and subsequently with the widely noted book referred to already in this chapter, *Occupational Prestige in Comparative Perspective*, published in 1977. His book eliminated the need for a succession of separate reports on prestige surveys from different countries, a prominent feature of the journals in earlier years (e.g., Sarapata and Wesolowski 1961; Thomas 1962; Armer 1968). Treiman's book is a forthright source to the assumptions guiding the analysis of occupational prestige in the 1960s–1970s period. "[M]an," and woman, "is an evaluative animal," he premised (1977, 19), drawing from Veblen and re-expressing the status-preoccupied theme seen in Counts. A theory of occupational prestige then unfolded emphasizing worldwide uniformities in the division of labour, that core sociological concept from Durkheim, notions of functional imperatives from Parsons, and a recognition of occupations as sources of power from Lenski. For Donald Treiman there were good and necessary reasons why respondents on surveys can differentiate by prestige between different occupations, and these reasons also explained why a prestige scale from one country looks much like one from another.

That finding resounds throughout Treiman's book, whether it be the recurrent correlation of 0.8 or more between scales compared cross-nationally for sixty societies, even higher correlations for internal analysis comparing social groups and categories within societies, or ingenious attempts to decipher the prestige hierarchy of societies dating back to the European industrialization beginning two and a half centuries ago. Congruent prestige is a theme already familiar in our review, but it was Treiman who insisted most forcefully on the implications of these data for the theory of social inequality. Although he did report some anomalies, such as an upgrading of the prestige of manual labour in Eastern European societies (1977, 146), these for him were minor "exceptions that prove the rule" (141).

In the section below I review some later criticisms of Treiman's consensualist, structural-functionalist interpretation of prestige data. Much of the controversy revolves around issues of the meaning of different statistical summaries that might be made of prestige data. Treiman and colleagues within the "'Chicago school' ... of conventional stratification theorists" (Coxon and Davies 1986, 43) placed great meaning in the correlation between scales already summed across respondents in a survey sample. It was true in 1925 and in 1965, and it is true today that such a form of analysis produces high correlations suggestive of structural uniformities within the division of labour and dismissive of cultural or individual uniqueness. Although there was some leverage due to time or place even with the correlational approach, the elasticity was low. My chapter 7 will give illustrations. Hodge, Siegel, and Rossi (1966, 329), for example, had in their longitudinal article acknowledged that "[s]light though the variation in correlations ... may be, it is noteworthy that the observed variation is apparently a function of lapsed time." The correlation between scales from different years in the United States dropped by an average of one point every seven or eight years. The later Nakao and Treas (1994) 1964–89 comparison, with $r = .97$, adheres to the same rule of thumb. In another example of gradual change, Treiman (1977) included a chapter on "prestige and industrialization," with an analysis showing that the correlation between the prestige scale for the United States and any other country in the world increased by about seven points for every $1,000 (early post-World War II dollars) per capita gross national product.

The Pineo-Porter Study

In the first half of the 1960s, Pineo and Porter were preparing for the field their national survey on occupational prestige in Canada. Peter Pineo, then a young assistant professor with a 1959 doctorate from Chicago, and John Porter, who at that time would have been putting finishing touches on the legendary *Vertical Mosaic*, approached the issue of prestige "from the need for a standardized indicator of social class or measure of socio-economic status"

(Pineo and Porter 1967, 24). Pineo (1981, 620) reiterated this measurement theme in his retrospective piece on the 1965 study, written shortly after Porter's death. The two Canadians took note of the vocational guidance motif for prestige studies, which had begun with Counts and was continued in Jacob Tuckman's (1947) Montreal study, but argued that this emphasis had led research in the direction of samples of people unrepresentative of the general population and samples of occupations overrepresentative of the professions. In the 1967 *Canadian Review of Sociology and Anthropology* article, a citation classic in Canadian social science, NORC's work with representative samples received favourable comment, and notice was taken of the "small variation between the major sub-groupings" denoting "a remarkable consistency in the prestige of occupations, enough to indicate a general ranking consensus for the society" (Pineo and Porter 1967, 24).

The data that Pineo and Porter collected between April and December of 1965 brought Canada into the front rank of the international movement to analyse industrial societies worldwide by means of comparing the hierarchy and consensual structure of occupational stratification as perceived within the minds of citizens. Treiman (1977, 32) considered the Canadian data one of the higher quality studies in his cross-national data bank. Sixteen years after the fieldwork, Pineo (1981) recalled that one of Porter's motives for the research had been to stimulate national-level survey research of high methodological quality in his own country. Prestige was attractive to Porter in part because the record of high agreement between studies already conducted in other countries made the research "unadventuresome" (Pineo 1981, 620) in a way that would help validate the survey method in the eyes of Canadian social scientists. The investment in quality was detectable in a key correlation: the Canada-U.S. scales collected in 1965 and 1964 respectively agreed to the extent of r = .98. For the subset of 165 titles considered "identical" in a re-examination by Guppy (1984, 74–5), the correlation crept to within one point of perfect interchangeability.

Re-Interpretations of Occupational Prestige: British

In step with growing international interest during the 1970s with surveys on occupational mobility and attainment, several teams of researchers in British universities considered issues of the prestige and scaling of occupations. At Oxford, John Goldthorpe and Keith Hope (1974) published the results of an innovative study entitled *The Social Grading of Occupations: A New Approach and Scale*. Turning the American interpretation of NORC data on its head, these British sociologists saw the routinely high correlations between scales compared across subgroups not as convincing evidence of a collective conscience but as a warning sign of poorly conceived research. The Oxford approach was consciously non-structural-functionalist (Goldthorpe and Hope 1974, 13), critical of the meaning of NORC-style prestige data. Since research has demonstrated that "values and symbols do vary with socioeconomic status in modern industrial societies," Goldthorpe and Hope (1944, 6) said, differences should be detectable in the occupational prestige ratings made by people at these different socioeconomic status levels. The point being made here rested on a view that prestige relating to occupations is well separated from economic rewards. "Relative advantage and power in terms of prestige," argued Goldthorpe and Hope (1974, 5), in a passage reminiscent of the passages from Le Bon noted above, "stem from the ability of an actor to exploit and benefit from *meanings* and *values* – rather than, say, economic resources, authority or physical force." Such arguments led the two Oxford authors to the interpretation that NORC-type studies do not elicit these "symbolic indications of social superiority or inferiority" properly associated with the term prestige ratings, but rather mental reports labeled "general desirability" by Goldthorpe and Hope (1974, 11–12). Ten years earlier, Gusfield and Schwartz (1963, 266) had anticipated that one job being simply "better" than another was one dimension of occupational prestige. This "rather unspecific 'better-worse' dimension" came, Goldthorpe and Hope suggested, from respondents' knowledge of "a *variety* of more 'objective' occupational attributes – most often, perhaps, job rewards or requirements.

Treiman (1977, 26–7) addressed these criticisms, in the book cited earlier, making two points. The British pair had stressed that respondents, when asked what criteria they used in rating occupations, seldom named "social prestige." The American countered with the plausible point that "most respondents no doubt failed to name 'prestige' because they thought it synonymous with the criterion of evaluation, 'social standing.'" If the respondents named factors such as skill or income, they were merely giving to the researchers an account of where the more symbolic evaluations come from. Treiman (1977, 27) also found the distinction between prestige and deference thin: "Inexplicably, Goldthorpe and Hodge believe that the things people regard as desirable about jobs will be invariant from place to place and group to group while the degree to which occupations command deference will strongly reflect differences in values."

It never is mentioned in the scholarly exchanges, but the points being raised perhaps revealed more about social inequality in Great Britain compared with the United States than about sociological theory. It is easy to believe that the symbolic aspect of inequality, factoring out skill, pay, etc., would be more important east of the Atlantic ocean than to the west. Britain after all is the land where not so many generations ago there was a "contempt of commerce entertained by young men having some pretence to gentility" (Sir Walter Scott 1819, ix). Even if that world has vanished, I would not be the first to observe that Britain remains a unique natural laboratory for the subtle nuances of status.

Goldthorpe and Hope (1974, 14–17) acted on their assessment that survey respondents took "social standing" to mean objective traits of occupations by asking a pilot sample in Oxford for ratings of forty occupations along four criteria: standard of living, power and influence over other people, level of qualifications, and value to society. Remeasurements were taken two to three months later, yielding a test-retest correlation of 0.73 (Goldthorpe and Hope 1977, 156). While some differentiation between the four criteria was made by the pool of respondents, notably with value to society being only weakly ($r = 0.47$) related to standard of living, the cumulative hierarchy of occupations averaged across all the four dimensions agreed closely (97 percent variance explained) with those from conventional "social standing" ratings of the same occupations conducted by a second pilot sample of Oxford residents. It was the same simple old phrase "social standing" from American work that the Oxford researchers adopted for their main national-level prestige survey (Goldthorpe and Hope 1974, 182).

Thames Valley concerns about the "symbolic" (Goldthorpe and Hope 1974, 11) aspects of one trade or another, and possible implications for "some underlying structure of social relations" (1974, 12) had melted away in face, perhaps, of the exigencies of mounting a study of occupational mobility in Britain. About the same time, however, researchers at Oxford's ancient rival, Cambridge University, were working on a scale based almost brutally on the behavioural structure of social relations. Ken Prandy and colleagues Stewart and Blackburn asked survey respondents about the occupations of four persons "with whom they are friendly" (Prandy 1990, 640). From these simple data the Cambridge group proceeded with an ingenious analysis leading to a "relational" (Stewart et al. 1980, 27) scale based on the distribution of occupations of friends of respondents in different types of occupation. After computing a dissimilarity statistic for each pair of occupations in the comparison (in the Cambridge data this was forty occupations meeting the criterion of containing at least ten respondents), the matrix of dissimilarities became the input into a multidimensional scaling program. The scaling analysis addressed the number of dimensions of dissimilarities in the matrix and produced a first dimension turning the occupations into a hierarchy looking much like the "reputational" (Stewart et al. 1980, 24) one from NORC. The approach has some similarities to the more recent work by Rytina (1992), in which a scale (the one maximizing the association between generations) was extracted from a detailed occupational mobility transition table. Grusky and Rompaey (1992, 1716–17) have a good chart mapping these different scaling traditions.

Like their Oxford counterparts, albeit only after scoring some debating points at the expense of Goldthorpe and Hope, the Cambridge group approached occupational scoring from the viewpoint that the NORC work was conceptually empty. "[A]lmost all of the discussion is conducted as if the meaning of occupation were unproblematic," they contended (Stewart et al. 1980, 1). Discussion about "consensus" in ratings, for example, was bound to prove unproductive because "[t]he social system is ... experienced merely as the sum of inter-personal relationships" (Stewart et al. 1980, 6). NORC-type scales of occupational social standing, they felt (72), "measure basic similarities of life-style."

A third group of British researchers interested in occupational prestige took yet another slant, but again within the theme of attention to the meaning of occupational hierarchy. Thus, Coxon and Jones, working at the University of Edinburgh, examined the distinction between "cognition" and "evaluation" in occupational ratings. Cognition, argued Coxon and Jones, concerns such issues as the *kinds of* distinctions people might draw about occupations.

They experimented with cognitive tasks like presenting respondents with titles of occupations and asking for a sorting into as many piles as the respondent thought appropriate. Could the piles be named by respondents, and what were the criteria by which they might be ordered? Such tasks, argued Coxon and Jones (1978), should precede the evaluative stage of rating or ranking by prestige or social standing. Their critique thus held that earlier work had proceeded too hastily to the final stage of evaluation, neglecting (and therefore implicitly pre-imposing onto respondents) the prior cognitive work. Since the research community gathers together those who tend to have excelled in school, who hold a strong work ethic, and who would not see their ideas in print unless they could play the prestige games of academe, more egalitarian outlooks within the general population were underemphasized. Illustrative of this is Ollivier's (2000, 451) comparison between samples of university professors and electricians regarding comments they made during a Coxon and Jones-like sorting task for occupations.

Attention to cognitive issues preceding evaluation was also taking place in Israel, in research by Kraus and Schild, along with Robert Hodge from the United States. In work probably independent of and simultaneous with the Scottish project, judging from publication dates, Kraus et al. (1978, 902) raised many of Coxon and Jones's points and indeed traced the lineage of free-sorting tasks informing about occupational cognition back to a Harvard PhD thesis dating from 1952.[3] But despite the similar research designs, conclusions from the Scottish and the Israeli-American projects were divergent. Having discovered just one important dimension in a multivariate analysis of the free-sort data (probability of any two occupations being sorted into same group), along with dimensions being defined similarly across subgroups, Kraus et al. ended their piece with, "[w]e do not doubt that prestige is in the collective conscience" (915).

Coxon and Jones were less "Durkheimian" in their perspective on occupation prestige. Early in the first of their three books on the topic (see also Coxon and Jones 1979a, b), reference is made to the "profile fallacy" of drawing conclusions about what lies within the minds of individuals from data aggregated across multiples of people (Coxon and Jones 1978, 9). Marxist theory receives mention a few pages later in Coxon and Jones, if not with full approval, still as an important perspective to be included in a "compromise account"

(13). For Coxon and Jones (193), "occupational images" had free-standing *sui generis* status as things-in-themselves, but not in Durkheim's consensual sense. Their empirical design was distinctive for rigorous statistical work using multi-dimensional scaling of various types of cognitive and evaluative data to show that "occupational images do in fact differ, not only from individual to individual but also from group to group."

Reinterpretations: North American

Not all sociologists in North America allowed the conceptual importance claimed by some for the Treiman constant. Nosánchuk (1972), in Canada, was one early skeptic. In the late 1970s and early 1980s, debate quickened as the journal *Social Forces* became an important medium for discussion about the meaning of occupational prestige. A pair of studies (Kraus et al. 1978, already mentioned, and Balkwell et al. 1980) underlined the consensus around prestige ratings, the Balkwell group emphasizing how this interpretation validated "a key assumption underlying the 'Wisconsin Model' of status attainment." Guppy (1982) linked results from the Kraus et al. and Balkwell et al. studies and drew a provocative implication. Both teams had computed the average individual with individual correlation in prestige ratings (that is, each respondent's scaling is treated separately and compared to any other randomly selected respondent's). It had been realized back to Counts's (1925, 24) time that "while groups agree, individuals tend to disagree." Treiman (1977, 60) had considered this issue of dissensus at the level of individuals in his international data base. "There is," he concluded, "a relatively large idiosyncratic component in the prestige ratings made by each individual, so that the typical correlation in the ratings made by any pair of individuals is about .6." Several such correlations were in the literature (e.g., r = .46 in Goldthorpe and Hope 1974, 163). Guppy noticed a pattern: in middle-class samples such as the university students surveyed by Balkwell and colleagues, the average individual-with-individual correlation was much higher than for general cross-sections that would include respondents of lower socioeconomic status. In reanalysis of NORC data, he showed that this indicator of dissensus, the average inter-individual correlation, indeed was higher among university-educated pairs than among the less educated. Here was an answer to the consensualist claims (e.g., Treiman 1977, 60) that the dissensus between individual and individual had no social structuring to it and was therefore unimportant.

Balkwell et al. (1982, 1185) replied that Guppy's finding was trivial, merely reflecting the "low levels of cognitive skills" among the less educated. A similar interpretation had appeared in the earlier work by Reiss (1961, 11–18, 183). Likewise, Hodge, Kraus, and Schild's (1982, 1195) commentary cited the "lower levels of measured intelligence" of lower status groups and their tendency to "know less about the occupational world." The low correlations for lower SES (i.e., socioeconomic status) raters were simply "error."

Guppy and Goyder (1984) attempted "a reassessment of the evidence" on these issues of consensus and dissensus. We began with a definitional issue. Parsonian consensus implies not just empirical similarities in ratings for occupation titles but consciousness among people that agreement is high because the uniform ratings are of the culture, not just of the individual. The data from occupational prestige studies were, we felt, being asked to do too much work in service of structural-functional theory. The dismissal of low inter-individual correlations as measurement error seemed elitist and unmindful of the larger body of knowledge about social inequality. With the British work in mind, especially that of Coxon and Jones (above), it seemed wrong to dismiss lower SES respondents as ignorant, and more sociologically sensitive to recall research on the cross-pressures and competing ideologies to which those near the bottom of the heap are subject. Ollivier's (2000) more recent Canadian study shows that the overlap between dimensions in a free-sorting of occupations into piles à la Coxon and Jones declines from higher to lower SES respondents, suggesting from another angle that the lower strata are dealing with mixed ideologies rather than simply suffering from ignorance. Pineo and I (Goyder and Pineo 1977) had some years earlier looked at how respondents protected their self-respect when they encountered their own lower-status occupation on a prestige-rating survey by allowing themselves bonus points. That was not error, nor from the error perspective was it comprehensible that, paradoxically, the Canadian population (of lower education, nationwide, than the U.S. population, thus more "error-prone") had higher across-individual correlations than did comparable Americans (Guppy 1984).

Another viewpoint from outside the U.S. orbit was expressed by the long-time University of Alberta sociologist Nico Stehr, reporting in the *British Journal of Sociology* on German data collected in 1967. Stehr (1974, 410) echoed the "preoccupation" with consensus among some of the leading U.S. researchers, pointing out the importance of timing, how key NORC research appeared during the "zenith" (411) of the functional theory of stratification. Arguing that the nuances of occupational prestige become most visible when sampling titles of roughly equivalent socioeconomic status in terms of educational prerequisites and income returns, Stehr selected sets of natural science (physicist, chemist, mathematician, biologist) and non-science (physician, lawyer, banker, plus nine other) occupations. A sample of the (then West) German elite was approached for prestige rankings (not ratings, in this study), with analysis organized along the hypothesis that "proximity" of raters to occupations, whether in terms of social interaction or ideological (i.e., favourability to science and technology) closeness, would affect rank given to an occupation (418). And indeed, respondents favourable toward science gave higher prestige to a physicist, for example, than to a banker in 56 percent of comparisons, against 42 percent among those with negative attitudes toward science. Thus, when the sampling plan of titles and respondents is sensitive to the possibility of inter-individual variations among raters, the differences are there, and in logical, interpretable form.

Doubts about the 1960s era structural-functionalist interpretation of occupational prestige data were reinforced as gender was increasingly added to discussions. In the era when the study of occupational prestige first got under way, differences by gender were considered unimportant. The labour force at mid-twentieth century was predominately male, and the women who did work in paid employment were concentrated in the "sex-stereotyped" jobs such as nurse, elementary school teacher, or stenographer. Pineo and Porter (1967) were addressing this labour force in their work in the 1960s. By a decade later, the implications of gender for occupational prestige had gained complexity with the female labour force participation rate moving from just under one-third in the mid-sixties to over 45 percent by 1975. Table 2.3, in chapter 2, gives the time series. Consciousness had increased of gender as an ascribed factor in the worlds of work and pay. Occupational-prestige researchers now had to consider whether assessments of the social standing of jobs depended on whether the worker was male or female. Commentators such as Haug (1973) articulated the need.

A new conceptual issue had emerged: is the prestige that members of the public accord an occupation something adhering to the status-position and its role content, no matter what the social characteristics of the holder might be, or, in contrast, is prestige in part a reflection of the kind of person typically engaging in the occupation? The former view was perhaps more widely accepted, and in Canada had the authority of Bernard Blishen's view that "the unit of analysis in socioeconomic indexing is not the individual incumbent in an occupation, but the occupation itself" (Blishen et al. 1987, 468). The importance of this distinction between position and person is underlined in Wegener's review article on prestige (1992, 255).

The issue of gender and occupational prestige was investigated by Guppy and Siltanen, then two University of Waterloo graduate students, in survey fieldwork conducted in Kitchener-Waterloo in the summer of 1975. Although of modest scale and geographic coverage, the study was rather unique for its time. In the key finding of the research, occupations specified as practised by a male were attributed exactly 5.0 more points – about one-quarter of a standard deviation – on a 0–100 scale than the same occupation for a female worker (Guppy and Siltanen 1977, 327). It had thus been demonstrated that, whatever the textbook logic behind the status, role, and prestige of occupations might be, in the community people indeed did adjust the prestige to be accorded occupations according to the gender of the incumbent. Further analysis suggested that the differential was more a "sex as role" than "sex as status" phenomenon: "esteem" was granted to or withheld from women workers based on an evaluation of whether a job was congruent with their role as women. Similarly, the premium given to male incumbents was not across the board, but rather at its greatest in male-dominated (thus incongruent with the female role) occupations. Guppy and Siltanen found that their 5.0 gender difference shrunk to 2.8 points when computed just for the "mixed sex occupations" (328). It was within the male-dominated occupations where raters considered a female incumbent to be deviant that the gap widened to 8.6 prestige points.

Once occupation ratings are conceived as related to the gender of the incumbent, a new slant on the issues being discussed in this chapter arises. With a gendered labour force, rather than assuming the prestige of occupations to be longitudinally static and highly consensual, one must theorize in a social-change framework that acknowledges how over the past quarter century, the occupational gender mix has shifted as rapidly as perhaps any of the important social indicators. With gender-specified occupational prestige so sharply reactive to the gender distribution within occupations, Fox and Suschnigg (1989, 358) concluded that "the failure of 'prestige' to capture the profound occupational disparities between men and women suggests that the concept should be removed from its central role in research on stratification." In a year 2000 replication of Guppy and Siltanen's 1975 fieldwork, it was both predicted and found that the additional prestige due to an occupation having a male rather than a female incumbent had disappeared (Goyder et al. 2003). So, paradoxically, social changes over the latter quarter of the twentieth century have helped restore the notion of occupations per se holding prestige.

Concurrently with Guppy and Siltanen, researchers in the United States were asking some of the same questions about gender and occupation. It did not seem to be noticed how deeply the assumption of consensus was being undercut when, for example, Bose and Rossi (1983, 318) wrote, "prestige scores cannot be utilized in any circumstance because the ratings vary with both the sex of the rater and the sex of the job incumbent." The researchers at the time were not reflecting backward to the 1960s consensus school but forward to how occupations should be scored in studies of gender inequality in the 1970s and 1980s (e.g., Powell and Jacobs 1984, 175). Occupational scales in which the premium educational qualifications of women were neutralized by their lower earnings relative to men, giving the appearance of equal scores for men and women, were an instance of "vacuous sex equality," in the often quoted words of Paula England (1979). It was not until the 1990s that the connection between the gender factor and the hypothesis of high consensus around prestige was explored more critically. Saltiel (1990) replicated the Kraus et al. (1978) procedure but used paired comparisons of occupations instead of the free sort into unnamed piles. This methodological variation, which Coxon and Jones had also exploited in some of their research, suggested a more complex dimensionality than Kraus et al. (1978) had detected while arguing for the primacy of the prestige dimension. Much of the meaning of secondary dimensions seemed to revolve around sex typing (Saltiel 1990, 293).

Commentaries on occupational prestige in the 1990s tended to show fatigue with the *Sturm und Drang* of consensus and dissensus, one dimension or many, and the meaning of prestige. Despite effort at measuring the evaluated prestige of a large and representative slice of the u.s. labour force by Nakao and Treas (1994), attention seemed to be shifting to the least ambiguously observed traits of occupations, such as education and earnings, or to selected "non-monetary characteristics of jobs" (Perman 1991). Wegener (1992, 254) noticed the drift in his commentary. As Hauser and Warren (1997, 251) concluded in an influential review article, "[w]e would do better – in studies of the stratification process – to index occupations by their educational level alone than by any of the usual, weighted combinations of educational level and earnings ... the global concept of occupational status is scientifically obsolete." It was an approach well suited to resolving the impasse England (1979) had noted around scoring the socioeconomic status of men and women, but to accept so objectivist a stance was a pragmatic rather than a conceptually informed solution. As Neil MacKinnon had observed with co-author Tom Langford in the mid-1990s (MacKinnon and Langford 1994), the data collected in occupational-prestige studies reflect *affect* as well as cognition. Were affect non-existent, one could agree that dissensus among raters results from mis-cognition (the error interpretation noted above). We would indeed proceed directly to the census tabulations on average educational preparation of job incumbents, ignoring the mistake-prone cognitions of human subjects. By placing their research within the well-established tradition of affect control theory (e.g., Heise 1979), MacKinnon and Langford (1994) could underline the position that many students of prestige scoring have intuited, from Counts onward: occupational identities have strong affective connotations, and within the *evaluation, potency, activity* (EPA) scheme from affect control theory, the strongest factor is potency, meaning potential for exercising power.

PRESTIGE AND SCALES OF OCCUPATIONAL SES

Prestige surveys have implications for the scales of occupational socioeconomic status that researchers use throughout the academic social sciences, market research, and policy analysis by governments. The Hauser and Warren (1997) piece just mentioned was exploring that connection. Prestige surveys did not originate from scaling considerations, as the earlier discussion on George Counts shows. Prestige did, however, become important to occupational scaling through the work of Otis Dudley Duncan, the eminent sociologist and demographer who co-authored *The American Occupational Structure* with Peter Blau (Blau and Duncan 1967). Before Duncan's work, occupations were classified into groups such as "professional," "managerial," "clerical and sales," "skilled labour," "semi-skilled," "unskilled," and "farm." In the United States, this approach was associated with Alba Edwards, working for the u.s. Census Bureau. Wegener (1992, 261) refers to the "Edwards paradigm" and gives some details on the Edwards (1938) scale for occupations. It was a common sense approach suitable for a pre-computer age, when statistical work was mainly cross-tabular, using sorting machines for IBM cards. The convergence of NORC prestige surveys with occupational scaling came within the field of social inequality dealing with occupational mobility. Research on status continuity over generations had been under way since the 1920s (Sorokin 1927), but Duncan combined new accessibility to mainframe computers with his ideas about statistical problems with mobility analysis, reorienting research into an approach that became known as "status attainment."

Attention shifted from the cross-tabulation of parent's and child's occupation in Edwards's groups to a regression analysis. I attempted a comparison of the mobility and attainment approaches in Goyder (1984). As Duncan noted in a foundational paper with Hodge (Duncan and Hodge 1963, 630), "[t]he regression approach requires one fundamental assumption ... that occupations can be assigned values on the scale of a quantitative variable." Prestige scores alone were insufficient for the task, for at the time Duncan was working with only a few dozen out of hundreds of names of occupations that had been rated in NORC samples. He ingeniously tapped into u.s. census data on all occupations by linking the average education and income of incumbents of occupations in the detailed census classification to prestige scores for forty-five occupations from the NORC list that he deemed close fits to census occupation titles (Duncan 1961). Predicting prestige from census education and income data for occupations was "[t]antamount to a prediction of the prestige rating they would receive if included in a survey" (Duncan and Hodge 1963, 631). The resulting "Duncan scale" of occupational SES has been used, modified, and updated ever since. Hauser and Warren (1997) discuss the evolution.

The notion of combining census data on education and income for occupations to construct a socioeconomic scale was in fact a Canadian innovation made before Duncan by Blishen (1958). Blishen (1967) then adopted Duncan's idea of linking the census data to prestige scores, using the newly published Pineo and Porter (1967) scale. The Blishen scale, like Duncan's, was periodically updated (Blishen and McRoberts 1976; Blishen et al. 1987). Today, prestige and occupational SES scales have become decoupled, and reasons why become clear later in this book. Canadian researchers early in the twenty-first century can choose an all-prestige concept for occupational scaling (Goyder and Frank 2007) or a no-prestige approach by Boyd (2008), which, with some tweaking, reverts to Blishen's original notion of assigning 50/50 weights to the educational preparation and income rewards of incumbents of occupations, summing the two into an index. Later in the book I shall return to how prestige can inform the census-based scales of occupational SES.

Various themes and emphases from over eighty years of research into occupational prestige have now been reviewed. I have not attempted to outline every single study on occupational prestige, but sources such as Blaikie (1977) and Wegener (1992) have good review discussions and bibliographies. The next section categorizes these into modules to support a research program on the relationship between social change and the prestige of occupations.

A RESEARCH AGENDA

We have seen how the shifting social-theory climate over the twentieth century prompted successive researchers to ask new questions of their data on occupational prestige and that these led to innovations in survey research design and statistical approaches. In reviewing the literature we become sensitized that there is no single statistic for defining whether occupational prestige is static or dynamic. A summary chart for the main perspectives examined, along with notes on analytical implications, appears in table 1.1.

Table 1.1
The Literature on Occupational Prestige, 1925–2005: Main Conceptual Perspectives and Analytical Implications

Perspective	*Implications*
Occupational prestige as a social problem: A prestige-obsessed society presents a dilemma for vocational guidance counsellors.	Examine mean score changes and distribution of scores changes (chapters 4 and 6).
Occupational prestige as a necessity: A steep, stable hierarchy is normal to, and necessary for, advanced industrial societies.	Compute correlations of scales between aggregates, across time. Examine change in prestige scores by change in occupational education and income information (chapters 4 and 7).
Occupational prestige as ambiguous and non-consensual: Attention to characteristics of raters.	Explore criteria for ratings. Treat the individual respondent as unit of analysis (chapters 3, 5, 6 and 7).

Initial work had Counts's *social problems* motif, serving vocational guidance purposes. The theoretical background, largely left unstated, concerned the psychic reward system for the white collar and professional occupations that were becoming a factor in the post-World War I labour force. Contrary to initial doubts about declining status for professions such as school teaching, Counts (1925, 27) found the main problem of the growing industrial society of the mid-1920s to be how, "in spite of what is said about the dignity of labor, many occupations which are clearly necessary to the promotion of the common good are stamped as unworthy and are thus given an essentially negative social standing." It was the flip side of the famous or notorious functional importance argument by Davis and Moore (1945), stressing the need to motivate people to undertake the most important and cognitively difficult occupations. The psychologist Jacob Tuckman (1947, 74), in the study from Montreal quoted earlier, caught the implications of the status-race for prestigious jobs noting the "frustration and job dissatisfaction" among those ill-equipped through native ability or family advantage to reach the top – an early expression of the anomie theme from Merton (1957). One of the analytic implications of this vocational guidance perspective is that the shape of the distribution for occupational-prestige hierarchies should receive renewed attention. Chapter 6 will show that in recent Canadian data the bottom end of the prestige distribution has squeezed into the middle.

From prestige inequality as a problem for vocational guidance, theory and research moved into the view that a stable hierarchy was a *necessity* in advanced industrial society. In the theoretical climate in the United States circa 1960, "the 'prestige dimension'" became, as Coxon and Davies (1986, 42) contended, "more a presupposition of such studies rather than an empirical finding." Treiman (1977) recognizes the Counts problem only on the second to last of his 234-page account of international consensus about the occupational-status ladder. John Porter in Canada, while not greatly a self-identified structural-functionalist (Marion Porter 1981, 629), echoed many of its assumptions in his work in the 1960s and early 1970s. Some indicators appear in the article with Peter Pineo (Pineo and Porter 1967, 31) and more explicitly in Porter's (1968: e.g., 11) *American Sociological Review* piece, in which he stressed the need for high occupational aspiration among youth in advanced industrial society. The definitive statistic for workers within this functionalist school was the correlation summarizing the congruency between mean scores for one group of survey respondents and another, one of my topics in chapter 7. These groups could equally represent different nation-states, regions within a country, city types, or any of the other socio-demographic variables of sociological interest.

Researchers encountering prestige research in the later 1970s and early 1980s were wearing the more conflict-sensitive theoretical lenses typical in sociology graduate departments by this period, and saw the prestige literature as *ambiguous and non-consensual*. The dissensus previously buried within standard deviation tabulations or occasional looks at specific occupation titles now seemed just as important as the evidence of consensus undeniably present in across-group or across-society comparisons of aggregate scores. A common theme across the British research stressed the need to parse the meaning of terms such as "prestige" and "social standing." A drive toward more innovative measurement of cognition and affect around occupation resulted. Canadian research emphasized the importance of the weak agreement found from one member of the public to another, vis-à-vis the prestige of occupations. Here, contrary to the "profile correlations" suggested by the inequality-as-necessary perspective, there was variation by the standard categories of social structure, such as education level, or by attitudinal factors as revealed by Stehr. The analytical weapons of choice from this prestige-as-ambiguous perspective are (1) innovations in survey design, as seen in the British research reviewed, and (2) redirection of attention from the aggregate to the individual as unit of analysis when computing correlations. Chapters 5 and part of 7 herein focus on the individual rater.

The occupational-prestige literature is varied and often at odds with itself, but is by no means in a state of chaos in which researchers of different theoretical perspectives cannot speak to one another. To assess the effect of social change on prestige scores, all three perspectives and implied analytical models for computation need to be examined. There is some inertia and stability, as scholars such as Treiman have rightly noted, and it is not helpful to the advancement of knowledge to key in on a few individual titles chosen *post hoc* and over-interpret their movement. We know already that scores will shuffle somewhat in any longitudinal data on prestige (Reiss 1961; Nakao and Treas 1994, table 3), and such change in scores must be evaluated in the context of overall change/stability. But equally, for a balanced interpretation, the traditional correlations in the "high 90s" so typical of reports on prestige data need re-appraisal. It was Coxon and Jones (1978, 38–9, 57) who argued that these "profile correlations" mislead because conceptually revealing prestige differences for small clusters of occupations are "swamped" by many titles capturing the agreement that skilled jobs are "better than unskilled jobs." Perhaps differences between the profile correlations are therefore sociological micrometer readings in which small variations have big meaning. As already noted above in the discussion on work by figures such as Hodge, Siegel, Rossi, and Treiman, there is some elasticity to prestige hierarchies even in the most conservative forms of computation. One pattern to look for is gradual but consistent downward drift in the congruency between the most current scale and earlier ones. Even if the erosion is just a point of correlation every seven or eight years (Hodge, Siegel, and Rossi 1966, 329), such a trend, if sustained over many years, would become meaningful.

The international dimensions of research on occupational prestige perhaps was apparent in my sketch of research since the Counts study of 1925. Canadian work, especially, is inextricably tied up with American, both empirically and conceptually. The mid-1940s study by the Canadian Jacob Tuckman took Counts's work in the United States as its reference point, and the important Pineo-Porter study of ratings of occupational prestige by a national sample of Canadians in 1965 was closely modelled on NORC's work between 1947 and 1964. The best pre-1960s data come from the United States, and in later pages herein receive some re-examination. The focus in the present work is therefore North American. Canada in 1965 had an occupational-prestige regime virtually identical to that of the United States. The following chapters will show that prestige in Canada has changed greatly in the meantime, and so it seems plausible that the same has happened in the United States. I hope the present work will stimulate American researchers to replicate the last prestige study south of the border, from 1989, and find out if I am right.

The next chapter offers a brief synopsis of social changes over the past three-quarters of a century in both Canada and the United States, drawing attention to the transition from industrial to post-industrial society. Chapter 3 describes the data sets employed, briefly noting details on the NORC surveys mentioned above, then proceeding to more extended description of two new Canadian surveys on occupational prestige. Chapters 4 to 7 compare changes between 1965 and 2005 along the three dimensions outlined in figure 1.1: chapter 4 is concerned with the changes in mean score for occupations rated in both 1965 and 2005; chapter 5 with the scores individual respondents in 1965 and 2005 gave occupations. Chapter 6 addresses occupational prestige as an inequality distribution. Consensus in prestige, both at the societal level and across individuals, is the topic of chapter 7. Interpretations of the recurrent theme of a prestige squeeze are developed in the concluding chapter 8.

A NOTE ON TERMINOLOGY

"Prestige" here will refer to the core concept being examined, "social standing" being a prestige synonym often used in survey questions. While it is colloquial to refer to high or low "status" or "social status," I shall usually avoid that usage because, sociologically, status has two meanings, one of position in the social structure and the second as another term for prestige (Jary and Jary 1991, 494). A cluster of other terms recur in the research literature on occupational prestige. "Esteem" for some researchers is simply another word for prestige. For example, "[t]he currency of moral worth is prestige, known synonymously as honor, regard, respect, standing, and esteem" (Treiman 1977, 20). A similar sentence appears in Laumann (1966, 3). A more nuanced usage, followed herein, is to specify prestige as referring to positions, esteem to the way a position is performed by an incumbent (Davis 1942, 312; Hatt 1950, 533). As Kingsley Davis says, "a person may hold a position of high prestige, and yet, by virtue of his [or her] ... behavior in that position, enjoy little esteem." In one of the foundational works of the occupational-prestige literature, Reiss (1961, 240) agreed that esteem refers to how the individual job-holder behaves. This usage has been accepted by several researchers working on occupational scaling (e.g., Blishen et al. 1987, 468). Another term, "deference," as Shils (1968, 105) specifies, is "closely related to such phenomena as prestige, honour, and respect." The difference between deference and prestige for Shils, in a usage I shall adopt, is that deference refers to an action, prestige to a thought. Possession of prestige entitles a person to acts of deference, as Lewis and Haller (1964, 26) have noted. "[S]upplicants give deference to those in positions which command it" (Hodge and Rossi 1978, B63). Part of the Goldthorpe and Hope (1974, 132) critique of prestige studies, outlined earlier in this chapter, was based on the contention that the ratings did not correspond to "social relations of deference."

2

Changing Society, Changing Prestige?

For over a century, observers have remarked on the increasing pace of social change in North America. The historian Arthur Schlesinger Sr (1922, chap. 11) saw acceleration from as far back as the close of the American Civil War. William Ogburn's (1966 [1922], xiii) early post-Great War writing referred to "the vast social changes which characterize our age." A sense of transformation was in the air following the war against Hitler, with an "other-directed" (Riesman 1953 [1950]) personality holding a new "social ethic" (Whyte 1957 [1956], 7) emerging in the United States. Bureaucracy had tightened its hold in the "managerial revolution" (Burnham 1941), in which a corporate "new industrial state" (Galbraith 1967) replaced the family entrepreneurships of earlier generations. Alvin Toffler's *Future Shock,* discussing the stresses on human beings in a period of hyper-change, appeared in 1970 and John Naisbitt's pop-soc *Megatrends* of 1982 has been followed by later editions and similar volumes by other authors (e.g., Celente 1997). Caplow (1991, 49) is among those who rightly remind the present-day reader that the whole twentieth century was an era of change, not just the 1980s and 1990s period of the computer chip.[1]

This chapter lays out expectations about change in occupational-prestige rating between the mid-1960s and the mid-2000s, drawing from the sociological repertoire of images of society in their shifting form as social change has unfolded. Several statistical time series for social indicators are given to document the extent of social transformations over the period of recent history spanned by research on occupational prestige. A running comparison between Canada and the United States is included most of the way, because the 2005 Canadian results have implications for prestige in Western societies in general. With the United States being the birthplace of occupational-prestige research, in the work dating back to Counts, I again note that it is the logical reference to compare Canadian society against. Rural-agricultural society is noted briefly. Even though largely vanished today, this would have been the formative experience for many mid-1960s survey respondents. Industrial society has been the dominant context for most research on occupational prestige, but the more recent post-industrial and information societies raise the issue of whether the stable prestige hierarchy of the 1960s can be expected to persist into the twenty-first century.

OFF-FARM MIGRATION: MARKING THE RISE OF INDUSTRIAL SOCIETY

Social trends can begin imperceptibly, but then gather momentum and dominate the sociological landscape as though they had always been present. Eventually, however, diffusion curves exhaust themselves and "top out" (Caplow 1991, 23). Then the once familiar phenomenon quietly disappears from notice and from statistical abstracts. Off-farm migration is one such late-phase trend that at one time captured much of the essence of Canadian and United States society. As of the early 1930s, it was "the most dramatic single movement" in occupations, according to the U.S. President's Research Committee on Social Trends (1933, 282). John Porter (1965, 140), in his Canadian sociological classic of the 1960s, termed the movement off farms the "loadstone" of population migration in the first half of the twentieth century. Blau and Duncan's (1967) *The American Occupational Structure*, one of the key quantitative sociological works of the 1960s, devoted a full chapter to farm background and occupational achievement. It was only with the 1995 edition that a long-standing table dividing the labour force into farm and non-farm was discontinued in the *Statistical Abstract of the United States*. In Canada, the Pineo-Porter study of occupational prestige in 1965 carried no fewer than seven agriculture-related titles. The 2005 study described in the next chapter had just four.

The decline of farming, and especially the small-holding owner-farmer, was a theme for Mills (1956 [1951], 16) in *White Collar*. In 1880, Mills noted, half the U.S. labour force was still in farming. As

Table 2.1
Percentage of Labour Force in Agriculture, Canada and the U.S., 1921–2000

Year	Canada	United States
1921 (Canada)/1920 (U.S.)	30.8	25.0
1931/1930	28.5	21.2
1941/1940	23.5	17.0
1951/1950	14.6	12.2
1961/1960	9.2	8.3
1971/1970	7.9	4.4
1981/1980	4.4	3.4
1991/1990	3.6	2.7
2001/2000	2.2	0.8

Sources: Canada: Kubat and Thornton (1974, table J3), with additions and re-arrangements; Statistics Canada Cat. 71–201-XPB (historical statistics), and *Canada Year Book* for 1997 and 2007. U.S.: *Historical Statistics of the U.S.* (Washington: Department of Commerce 1975), table D1–10; United States Bureau of the Census, *Statistical Abstract of the U.S.* (Washington, DC), various years.
Definitions: U.S.: Civilian employed labor force, aged 14 and over, up to and including 1940, then age 16 and over. Canada: Civilian employed labor force aged 15 and over.

of 1910, the number began to decrease absolutely as well as relatively, as a proportion of the U.S. labour force (President's Research Committee on Social Trends 1933, 283). By the 1920 U.S. census, the point where the time series presented in table 2.1 begins, the expansion of urban-based work already had momentum. Only 25 percent of the workforce remained in farming. In the world of occupations in the United States that Counts set out to examine in 1925, the complexity of the division of labour was in a phase of rapid increase, and substitution for farming was a driving force. Steadily with each passing decade, the agricultural component of the workforce eroded, so that by the beginning of the 1970s in the United States and the beginning of the 1980s in Canada, the percentages had dipped below 5 percent. Even within the 1947–63 period examined in the early NORC research, farming dipped below the 10 percent mark in the U.S. labour force.

If issues of skill and the technological content of jobs were set constant and a pure competition market imagined, declining sectors of the labour market ought to lose prestige; lesser labour force demand would signify lesser importance for the function. Farming carried the nineteenth-century economies of Canada and the United States much as the technology sector does today and the title "farmer" ranked quite high in the Counts data, sixteenth of forty-five occupations. As the importance of agriculture for GNP slipped and as migration out of the farm sector accelerated, the prestige of those remaining on the land might have suffered. Applying ideas from Merton's (1957, 236–41) theory of reference groups, expectations damaging for those who remained on the farm might have been created by the intense out-migration, in the same way that in research noted by Merton, morale was low in military units having high rates of promotion. This could hold even though the occupational mobility taking place among sons of farmers was in reality more lateral in socioeconomic status than upward, more into the unskilled manual sector than into the skilled white collar (Blau and Duncan 1967, 62, 259, 285). As late as NORC's 1947 data, perhaps reflecting a lag back to the time when farming was a more central feature of the U.S. economy, farming had higher prestige than would have been expected from a prediction based on education and income of practitioners (Blau and Duncan 1967, 286). In the United States, perhaps not so much in Canada, farming has enjoyed a privileged position, representing, so some historians say, the Jeffersonian ideal of what the American republic was all about; a nation of small farmers, politically aware and vigilant in the protection of democracy. As a frequently quoted passage from Jefferson reads, "those who labour in the earth are the chosen people of God" (Yarbrough 1998, 56). In chapter 4 we can further track the prestige of farming over the second half of the twentieth century and into the twenty-first.

THE HIGH NOON OF INDUSTRIAL SOCIETY

At mid-twentieth century, the amount of energy consumed per capita gave a useful index of industrialization. Treiman (1977, 133) used this indicator in his analysis of occupational prestige scores. Energy of all types could easily be converted into a common unit such as kilograms of coal equivalent. Where indicators such as education could be hard to norm across societies, energy consumption was well adapted to cross-national comparisons, such as one by Hazelrigg and Garnier (1976), linking rate of per capita consumption of energy with rate of intergenerational mobility across occupations.

Energy consumption at mid-century and through the 1960s clearly articulated the extent to which Canada lagged behind the United States in the transition toward full industrialization. Pineo

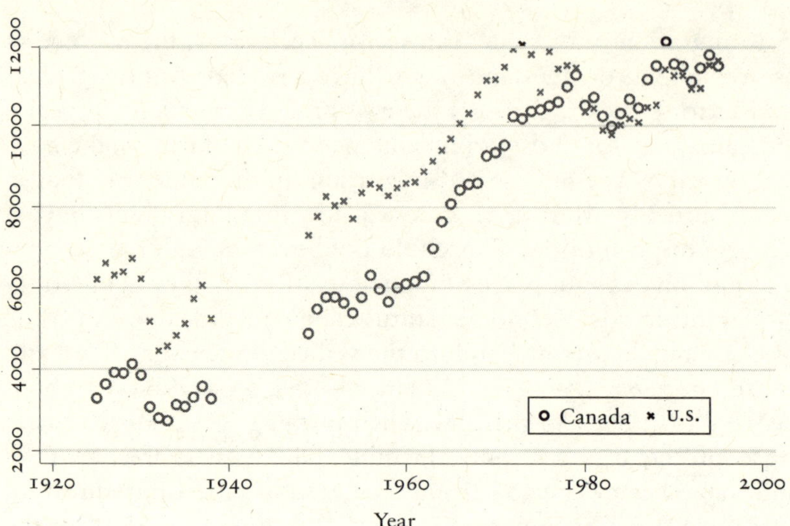

Year

Fig. 2.1   Energy consumption per capita, Canada and the U.S., 1925–1999. *Sources*: Darmstadter (1971, 653); personal communication from Resources for the Future, Inc. (Joel Darmstadter); Schurr and Netschert (1960, 524–5); *Canada Year Book*, 2000, and other years; *Statistical Abstract of the United States*, 1969, and other years. For consistency, all sources are spliced to the Darmstadter time series, using linking adjustments

and Porter (1967, 31) reasoned out possible consequences for occupational-prestige ratings in the two societies. As the graph in figure 2.1 documents, Canada before the 1940s had only about half the per capita energy consumption of the United States, but by the end of the 1970s near parity had occurred. Thus by the time national-level comparisons of occupational-prestige in the two countries were available (i.e., NORC's 1964 U.S. study and Pineo and Porter's 1965 work in Canada), the two societies had narrowed in terms of economic development. The war effort against Hitler had stimulated Canada's growth as an industrial society and helped produce some of the sameness with the United States chronicled in the famous lament by George Grant (1965).

By the mid-1970s, the meaning behind energy consumption as an economic indicator was changing, in part owing to the oil supply crisis of 1973. As of the early 1980s, the graphs for energy consumption and gross domestic product, previously close overlays of one another, were diverging.[2] Some of the most productive part of the industrial economy was becoming more energy-efficient (Meyers and Schipper 1992, 469), and well under way was the transition into a new kind of economy in which the sheer quantity of energy played a lesser role. As with decline in the farm sector, the period of sharp rise in per capita energy consumption in Canada and the United States captured a trend that by century's end was exhausted. The prestige of workers in the smokestack industries should have been peaking at the time the 1960s set of NORC prestige studies were in the field. Kerr et al. (1964, 17), in one of the most-noted of 1960s interpretations of industrial society, commented that the Marxian prediction of eroding skill levels as industrialization proceeded had not happened. Instead, "[i]ndustrialism in fact develops and depends upon a concentrated, disciplined industrial work force – a work force with new skills and a wide variety of skills, with high skill levels and constantly changing skill requirements." Thus "[t]he absence of a highly qualified labor force" was a more serious "impediment" than de-skilling. Even if Kerr et al. were wrong (and Braverman 1974, right), such that industrialization did on balance precipitate skill loss from the pre-industrial trades,[3] 1965 was not greatly distant from the essentially pre-industrial Canada pre- the 1914 war. A thirty-five-year-old in 1965, thus born in 1930, might have had parents born around the turn of the century. Even in Europe, where industrialization came sooner than in Canada, early sociological writers such as Durkheim and Weber were bearing witness to the recent transition from agrarian and small-scale craft to mass production (perhaps de-skilled) industrial society (e.g., Durkheim 1964 [1893], 39). Russia, for example, did not have "first-generation proletarians" until around 1917 (Brzezinski and Huntington 1965, 28). Late in the first decade of the twenty-first century, it is nearly two more generations removed from first-hand memories of pre-industrial society. If prestige is part of the culture that lags behind material changes, craft occupations circa 1965 may still have been carrying some halo from an earlier, greater prestige-entitling, era.

The post-World War Two convergence between Canadian and American energy consumption was the kind of pattern noted during the high noon of industrial society in support of the general convergence theory of industrial society. In arguing that industrialization carries a logic that pushes cultures toward a common form, convergence theory was compatible with Cold War needs. It was reassuring to believe that tensions between the divergent political systems in the United States and the USSR might with time abate owing to the similar force of industrialization in each society. Convergence owing to industrialization was the engine believed partly responsible for the longitudinal stability attributed to prestige ratings by 1960s researchers (Feldman and Moore 1962, 165; Treiman 1977, 133).

Best to pull back, however, for two reasons, from too tight a reliance on an industrial-society theory of occupational prestige. First, Treiman (1977, 12, 23, etc.) stipulated that the pattern of longitudinal and cross-national invariance traced back to *complex* society not just *industrial* society. Haller and Lewis (1966) had said the same thing, even though their commentary was critical of the Treiman constant argument. Uniformity in prestige ratings, from both authors, came not from a cultural homogeneity arising from the deployment of science and technology in service of industrialization (Ellul 1967), but more specifically from the division of labour arising as soon as a society moved from a tribal or totally agrarian state toward greater differentiation. Secondly, a look back at the convergence literature recalls that scholars at the time keenly debated the extent to which the convergence argument held (cf. Feldman and Moore 1962; Moore 1963; Brzezinski and Huntington 1965; Aron 1967). Moore (1963, 111–12) perhaps was representative in noting that industrialism was not "a stable destination"; rather, all societies were changing all the time. Kerr et al. (1964), whose book readers tend nowadays to depict as the quintessential document arguing convergence, throughout emphasized the differential social forms of industrial society arising from which kind of "industrializing elite" drove the transformation out of agrarian society. To be sure, they also recurrently noted convergence themes such as "universals" of industrialism (15), the decline of "cultural and national differences" (25), "the new culture" (44), and the "culture of industrialization" (78 and 88). But even so, a reread of *Industrialism and Industrial Man* moves thinking about occupational prestige and industrialization somewhat away from the resolutely structural-functionalist interpretation reviewed in chapter 1 (discussion on Hodge, Siegel, and Rossi 1966). Structural-functionalism "never pretended" to be a theory of social change and therefore when applied to interpreting occupational-prestige data was predisposed to hypotheses about stability in the scores. Writers such as Moore (1963) and Kerr et al. (1964), in contrast, were examining social change, dissecting the transition from agrarian to industrial society. As stressed as far back as Weber

(1958 [1904]), the coming of industrial society was not automatic. Pre-industrial values needed to be shifted and elites needed to emerge to drive on the process, sometimes over resistance (Kerr et al. 1964, 66). Principalities had to meld into nation-states (76) in order to "conquer the old and create the new culture" (44). This part of the literature on industrial society is stressing the *revolution* in Industrial Revolution (43). It is from such sources that any 1960s-era predictions of shift in prestige scales must derive.

Even with the interpretations of industrial society seen in a source such as Hodge, Siegel, and Rossi (1966) or Treiman (1977), contrasted with others just examined, synthesis can be made that helps show how researchers in the 1960s viewed occupational prestige. Thus Kerr et al. (1964, 50–1) stressed that industrialization driven by a middle class was distinctive among four other types. An industrial revolution orchestrated by the middle class relies "on markets and elected governments to determine the pace of industrialization" and "the principal means of motivating the labor force is resort to monetary incentives and to individualistic ethical values." A culture of "discipline" holds around work and occupation (all from 104), making a "committed" (145) workforce. That image of individuals making work decisions within a labour market resonates clearly with the structural-functionalist notion of workers "induced" and "motivated" (Davis and Moore 1945, 242) through the "unconsciously evolved device" (243) of differential rewards whereby high consensus is reached about the prestige of each occupation.

POST-INDUSTRIAL SOCIETY

The realization that a stage beyond industrial society, a "post-industrial society," was dawning following the end of World War Two can be detected as far back as Feldman and Moore's (1962) examination of convergence theory. Caplow and Mendras (1994, 7), in retrospect from the 1990s, saw signs of deindustrialization as early as 1965, the date of Pineo and Porter's (1967) study of Canadian occupational prestige. Early in the 1970s two books appeared making explicit reference in their titles to this term "post-industrial society." Alain Touraine's (1971) study addressed the class status of the new generation of highly educated "technocrats," while Daniel Bell's (1973) *The Coming of Post-Industrial Society* dealt more with the centrality of theoretical knowledge as the source of

Table 2.2
Count of People Enrolled in Colleges or Universities per 1,000 Population, Canada and
the U.S., 1920–21 to 1999–2000

Year	Canada	U.S.
1920–21	2.6	5.6
1930–31	3.2	8.9
1940–41	3.2	11.3
1950–51	4.9	17.5
1960–61	6.4	17.8
1970–71	21.6	41.8
1980–81	35.9	53.1
1990–91	41.9	55.3
1999–2000, Canada; 2000–1 U.S.	51.3	54.2

Sources: *Canada Yearbook*, 1999, tables 3.2 and 5.13, and equivalent tables for other years; for 1999, *Education Quarterly Review*, 2003, volume 9, number 3, 27–8; *Statistical Abstract of the United States*, 1999, table 253 and equivalents for other years.

innovation and policy formation. Either way, the shift was "technetronic," Brzezinski's (1970) phrase. Both Touraine and Bell were reacting to the rising importance of formal education in the economy and workforce. As energy consumption began changing from an indicator of economic vitality into a test for ecological wastefulness, the human capital increments resulting from education became a crucial index of progress.[4] Table 2.2 takes the number of people enrolled in college or university at the beginning of each decade since 1920 per 1,000 population in Canada and the United States. The massive increase of post-secondary enrolment between 1960 and 1970, the post-Sputnik decade in which Kennedy committed the United States to land a person on the moon by 1969, is clear in the figures for both countries. An echo of the convergence theme seen in energy data reappears with the education figures. Earlier in the twentieth century, one of the clearest distinctions between the two societies north and south of the forty-ninth parallel was the higher level of formal education in the United States. The size of the margin drew frequent comment within Canadian sociology (e.g., Porter 1987 [1979], 191). As table 2.2 shows, however, the two societies began closing with respect to education after 1970. In the 1970–71 academic year, Canada's count of students enrolled in college or university was only just over half of America's; by 1999-2000 the Canadian rate had reached some 95 percent of the U.S. figure. As other commentaries have noticed, in the

United States "[e]ducational progress ... virtually ceased in the early 1970s" (Caplow 1991, 123).

Admittedly, the increment in human capital may not be quite so impressive as the early post-World War II education figures suggest, for, along with criticism of the erosion of academic standards, a lament that continues to this day, the 1960s were times of growing alternative opportunities to the traditional full-time, unbroken three- or four-year stint in university by a young man or woman typically in or near the eighteen to twenty-one age range. Various options, such as junior colleges in the United States and community colleges in Canada, were expanding. Some of these programs allowed for university transfer and others not. Post-secondary education on a part-time basis, often involving "mature students" in their later twenties or beyond, was no longer abnormal. The compilers of the *Canada Year Book* of 1969 did not find it necessary to tabulate post-secondary enrolments by full- versus part-time (Dominion Bureau of Statistics 1969). A later edition remarks that it was in "the early 1970s" that "[p]art-time students began to increase more rapidly than those registered for full-time study" (Statistics Canada 1985, 130). The matter of over-credentialing need not be resolved here, but no matter whether one takes a disparaging view or not of higher education in the 1960s, mean education levels in the population were moving up fast, with post-secondary qualifications of some sort replacing high school graduation as the norm. If the prestige of education-intensive science and technology-related occupations increased during the decade of the race to the moon, the trend might be captured for the period bounded by the 1947 and 1989 NORC studies.

One of the most important features of post-industrial society was the maturing of a long-standing trend toward women's involvement in the paid labour force. In both countries, it was not until between 1975 and 1980 that participation by women in the workforce exceeded 50 percent (table 2.3). Again, convergence occurred between Britain's two former colonies in North America, the formerly lower Canadian percentage of working women drawing level to the U.S. rate by the mid-1970s.

Trends in the sex segregation of occupations appear in table 2.4, using the index of dissimilarity (IOD), the statistic often seen in this research. Even though alternative and perhaps better indexes exist (Blackburn et al. 2000, 120), the IOD has been used so often that a

Table 2.3
Labour Force Participation Rates for Women, Canada and the U.S., 1950–2000
Percentages

Year	Canada	United States
1951 (Canada)/1950 (U.S.)	23.8	33.9
1956/1955	24.9	35.7
1961/1960	28.7	37.8
1966/1965	32.8	39.3
1971/1970	39.9	43.4
1976/1975	45.6	46.3
1981/1980	52.3	51.5
1986/1985	55.8	54.5
1991/1990	58.5	57.5
1996/1995	57.6	58.9
2001/2000	59.7	59.8

Sources: *Canada Year Book* 2000, 237, and 2007, 330; *Statistical Abstract of the United States*, 1969, table 307 and equivalents from later years.

Table 2.4
Occupational Sex Segregation in Canada and the U.S., 1900–80s

	Change in Index of Dissimilarity per Ten Years	
Interval	Canada	United States
1900–50		0.5
1931–41	0.4	
1941–51	–1.3	
1950s		1.2
1951–61	–0.8	
1960s		–2.7
1961–71	–5.3	
1970s		–7.9
1971–81	–6.3	
1980s		–4.6

Sources: Canada, Fox and Fox (1987, 384); United States, 1900–50, from Jacobs (1989, 168), for other decades, medians computed from Cotter et al. (1995, 5–6, 13).

rich historical legacy of data on occupational sex segregation has accumulated. The authors of sources consulted in compiling the table note how gender distributions are difficult to compare over time owing to evolution in the classification of occupations. The classificatory issues in turn arise partly from the decline of some occupations and the creation of new ones. The Canadian data by Fox and Fox (1987) compared sets of titles matching at the beginning and end of each census decade. In the United States, the consequences of coding older censuses such as that for 1900 into later occupation classifications (e.g., Jacobs 1989) have been explored, and multiple estimates exist for each decade between 1950 and 1990. The u.s. column in table 2.4 therefore reports the median change in the index of dissimilarity over several studies from each decade. After decades of little change in the occupational distributions of men and women, a more dramatic pattern began after about 1960. Trends for the two countries agree in detecting continuing convergence in sex segregation of occupation structures. For occupational prestige, this means considerable churning in the gender proportions within occupations between the 1960s and 2005. I examine the implications of gender composition of occupations for prestige scores in chapter 4, considering whether the more feminized an occupation became, 1965 to 2005, the greater the prestige loss.

Growing ambiguity around social class is part of the story of post-industrial society, this first stage beyond industrial society. Trend data capturing all the importance of social class are difficult to compile because of the complexity and multiple meanings of the concept. Nevertheless, a number of voices over the years have come together in detecting long-term shifts. Even at mid-century, observers such as Robert Nisbet (1959) had sensed a growing fuzziness to class differentiation and later Aronowitz (1992, 8) described the "displacement" of class by other bases for identification. It was during the 1950s that research attention to status "inconsistency" or "crystallization" became intensive (e.g., Lenski 1954, 1956), referring to statuses out of line with each other, thus lessening the clarity of class lines. In the Middletown III investigation of an American community, Caplow et al. (1982, 15) found that in terms of lifestyle "most of the differences that the Lynds observed between business-class families and working-class families half a century ago have by now been eroded away." Higher education ceased to be so exclusively the privilege of sons and daughters of the business owners, and new fortunes were made to dilute the influence of the old local industrial elite. Lifestyle markers such as the employing of domestic servants died out for all but the very richest families. "Lifestyles were becoming more homogeneous" (Caplow et al. 1982, 13), as well, in terms of working-class home ownership and access to labour-saving consumer goods. Admittedly, research into occupational mobility has been equivocal as to whether rates increased or not during the late twentieth century. By some definitions, intergenerational mobility increased both in Canada (Boyd et al. 1985, ch. 5; Wanner 2005, 459) and the United States (Featherman and Hauser 1978, ch. 3). As a net rather than occupational structure-derived trend, however, evidence of change is less distinct (Featherman and Hauser 1978, ch. 4).

Some insight into class as an in-the-mind phenomenon comes from the social-class identification question posed many times in surveys beginning in the 1930s and developed in the work of Richard Centers (1961 [1949], 76), who re-framed an earlier middle class-biassed question to read, "If you were asked to use one of these four names for your social class, which would you say you belonged in: the middle class, lower class, working class or upper class?" Table 2.5 assembles a time series of correlations between this "Centers question," asked of men and women in national samples, and occupation. Occupational status is coded into seven major groups, for household main earners in the earlier surveys and for respondents from 1984 on. Several of the later surveys for the United States used a substantially altered wording involving a filter question to cue the respondent: "There's been some talk these days about different social classes," the preamble for this version developed for election studies at the University of Michigan Survey Research Centre (SRC) begins. "Most people say they belong either to the middle class or the working class. Do you ever think of yourself as belonging in one of these classes?" Since two studies for the United States in the year 1964, by NORC and by the University of Michigan Survey Research Centre, carried the Centers and SRC variants respectively, giving r = .36 and .43, one can step down the SRC-version results later in the table by the factor .36/.43, and this has been applied to several of the estimates in table 2.5, as the notes to the table explain. The question for the U.S. figure for 1997 is more leading than the original Centers format and probably should be adjusted down by a few points, although the exact amount needed for the correction is unknown. The Canadian surveys in the series essentially follow the Centers wording, although in both countries the label "upper middle class" enters question designs beginning in the 1960s.

In this time series, something about class indeed has declined, but exactly what does this correlation between occupation, the "objective" component, with class identification from the "subjective" domain, mean? For Jackman and Jackman (1983, 70) it reflected

Table 2.5
Pearsonian Correlations between Self-Identified Social Class and Occupational Group,
Canada and the U.S., 1945–97

Year	Canada	United States
1945		.52
1946		.50
1947/48		.47
1949		.37
1950		.40
1952		.39
1956		.36[a]
1960		.35[a]
1964		.36
1965	.38	
1968		.34[a]
1969		.33
1974	.35	
1975		.34
1984	.33/.35[b]	.27/.25[a,b]
1997		[.31[b]][c]

Source: Goyder (1975, 104) for U.S. results up to 1969; U.S. 1975 computed from Jackman and
Jackman (1983) table 4.1. Other results computed from micro data sets available through the
Tri-Universities Data Resource run by the University of Guelph, University of Waterloo, and
Wilfrid Laurier University. Several of the U.S. sets originate from the Inter-University Consortium
for Political and Social Research.

Note: The 1952 correlation has been stepped up by one point to compensate for cruder coding of
occupation than in other studies.

[a] These samples used the University of Michigan SRC wording. Correlations have been adjusted by a
factor of 36/43.

[b] Respondent's, rather than main earner's or "head's" occupation group.

[c] From World Values Survey, with non-standard class identification question reading: "People
sometimes describe themselves as belonging to the working class, the middle class, or the upper or
lower class. Would you describe yourself as belonging to the ..."

"how people convert their own experience into an identification
with a social class," but we have here a far from error-free measure
of class consciousness (from the size of correlation) or false consciousness (from unexplained variance left behind by the correlation). Even in the most Weberian conception of social class, no-one
would claim that occupational group translates one-to-one into an
"objective" class position that can then be collated against "class
awareness" (Morris and Murphy 1966, box 3), the "ability to place
self and others." While the measurement error and conceptual
ambiguities around class identification may be too great to allow
access to even a low grade of class consciousness, the correlations
do indicate a revealing aspect of class crystallization, the above-

mentioned concept from Lenski (1954), referring to the congruency between dimensions of social inequality.

These changes in how social class is perceived for self may help inform people's prestige ratings of their own occupation or the cluster of occupations to which theirs belongs. When a later chapter demonstrates a decline in the consensus around ratings of the respondent's own occupational prestige, one articulation of a general separation of self from the stratification system is, I think, being encountered.

THE INFORMATION SOCIETY

The 1970s became the 1980s. The meaning of post-industrial society was debated and new descriptors such as "information society" were coined (e.g., Lyon 1986) to help capture the continuing flow of social changes. Kumar (1995, 3) saw this information emphasis as just one of several conceptualizations of society beyond the post-industrial stage. Indeed, he reserved the "information" moniker for the most optimistic, technology-cheerleading side of turn of twentieth-to-twenty-first-century society. For along with such information society themes as computers eroding older workplace hierarchies, blurring the distinction between manufacturing and service and moving emphasis from the skill of jobs to the skill of workers (Kumar 1995, 3–25), the new society – whatever it was best to be called, Giddens (1991) suggested "late modern" – brought a complex basket of traits. There was a "post-Fordist" aspect, referring to the proliferation of small-scale, high-technology, "flexible" manufacturing with complex subcontracting networks. This same small-scale manufacturing was also a theme in Toffler's *Third Wave* from 1980, but for post-Fordists the changes were not necessarily one hundred percent beneficial for workers. Economic globalization, the notion given wide exposure in Friedman's (2005) *The World is Flat*, with connotations of frantic corporate competition and shifting of jobs to the cheapest labour markets, was part of the post-Fordist story. Societies of the Western world had also become *postmodern*, that familiar social science phrase, by around the year 2000. For Kumar (1995), this was yet another conceptualization of post-post-industrial society, this one bringing out the ideological fragmentation, the cultural pluralism, and the ethos of individualism in late-twentieth-century life within the developed world.

Table 2.6
The Service Sector as a Percentage of the Labour Force, Canada and the U.S., 1960–61
to 2000–1

Year	Canada	U.S.
1961 (Canada)/1960 (U.S.)	54.3	58.1
1966/1965	56.9	60.5
1971/1970	62.0	63.3
1976/1975	64.4	65.3
1981/1980	66.3	65.9
1986/1985	69.9	68.8
1991/1990	72.4	70.9
1996/1995	74.1	73.1
2001/2000	74.7	[a]
2005	75.3	[a]

Sources: *Labour Force Statistics 1959–1970* (Paris: OECD 1961) and later versions of the same
publication. Figures are for civilian employment.

[a] For these years, the needed data for the U.S. were not reported in the OECD labour force statistics,
and their standardization of definitions is needed for the comparison.

Yet another adjective designed to specify the meaning of "information society" was "new economy," a term (see chapter 1) originating from the United States in the 1990s, prior to the technology stock crash at decade's end. "New economy" drew attention to the surge of prosperity with low inflation seeming (until the tech-stock implosion of 2000 and general recession of 2009) to result from information technology and to the new service sector class of highly paid, highly skilled "symbolic analysts" (Reich 1991). Schumacher (1973, 125), of *Small Is Beautiful* fame, suggested that these analysts would enjoy high prestige: "The prestige carried by people ... varies in inverse proportion to their closeness to actual production." While only about 10 percent of the workforce of a modern economy falls within the service sector in the most literal sense of domestic employees and workers in food, accommodation, retail trade, and recreation, over 70 percent is service when the sector is defined to encompass handlers of information (Goyder 2005a, 122). Figures using this latter broad understanding of the service economy are assembled yearly by the OECD, and the Canadian and U.S. time series beginning with 1960–61 appears in table 2.6. In Canada, the service sector crested the 50 percent mark between the 1956 and 1961 censuses. The U.S. figures were about four percentage points higher at that time, but the two societies had converged by 1980. Canada's Social Sciences and Humanities Research

Council (SSHRC) took up the new economy as an important topic of study with the announcement of an Initiative on the New Economy "to help Canada and Canadians adapt successfully to and benefit from the new economy."[5] It was unclear to some, such as Heather Menzies (1996), that the new economy was destined to be a success and benefit to all Canadians. The fall 2008 world banking crisis and stock market crash revealed vulnerabilities in the new economy not realized earlier in the 2000s. I shall return to the paradox of heightened inequality in the new economy/information society in chapter 8.

Another aspect of the late-twentieth-century social changes of at least ambiguous desirability was that life became less structured and predictable, more anomic. Mention of that theme traces back to the final stage of industrial society. In the late 1960s work *Collective Search for Identity*, Klapp (1969, 329) argued that "identity problems emerge as a common man's problem in advanced technological societies." The passage is prophetic in light of the complexities in the present day of multiple and fictitious social identities tied up with the Internet. R.H. Turner (1976) described late-twentieth-century life as an especially ambiguous existence in which the "real self" shifted from "institution to impulse." Snow and Phillips (1982, 473), too, talked of a growing "impulse orientation." The modern self has been termed "improvised" (McCall and Simmons 1982, 38) and "processual" (Burke 1991, 847); "saturated" (Gergen 1991) and "displaced" (Aronowitz 1992, 8). Giddens (1991, 169) chose the adjectives "frail, brittle, fractured, fragmented" when describing "the self in modern society." In the language of family systems theory, the modern self may be less "differentiated" than it once was (Kerr 1988, 41–47).

An economist interested in long swings in the business cycle has ventured similar speculations: Gerhard Mensch (1979, 88) contended in the 1970s that the Western world was nearing the closing stages of a down cycle and suggested that stagnation brings a form of "identity crisis" with "feelings of depression and victimization" (90) and an "alienation" that "increases sharply" (Mensch 1979, 92). More than once, Mensch mentions the "impulse personality" (90, 91) found in such anomic times. "The group behavior and market behavior of impulse personalities," he wrote, "are determined, on the one hand, by the barrage of stagnations and, on the other hand, by the onslaught of innovations that face them." The linkage between the business cycle and changing forms of identity is, as one colleague rightly warned me, "sheer speculation." The business cycle argument is not essential to the analysis of prestige scores, but the possible shifts in identity formation are relevant. It interests me that Mensch reached his conclusion about impulse personality seemingly without knowledge of the sociological literature on identity formation by writers such as R.H. Turner. The only social-identity source cited by Mensch (91) is an Eric Erikson work written in German and predating everything else cited in this paragraph.

One tap into some of these notions comes from applying the well-known Twenty Statements Test, or TST, an open-ended instrument for measuring identity that has been fielded for over fifty years now. A researcher applying the TST asks a group of subjects, often students, simply to write twenty statements answering the question "who am I?" or, in a slight variation, to write twenty statements beginning, "I am ..." Exactly what one learns from a TST is controversial among social psychologists (Wylie 1974, 242; Burke and Tully 1977, 882), in part because the instrument is completely dependent on the researcher's coding of the open-ended entries. Perhaps the most valuable aspect of TST research is the long historical record of data that has permitted certain trends to appear.

TST data often are coded by classifying each of the twenty statements into some scheme such as consensual vs. nonconsensual, the code developed by Manford Kuhn, a pioneer in the technique. "Consensual," for Kuhn (Kuhn and McPartland 1954), referred to statements such as "I am nineteen years old" or "I am a woman." They are verifiable, matters of record, rather than nonconsensual claims such as "I am lonely" or "I am sad." McPartland et al. (1961) later developed a more detailed version of Kuhn's code, differentiating modes A, B, C, and D, referring, respectively, to factual statements about self as a physical entity (e.g., "I weigh 150 pounds"), institutionalized statuses or roles (e.g., "I am a student"), ways of acting, feeling, or responding in social interaction (e.g., "I worry too much"), and existential statements such as "I am me." A and B are essentially sub-categories of Kuhn's consensual code, C and D forms of nonconsensual statement in Kuhn's scheme.

The structure of typical replies on a TST has shifted rather markedly over the years since mid-twentieth century. Table 2.7 assembles some of the well-known studies in this research, together with two

Table 2.7
The Structure of Responses to the Twenty-Statements Test, Canada and the U.S.,
Students in Introductory Sociology Courses, 1952–2002

Year	Place and Population	Cases	Number of "Consensual" Statements	Percentage A, B, or D Mode
1952	University of Iowa	151	10.8	
	(with additional cases)	151 + 137 = 288	9.5	
1957	A large midwestern university	1,653		69.0
1969	University of Texas at Austin	400		32.0
1969	Memorial University of Newfoundland	56	5.7	
1975–79	A southwestern university	1,125		31.6
1981	A midwestern university	484		12.0
1988	A university in rural north-western Pennsylvania	333		14.8
1993	University of Waterloo	231	4.9	
2002	University of Waterloo	104	5.6	22.1

Sources: 1952, Kuhn and McPartland (1954, 71 and 74); 1969 (NFLD), Hayes (1970); 1957 and 1969 (Texas), Zurcher (1977, 49); 1957 and 1975–79, Snow and Phillips (1982, 465–8); 1981, Roscoe and Peterson (1983); 1988, Babbitt and Burbach (1990, 474–7); 1993 and 2002, computed from data collected by author.

results of my own. For consistency, only samples of students in introductory sociology courses are included in the table, although the literature contains further supporting examples, such as the mean of 8.7 consensual statements from Schwiran's (1964, 53) sample of high school students circa 1962. The movement has been away from consensual or more specifically social, role-based B mode replies to the nonconsensual and especially C mode. Some of the studies gathered in table 2.7 were coded in the consensual/nonconsensual dichotomy and some in the fourfold A to D code, and the final one from 2002 in both. With either coding system the pattern away from consensual identities and toward the C mode is clear. The trend gives additional force to the persisting strength of occupational identity – a consensual or B mode identity – noted at the outset of chapter 1. The general trend away from B mode has been recognized since the early 1970s (Zurcher 1972; Spitzer and Parker 1976, 236) and is echoed in more recent research (Snow and Phillips 1982; Babbitt and Burbach 1990). The only reinterpretation called for from the 2002 data collection is that the trend now seems to have reached bottom, bouncing back, in fact, to the level

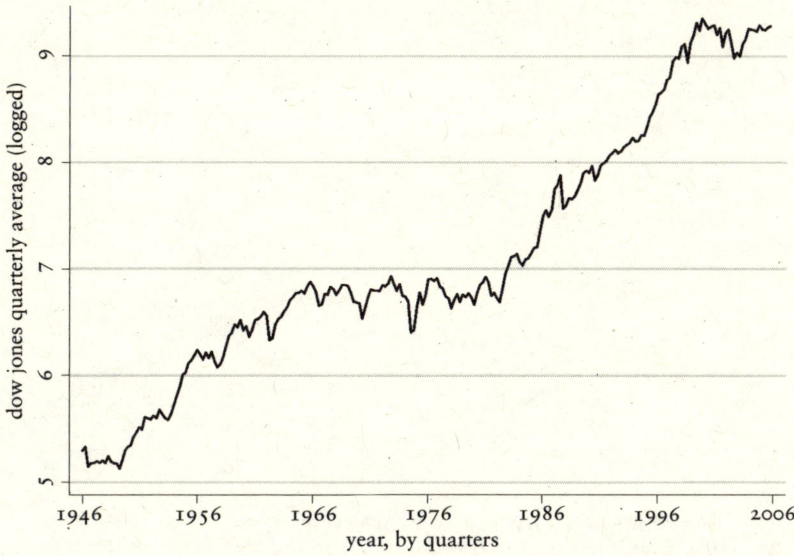

Fig. 2.2   Dow Jones Average (logged) for quarters from 1946 to 2005. *Source*: Data downloaded from www.dowjones.com

of a generation ago, although not of two generations ago (i.e., the 1950s). As noted, the trend has been linked to the economic cycle, which will now be examined briefly before inferring some suggestions about longitudinal patterns regarding consensus in the rating of occupational prestige.

Commenary on the TST by Snow and Phillips (1982, 471–4) emphasized the business cycle, the same factor noted by Mensch, discussed above. Citing the "highly unpredictable economy" of the 1970s, with "double digit inflation and, almost usurious interest rates, and an increasingly constricted labor market," Snow and Phillips (1982, 473) suggested that the "dominant institutions," most notably higher education, did not provide an attractive basis for identification for university students, leaving them to "take refuge in the self" as defined by the "impulse orientation." The stock market trend is examined in figure 2.2. The period of stagnation referred to by Mensch and by Snow-Phillips occurred from 1971 to 1979. After 1980, the market resumed mainly upward progress although the "technology crash" of 1999 and the perturbation from September 11th 2001 are easily visible. Putting the TST data together with the Dow Jones averages, the slight return to the more

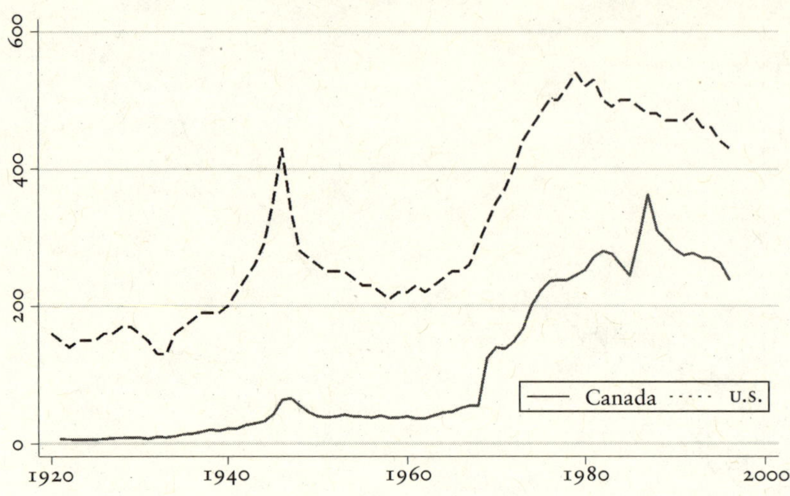

Fig. 2.3   Divorces per 100,000 population, Canada and the U.S., 1920-2000. *Sources*: Statistics Canada cat. 82–204 and later versions; *Historical Statistics of the United States* and various years of the U.S. *Statistical Abstract*.

socially structured identity by century's end may fit. The higher educational institutions were by the later 1990s indeed giving good returns to their graduates. Of course, even for those in the technical disciplines doing so spectacularly well, the technology-driven sector was not offering the secure lifetime career expected in the 1950s and 1960s. The technology-stock crash of 2000 demonstrated that vulnerability all too well. The crash of 2008 falls outside the historical period being examined here, up to 2005.

People by century's end were on the whole less firmly embedded into institutions such as the family, voluntary associations, or career-long employment, a theme becoming widely noted and discussed from the work of Robert Putnam (2000). The segmentation and anonymity is well described by Ollivier (2000, 444) writing with reference to occupational prestige. Some psychologists believed that such anomic trends were behind the seeming epidemic of psychiatric depression (e.g., Seligman 1989). Marital break-up is one of the most accessible empirical indicators of the more anomic social changes associated with post-industrial and information society, and allows a nice, long time series. As represented by number of divorced persons per 100,000 population, graphed in figure 2.3, the rates of divorce dipped during the early 1930s as the need for financial caution perhaps displaced marital dissatisfaction. The World

War Two years saw a spike in rates, and in both Canada and the United States rates of divorce accelerated during the 1970s in response to changing mores and new legislation around family law. Although useful for stretching the data back to the 1920s, presenting the divorce time series as a ratio to total population hides the full impact of the later figures. As is widely reported in the press and in sources such as introductory sociology textbooks, the divorce rates by century's end meant that some 30 to 40 percent of Canadian marriages and proportionately more in the United States would end in divorce (e.g., Kendall et al. 2000, 497).

One implication of these developments relevant to the present purpose is that people's psyches seem to have become more anxious and needing of respect, to pick up from the title of two early-twenty-first-century cultural interpretations (Sennet 2003; de Botton 2004). Consistent with a theme from Michael Young's (1958) prophetic *The Rise of the Meritocracy*, these two works form part of a recent cluster of cultural interpretations of life in the new economy stressing the quest for self-respect. Self-respect can be hard to maintain for those unsuccessful in a meritocracy. So there is a "fragile identity" about these days, "hooked on self-esteem" (Furedi 2004, 143) to an extent amounting to a "contemporary American fascination" (Hewitt 1998, xi). "My main priority is to raise Juliana to be confident with high self-esteem," a mother states in a *Globe and Mail* interview (6 July 2000, A8). In the wry comment of a *New York Times* reader (2 December 2007, "Week in Review," 12), "self-esteem should be based on something. We've created a cockeyed world where parents don't want the conflict of being adults and teaching their children real values lessons, and how to deal with hurt, and everyone else is supposed to praise kids just for existing." In another cultural document from the public domain, concern was raised in 2004 about the consequences of an advertisement "on the self-esteem of young people with false teeth" (*Globe and Mail*, 18 September, B6). I shall return to this theme in chapter 8, having meanwhile shown that twenty-first-century survey respondents in occupations of lower educational qualifications and pay enhance their ratings of their whole stratum of occupations as part, I shall suggest, of a quest for self-esteem within meritocracy.

Although my depiction has some gloomy aspects, there are also reasons for attributing an enhanced self-efficacy, increased personal power, and self-determination as part of turn-of-century (twentieth to twenty-first) society. The Internet, even though corporations were heavily involved, had many individually empowering aspects. A *Globe and Mail* column for 5 October 2002 (R12), for example, was headed "do-it-yourself-ism in the computer age." The first case of West Nile disease in 2002 was self-diagnosed by a truck driver who looked up his symptoms on the Internet after his physician doubted it was the virus (*Globe and Mail*, 7 September 2002, A5). As far back as his book *Powershift*, Alvin Toffler (1990, 7) was alert to the "fall from grace" of physicians owing to the new accessibility of medical knowledge. Such stories about people using the Internet for access to knowledge formerly part of the monopoly of the professions appear all the time in today's culture. There is a "cult of the amateur" (Keen 2007). As the professions are demystified, their prestige may suffer. Alongside that, cases of professional incompetence or dishonesty may receive wider publicity than they used to (see, for example, "Interview with William Mullins-Johnson," *Maclean's*, 6 March 2008).

If there is a case that the information society is qualitatively different from industrial society, not just an evolution, part of the argument comes from the progress of science and growth of technologies. The application of science and technology to the economy was as much part of the definition of industrial society as post-industrial (Aron 1967, 103–4), but the miniaturization of electronics may qualify as truly a new "defining technology" (Bolter 1984, 11), setting one period off from another. Zhou's (2005) twenty-first-century reinterpretation of 1960s theorizing about occupational prestige emphasized science and technology. Noting the paradox whereby prestige is all about differences, yet according to functionalist theory needs to be widely diffused throughout a population, he gives renewed importance to cultural factors, "the institutional realm of values and beliefs." Occupations commanding the highest prestige, Zhou (2005, 95) argued, are those that can splice their power and privileges into key aspects of the national value system. These key aspects are the most central, core beliefs that are strong enough to "naturalize" (i.e., make natural) prestige differences. The value society places on an occupation having a knowledge base rooted in science is an example of such a cultural factor. If association with science and technology is a basis for the prestige of occupations, the arrival of a new defining technology could help scramble the prestige hierarchy. Occupations that have adopted miniaturized electronic technologies, for example, might be prestige gainers.

The impact of the information society on social inequality clearly is complex, yet crucial to sorting out expectations about trends in occupational prestige scores. In some senses, the information society is an egalitarian society. Information technology often flattens organizational hierarchies (Dewett and Jones 2001; Meijer 2008), a theme noted early on by Toffler (1981, 68). E-mail, for example, gives easy access to those high up in an organizational chart, thus reducing the social distance between the chiefs and the Indians. In other respects, however, information technology has been a force for inequality. The phrase "digital divide," from the 1990s, captured this in terms of which countries and groups of people within countries had the best access to current technology. As noted earlier, writers such as Heather Menzies detected a widening in quality and income of occupations. Part of the large new-economy sector offered challenging, remunerating work to people with the educational skills of "symbolic analysts," the term from Reich (1991). Other service employment, however, meant the notorious "Mcjobs" of the "jobless recovery" after the early 1990s recession. Graham Lowe (2000, 37) assembled a collection of poll data revealing Canadians' perception of a growing class divide around work.

The most important demographic trend of all may be the evidence of growing income inequality in both Canada and the United States over the past forty years. If the world has become harsher, more competitive, less egalitarian over time in terms of income, the immediate prediction is for the ratings of occupational prestige to have followed suit. But as succeeding chapters shall show, that is precisely what did not happen in Canada between 1965 and 2005. The distribution of occupational prestige in Canada has become more bunched, clustered, or "squeezed." Given such a counter-intuitive main finding, it will be wise to take a close look at income data.

The non-expert quickly discovers that examination of financial inequality involves a labyrinth of alternative data sets and measures of dispersion and distinctions between income, wealth, consumption, pre-tax, post-tax, pre-transfer from government programs and post-transfer, individual incomes vs. family incomes. Much of the recent Canadian work appears in the journal *Canadian Public Policy* (*CPP*). Moore and Pacey (2003, 36), for example, examined census microfiles between 1981 and 1996 and saw in their data that "inequality in pre-tax household income has increased continually since 1980," seeing an especially large deterioration in equality between 1990 and 1995. Family income here is "equivalized" (2003, 36) for variations in family size by dividing by the square root of family size, because large families would draw some economies of scale. The Current Population Survey from the United States and the Survey of Consumer Finances for Canada were used by Johnson and Kuhn (2004, 162) in a *CPP* piece giving a comparative analysis of the two countries, with a focus on the role of hours worked for the wage and salary of non-self-employed individuals. From quintile comparisons, "earnings inequality increased in both countries" (166). Dhawal-Biswal, writing in the 2002 *CPP*, argued for consumption as a more stable measure than income, with its probability of ups and downs. Using the Family Expenditure Survey, his time series begins earlier than most, in 1969, and detects an improvement in equality up to 1978, after which a gradual climb in the Gini coefficient begins, extending to his final reference year, 1996. Although inequality has a lower reading using consumption than using family income, both consumption, pre-tax family income, and post-tax family income share the same overall trend.

The data for Canadian family income inequality presented in figure 2.4 is from the Statistics Canada Cansim data base giving a time series from 1976 to 2006. The Gini coefficient used here is the index of inequality that tends to be the common denominator across various studies. As several students of income inequality note, the Gini detects changes in the middle of the distribution (Moore and Pacey 2003, 36; Heisz 2007, 16), picking up the hollowing out of the middle noted for example by Urmetzer and Guppy (1999, 58–9) when they commented that "[s]urprisingly, perhaps, it is not the lowest of the quintiles, the point of focus of most poverty studies, where the majority of losses have occurred."

Reasons suggested for the growing inequality include problems of absorbing the large numbers of recent immigrants (Moore and Pacey 2003), a decrease in the demand for low-skill labour (Johnson and Kuhn 2004), a counter-cyclical relationship with the business cycle (meaning greater inequality during boom times), and the increase in lone-parent families, both points argued by Dhawal-Biswal (2002, 514). *Canadian Public Policy* devoted a January 2003 supplemental issue to "linkages between economic growth

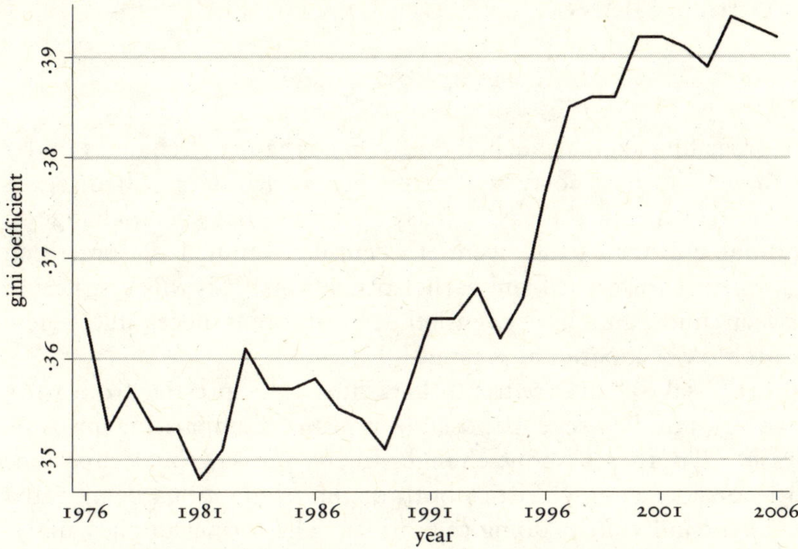

Fig. 2.4   Gini coefficients for family income (after tax) inequality, Canada, 1976–2006. *Source*: CANSIM series 202–0705

and inequality." Heisz (2007, 11) reminds us that recessions struck in 1981–82 and 1991–93, with recovery from the latter taking until 1996, and indeed spikes in the Gini coefficients in figure 2.4 do seem to coincide with those points.

Widening in the income distribution has received press notice in both Canada and the United States. The *New York Times* of 19 November 2006, B43, for example, noted that the share of national income in the United States earned by the top 1 percent of taxpayers was higher in 2004 than at any time since 1936. The explosion in salaries for corporate heads attracted comment in *Globe and Mail* stories such as "Feeding the Lead Dogs" (24 October 2003, C1) and became very prominent in media coverage of the fall 2008 banking crisis on Wall Street.

Compared against other developed countries, Canada has a middling level of inequality, whether assessed against twenty-five OECD countries (Sharpe 2003, S4) or in the more focussed comparison by Glatzer and Hauser (2002), examining not only pre- and post-tax family incomes for Canada, France, Germany, Spain, and the United States, but also poverty rates and wealth distribution.

SOCIAL CHANGE AND OCCUPATIONAL PRESTIGE

Types of Comparison

The preceding sketch touched on some of the many changes under way over the past forty and more years. Scholars will disagree on the details, but the case is easy to argue that social change in the final quarter of the twentieth century summed to something qualitatively different from earlier transitions. It is this distinction between mid- and late twentieth century that necessitates new research on occupational prestige.

A proposal to "analyse trends in occupational prestige from 1965 to 2005" bundles several possible types of comparison into one phrase. Hypotheses about changes in the prestige of occupations must consider characteristics both of the occupations being rated and of the individuals doing the ratings. The former implies analysis at the level of the occupation title, with ratings aggregated across all respondents; the latter needs disaggregated computations at the level of the individual respondent. Some issues can be examined at both levels, for traits of occupations can be coded onto a file of ratings by individuals (e.g., Zhou 2005), while socio-demographic data on individuals could be summarized and coded into a file of aggregated prestige scores for different years. Aggregation of prestige ratings dangerously obscures possibly meaningful variation among individuals, but confining all analysis to the level of the individual may leave overly fussy models that obscure relationships worth knowing about in a sea of inter-individual variance. A key benefit is gained by aggregation, because a panel can be created in which the same occupation is traced between 1965 and 2005. There is no panel equivalent at the individual level, since the 1965 and 2005 surveys examined here are cross-sections collected with no thought of attempting re-contact in 2005 of the still-surviving respondents from 1965.

Since the core data are *sets of scores* by respondents (rather than one score per respondent), three different tabulations are relevant to temporal change in occupational-prestige scores. As summarized in the accompanying list, right-hand column, a first issue is the score that any individual respondent gives any one occupation. The occupation-level equivalent, left-hand column, is the mean score for each occupation, summed across respondents. A second issue is, for the set of ratings by each respondent, are the scores scattered or clustered? Equivalently, for mean scores for all occupations rated, what is the variance in the scale? And as a third issue, what is the congruency between sets of ratings by individuals? That can be measured by computing the correlation between scales for randomly selected pairs of respondents. The occupation-level equivalent for issue three is the correlation between scales that researchers such as Treiman (1977) often report.

Issue	Tabulating for Occupations	Tabulating for Individual Respondents
1 Size of score	Mean score of jth occupation, by Σi's	Score of jth occupation, by i^{th} person
2 Variation in scores	Variance in total scale of Σj occupations	Variance of ith person's ratings of Σj occupations
3 Agreement in scores	Congruency between mean scores of Σj occupations, between sets of i's	Congruency between any two i's, in their ratings of Σj occupations

The list is a re-working into operational form of the thematic scheme suggested at the end of chapter 1.

Hypotheses

Here I shall gather points from earlier in the chapter into a more formal scheme.

ISSUE 1: SIZE OF SCORE

(a) Education. I could term this "the Porter hypothesis" in honour of John Porter's career-long stress on the importance of education as the master-variable of the social stratification system of societies: since highly rewarded occupations tend to have high educational prerequisites, occupations in which the typical educational level has increased over time should show increased prestige scores.

(b) Income. Here is the quintessentially visible and measurable occupational reward. Even though prestige is conceptually separable from income, decades of prestige research demonstrate the robust association between the two. Occupations gaining income

between 1965 and 2005 should have gained prestige too. To be sure, the causes of occupational income are varied, and that is one reason why the plot between income and prestige is not one-to-one. In part, the income level for an occupation responds to the relationship between demand and supply of incumbents (Freeman 1975, 288). If the ratio of demand to supply is structural, in the sense of being beyond the scope of manipulation by particular communities within a society, the explanation of occupational prestige fits into the classical pure-competition market model. Alternatively, demand and supply may reflect the efforts at image creation, control of the labour market, "incorporation processes" (Zhou 2005, 101), and other strategies pursued by occupational communities. Like education, income is a key marker within a larger causal chain, having the advantage of being accurately measured, whereas antecedent factors such as deliberate restriction of the number of workers is not.

(c) Gender. If ratings for occupations specified as having a female incumbent lose prestige (Bose and Rossi 1983; Jacobs and Powell 1985), then as the proportion female in an occupation rises over time the mean prestige might decline. The relationship between proportion female in an occupation and its prestige was investigated by England (1979), who found only a little such effect. The issue does not go away, however, research on the medical profession being one continuing focus (e.g., Harden 2001; Riska 2001). Since the present research covers a long period of transformation in the gender segregation of occupations, investigation of the gender composition of occupations was warranted.

(d) Skill set. Occupations gaining skill between 1965 and 2005 will show gains in prestige. We already have seen in the discussion above how tricky it is to gauge skill change consequent to technological change. Nevertheless, Human Resources and Skills Development Canada (HRSDC) has invested great effort into tracking skill change in occupations, and a later chapter will employ these measures.

(e) Occupational presentation. Occupations might gain prestige by improving their identification with the core institutional realm of values and beliefs that Zhou (2005) has discussed. They might, for example, change the occupational title from "sales clerk" to "sales associate." They might advertise in the mass media in order to emphasize their level of professionalism or their access to a scien-

tific knowledge base. There are not the data within the present analysis to be definitive here, but I do have a reading on how favourably or unfavourably occupations were represented in a national Canadian newspaper for 1964 and 2004. The hypothesis of course is that occupations receiving "better press" in the later period gained prestige.

(f) More generic shifts in functional importance. When it was suggested earlier that farming and trades occupations may have lost prestige over the latter twentieth century, and symbolic-analyst ones gained, the effect may be reflected through hypotheses (a) to (e), but not necessarily. Farmers, for example, may have up-graded their typical education level by increasing attendance at agricultural college. Technology may maintain the profitability of farming relative to some other occupations. The gender balance might not have shifted, and skills might have increased. Occupational presentation might have been maintained by farmers' associations. If a general perception prevailed among the public that farming was no longer very important, however, possibly owing to the availability of cheap food imported from outside Canada, the prestige score could still have dropped. For this kind of "hypothesis," scores must be examined title by title to see if commonsense expectations are reflected in the data.

(g) Characteristics of raters. Finally, for this sub-section, there is the possible impact of differences between 1965 and 2005 in the socio-demographic profile of the Canadian population. Occupational-prestige scores reflect not so much the people of a society speaking with one voice but, rather, a statistical summation of different viewpoints, ideologies, and levels of occupational knowledge. Change in the socio-demographic composition of a population, therefore, is a potential determinant of change in prestige ratings. Reiss (1961, 186), for example, hypothesized that young people, having high career aspirations, would down-rate humbler occupations. If older people are then more lenient in rating occupations, scores for occupations would rise over time, owing simply to the aging of the baby-boom generation. In another demographic possibility, in my pilot work highly educated respondents gave relatively severe prestige scores. Given the increase in education levels between 1965 and 2005 there could be a downward force, education-driven, on the scores due to this demographic alone. The cumulation of micro-sociological consequences is thus uncertain,

with both push and pull on the scores likely. As further examples, those in the labour force might give importance to work in general, translating into higher prestige scores. The increased female labour force participation rate between the mid-1960s and 2005 could thus create the conditions for rising prestige. The foreign-born may likewise especially value work, since it is a leading motivation for immigration. With work skills becoming increasingly important criteria for admission of immigrants over the forty years being examined, that too could factor into the rising prestige levels. Thinking about Canada's two main linguistic communities among the native-born, Pineo and Porter (1967, 31) believed that French-Canada would put less prestige "into the occupational structure" than English-speaking Canadians. Their grounds were that Francophone Canadian society shortly after World War II had scarcely industrialized. Given that modernization, secularization, and the rise of a distinct Quebec society has been part of the story of change in Canada since 1965 (Langlois 2006), there is another possible upward pressure on prestige scores.

ISSUE 2: VARIATION IN SCORES

From the growing inequality in family income, it would follow that prestige scores too would become more dispersed, related as they are to income. And yet countervailing themes to this in culture were noted above, namely, (a) the twenty-first-century quest for self-esteem, which suggests that raters of occupational prestige, and especially those from the lower strata, will avoid low scores to a greater degree than their predecessors did in 1965; (b) the heightened self-efficacy attributable to the demystification of much professional knowledge owing to the Internet. This should put downward pressure on professional occupations such as physician, lawyer, or accountant, helping further squeeze variance in the scores.

ISSUE 3: AGREEMENT IN SCORES

Declining consensus. The possible effect of postmodernism was noted above and suggests increasingly subjectivist, multiple, socially constructed realities for assorted identity groups (Zurcher 1977; Gergen 1991; Giddens 1991; Aronowitz 1992, Rosenau 1992). If this depiction is accurate, inter-rater consensus should have declined over the period examined, and this might carry over to affect correlations between aggregated scales for occupational prestige. Before drawing conclusions along these lines, it will be important to take into account as many of the socio-demographic social-structure changes as possible between 1965 and 2005. Chapter 7 will, for example, stress the impact of changing education levels for consensus.

SUMMARY

This chapter has looked at aspects of social change in North America, extracting hypotheses to guide analysis of the prestige surveys from 1965 and 2005. In a final preparatory task before showing results, the next chapter describes methods and procedures followed in assembling prestige data for secondary analysis and collecting new data for primary analysis.

3

Methods and Procedures

The analysis reported in the next chapters is based on sample survey cross-sections of population whose respondents were asked to rate lists of occupations based on their "social standing." Within the boundaries of the various types of error (Groves 1989, vi) encountered in any social survey, these random samples allow generalization to their parent population. The extent of bias owing to sampling-frame issues and nonresponse bias will be discussed later in this chapter.

Two of the surveys, collected in 2000 and 2005, are new. The historical data against which these two primary surveys are compared come from data banks, the entire inventory of occupational prestige data sets used in the present volume being itemized in table 3.1.[1] Most of these samples are old favourites for readers conversant with research on occupational prestige. Some natural pairings occur among the samples. As discussed earlier, careful effort was made by U.S. researchers in the 1960s to construct an accurate comparison between 1947 and 1963. A second twinning occurs between the next generation of NORC studies: those from 1964–65 and 1989. For this set the sampling technique was changed from quota to area probability and the number of titles rated was expanded. In Canada, an urban comparison is anchored by the 1975 sample for Kitchener-Waterloo (Ontario) collected by Guppy and Siltanen (1977). In the year 2000, I, along with Guppy and Thompson, replicated the earlier work. The latter study is referred

Table 3.1
Inventory of Data Examined

Identifier/ Bibliographic Source	Number of Titles Examined	Population Coverage	Response (%)	N of Raters, in Total, ( ) per Title
Counts/Counts (1925)	45	Mainly students	Unknown	450
NORC, 1947 / Hodge, Treiman, and Rossi (1966)	90	National U.S., quota sample	Not applicable	2,920
NORC, 1963 / As above	90	National U.S., quota sample	Not applicable	651
NORC, 1964, "Hodge, Siegel, Rossi" / Siegel (1971)	204	National, U.S.	79.4	923
NORC, 1965, "Supplementary" / Siegel (1971)	204	National, U.S.	About 79	1,519 (505–509)
Pineo and Porter, 1965/ Pineo and Porter (1967)	204	National, Canada	64.3	793
NORC, 1989/ Nakao and Treas (1994); Davis and Smith (1992, 54)	740	National, U.S.	77.6	1,166 (about 116)
Kitchener-Waterloo, Canada, 1975 / Guppy and Siltanen (1977)	93	An urban area	64.1	180 (about 60)
Kitchener-Waterloo, Canada, 2000 / ("KWMAS 2000) Goyder et al. (2003)	90	Same urban area as above, with slightly larger coverage	45.7	351 (about 115)
Occupational Prestige in Canada: 2005 / this chapter	214	National, Canada	51.0	2,053 (about 200)

Note: The surveys from 1965 (Pineo-Porter) 1989, 2000, and 2005 were analyzed in microdata form, the NORC 1989 survey being obtained via the Inter-University Consortium for Political and Social Research at the University of Michigan. All others used published results from the sources noted above, re-keyed.

to as KWMAS 2000, standing for Kitchener-Waterloo Metropolitan Area Survey, 2000. The fourth comparison is for Canada at the national level, examining the new survey I call Occupational Prestige in Canada: 2005, alongside the 1965 Pineo-Porter study.

DESIGNING OCCUPATIONAL PRESTIGE STUDIES IN THE TWENTY-FIRST CENTURY

Using the CAPI and CATI Methods

Urban Sample, by CAPI. Before computers were applied to survey fieldwork, occupational-prestige surveys were collected by personal (i.e., at the household) interviews using a "card and ladder" method whereby names of occupations were printed onto cards that the respondents then slotted onto a ladder representing a gradient of social standing. The card and ladder design appeared first in the 1964 NORC study and was adopted by Pineo and Porter (1967) in their 1965 Canadian study, since they were replicating the 1964 procedures as closely as possible. In the 1975 Canadian urban sample, Guppy and Siltanen, for continuity with Pineo-Porter, also used cards and ladder, as did Nakao and Treas (1994) in their 1989 replication of NORC work from the 1960s. The cards had been adopted as part of a program at NORC to improve the design of the foundational 1947 study. Siegel (1971) explains that, as part of the effort to secure ratings for a high proportion of occupation titles in the U.S. labour force, respondents were found to process more titles when presented in written form on the cards than if read off by a fieldworker. Svalastoga (1959, 47) reported the same in Denmark. The Chicago group had also considered but rejected the semantic differential technique as "too difficult for some respondents" (Siegel 1971, 34). Gusfield and Schwartz (1963) were able to explore the nuances captured by semantic differentials, but only by using a sample restricted to university students. Instead, Siegel and colleagues opted for the simple ladder gauging social standing, instead of the multiple dimensions that would have been captured with semantic differentials. The trade-off between the deepest rigour in measurement, some of the issues having been noted in chapter 1, and nationally representative samples is encountered recurrently in occupational-prestige research.

It was an objective for the Canadian project to convert to the more modern technology of computer-assisted interviewing while maintaining comparability with the card and ladder studies. Early in 2000, work began on designing an occupational-prestige study to be collected in CAPI (Computer Assisted Personal Interview) mode.

The prestige-rating question was set up in *Sawtooth Ci3* software as nearly as possible to a perfect replication of the NORC ladder. On the right-hand side of the screen of the laptop computers used by the fieldworkers, a vertical set of boxes appeared, reproducing the shape of a ladder. The "cards" were simulated by titles of occupations that flashed onto the upper left-hand portion of the screen. Respondents "placed" the card into the ladder by keying in a number between 1 (lowest social standing) and 9 (highest). Once the number was entered, a new screen presenting a new occupation appeared. Every screen had instructions advising the respondent to use the code "11" for occupations unrateable for one reason or another (e.g., "don't know"). A dividend from the CAPI technology was effortless automatic randomizing of the order of occupation titles. For Guppy and Siltanen (1977, 324), working with the traditional card and ladder technique standard in the mid-seventies, it was practical to run only two sequences of the cards. Randomization of the sequence of titles offsets the possibility of serial response set. Respondents might, for example, begin by avoiding the highest rung of the ladder but then decide they were being overly withholding of the highest social standing and, as further occupation titles came up, begin to use the top score more. Several such possible patterns to the use of the ladder could occur, including respondent fatigue (Reiss 1961, 7).

Promising though the CAPI approach seemed, pretesting during the summer of 2000 raised the question of whether every respondent could work with a computer screen rather than a physical ladder. Traditional kits of cards and cardboard ladder were therefore prepared for each fieldworker to hold in reserve, in case a respondent baulked at the computerized rating of titles. In fact, on the main fieldwork, no respondent needed the cardboard ladder, although fieldworkers carried it with them in case. We asked respondents to perform the ratings by taking over the laptop from the fieldworker, who had control of the machine at the outset of the interview in which questions about household composition were asked. The fieldworker's role normally was to observe and make notes on the behaviour of respondents and comments they made during the ratings, and this yielded some valuable qualitative field data. The fieldwork proceeded smoothly with the CAPI-format occupational-prestige rating. For 92 percent of the interviews, the respondent entered scores directly onto the laptop. For the rest of the cases, the respondent asked the fieldworker to read off the titles from the computer screen and handle the data entry.

As noted in chapter 1, Guppy and Siltanen mounted a quasi-experiment on gender-defined occupational roles Their plan of three versions was replicated in the 2000 KWMAS, with one gender-neutral, a second designating each title as explicitly held by a man or a woman, and a third reversing male and female from the second version. Thus, each occupation was rated by one random third of the sample understanding the incumbent to be male, one third presented with a female incumbent, and the other third performing the task without reference to gender. The Sawtooth program selected one of the three versions at random each time the program was opened. Naturally, the introductory phrasing for the two gendered versions had to be tailored. Our words were: "For each occupation, we ask you to imagine either a man or a woman in the position. The program alternates randomly between the sexes."

In keeping with the intention to replicate Guppy and Siltanen, as many occupation titles as possible from the 1975 study were retained. Some of the earlier titles, however, had become obsolete by 2000. A balancing was therefore attempted between pruning and modernization of titles, but not so much as to jeopardize the replication. The list of ninety titles used in the 2000 KWMAS is reported in Goyder et al. (2003). Of the forty-five "classic titles" (Coxon and Jones 1979b, 8) from the Counts project in 1925, sixteen survived in the 2000 list. Most of these had lineage through NORC 1947 and up through Pineo and Porter (1967). That sets aside duplicates in Counts, such as "elementary-school teacher" and "rural-school teacher," and of course some of the 1925 titles such as "teamster, drives horses" are non-applicable today.

Sampling for the 2000 fieldwork was by two-stage probability. All twenty-one Forward Sorting Areas (FSA) – given by the first three characters of Canada Post postal codes – for the Kitchener-Waterloo Census Metropolitan Area (which includes the town of Cambridge, along with Woolwich and North Dumfries Townships) were selected as primary units. Within FSAs the fourth to sixth characters for a postal code were randomly generated. About one in four were working ones that entered the sample. Forty percent of households within each code were then randomly selected for the sample. An alternative frame would have been the municipal assessment record, but the pubic versions of this began omitting dwelling-unit numbers for renters as of around 1998. In addition, the municipal assessments waste around 20 percent of sample draws because of wrong name, unoccupied dwellings, and other problems. Such errors are exacerbated by high migration rates into and out of the area. The postal codes were suitable because the fieldwork needed to be clustered owing to the personal interview mode of contact, and the final three postal digits identify quite small areas. The codes were attentive to newly built districts, important in as fast-growing an area such as Kitchener-Waterloo.

Unlike municipal taxation data bases, the postal codes do not identify occupants of households by name. Where possible, we extracted family surname(s) and telephone numbers from the city directory. The number was then called, allowing the name to be verified. At this stage, two routes were followed, alternating by random selection. For half the cases, the next-birthday method was followed so as to randomly select one household member. Interviewers would say, "I was hoping to speak with the person in the household who is over the age of eighteen and has their birth date closest to the first of ..." (a month pre-identified by a rotating order). For the other half, the interviewer simply asked to "speak with someone over the age of eighteen." The two versions were adopted owing to concerns that arose early in the fieldwork. The first week of contacts was scrapped and treated as a late pretest because of a very low response rate apparently attributable to the birthday method of within-household selection. We optimized response rate in one-half of the sample and randomness of within-household sampling in the other, thereby spreading risks of error.

For households having no traceable telephone number, interviewers made "cold" calls at the door. All sampled households had already been pre-contacted by means of a dropped-off introductory letter, together with a complimentary University of Waterloo Survey Research Centre coffee mug as prepaid non-monetary incentive (Willimack et al. 1995). At least two and up to five calls at the door were attempted. Failing contact, the cases were then put into the pool for a different method of contact. Such cases, along with all refusals, non-contacts, and missed appointments arising both from the contact by telephone and at-the-door contact, were sent the survey on a disk designed for self-completion. Naturally, this presupposed that householders had access to a computer, but figures from another recent survey in the area showed that about 70 percent of households indeed did (Goyder 2005a, 202). Concern about viruses was not quite so acute then as now. For those who did not have a computer, the letter accompanying the disk invited the householder to call the researchers so that a fieldworker could be dispatched. As incentive, all those involved in this phase of the survey were offered a draw in a raffle for $500. The rationale behind following up personal contact with self-administration was that people hold mode preferences about survey research. As a final follow-up, some eighty "soft" refusers were identified, and a third were re-contacted and offered a $10 cash payment to complete the survey.

Response rate on the survey was, despite these efforts, a disappointing raw figure of 45.7 percent, rising to 50 percent after weighting for the double-sampling involved in the refusal conversion attempts.[2] For the 1975 study of the same metropolitan area, slightly more narrowly defined, response was a much higher 64.1 percent. The problem in 2000 was refusals; non-contact accounted for 15 percent of cases in 1975 compared with 11 percent in 2000. Response rate for the next-birthday half sample from 2000 was about 10 percent lower (i.e., some 40 percent vs 50 percent) than for the interview-any-adult half, allowing some leverage on the impact of nonresponse on the prestige ratings.

National Study, by CAPI. The year 2000 study was both an investigation in its own right into the gender dimension of occupational prestige and a pilot test for a new national-level survey of occupational prestige in Canada. The pilot established that no decisive advantage in response rates was likely within the personal interview mode of contact, even though this has traditionally been believed to be the most effective, albeit costly, approach. Contact by telephone for occupational-prestige research was thus re-examined. A new pretest of one hundred sample draws from Kitchener was collected during the spring and summer of 2002. Contact was by telephone, using an experienced professional interviewer. Just twenty occupation titles were rated. The sampling frame was the Kitchener-Waterloo city directory; thus names of callees were known. The results were successful; using "cold calls" (i.e., no pre-contact), response was 56 percent. In the half of the sample receiving a pre-telephone-contact introductory letter containing $5 paid unconditionally, response rate (complete divided by [complete + refusal +

non-contact, with ineligibles owing to death, move, wrong address deleted]), the success rate reached 82 percent. People seemed to have no difficulty performing the rating task unassisted by the physical aid of the cardboard ladder. On the basis of these encouraging results, I approached SSHRC for funding under the Initiative on the New Economy program, for support for a national CATI (Computer Assisted Telephone Interview) survey of occupational prestige in Canada.

The strategy of rotating occupations across sub-samples in order to build up the number of titles rated was first used by Nakao and Treas (1994, 6) in their 1989 study in the United States. With ten samples of just over 100 respondents, each rating 110 titles, 40 of the occupation titles were common across all sub-samples in their study, 70 unique to just one. The study thus generated ratings for a total of 740 titles. That strategy was adapted for the Canadian study, modifying several of the parameters. Since the subdivision of titles worked well for Nakao and Treas, I used a much smaller common core of titles to be rated by all the sample, just four occupations, each to do with survey research (survey interviewer, survey statistician, supervisor of survey interviewers, director of a survey unit). These four were part of a sub-study within the overall design and provided a basis for checking whether any of the ten sub-samples were serious outliers from the others. Each sub-sample rated another 21 titles, so that 210, plus the 4 rated by all respondents, resulted in 214 occupational titles being given prestige scores in the Occupational Prestige in Canada: 2005 survey.

The Canadian research was mainly concerned with change since the 1965 Pineo-Porter study. It was not the objective to create a comprehensive prestige scale of occupation titles onto which all respondents on a survey could be scored. The need for a comprehensive scale based on prestige was addressed using a different approach in which the 2005 respondents rated the 26 major groups of the National Occupational Classification (NOC), dividing the task into four major groups to be rated by each sub-sample. The scale appears in Goyder and Frank (2007).

The list of occupation titles for 2005 carried over from Pineo-Porter 1965, together with those added and those from 1965 deleted in 2005 appears in table 3.2. Various explanatory notes are included in the table. I wanted to repeat as many titles as possible, and over 150 of the 204 titles from 1965 were repeated in 2005

Table 3.2
Information on Occupation Titles, 1965 and 2005 Surveys

2005 Titles That Were Retained Unchanged from 1965 (N = 153)	*Identifying Code*
Accountant	812
Administrative officer in federal civil service	303
Advertising executive	603
Advertising copy writer	1007
Airline pilot	602
Architect	1004
Author	904
Baker	315
Ballet dancer	601
Bank teller	312
Bank manager	804
Barber	115
Bartender	417
Bill collector	1017
Biologist	117
Book binder	206
Bookkeeper	113
Bricklayer	1001
Building contractor	309
Bus driver	1006
Butcher in a store	409
Carpenter's helper	810
Cashier in a supermarket	109
Catholic priest	321
Chemist	806
Chiropractor	1016
Civil engineer	402
Clerk in an office	901
Coal miner	509
Cod fisherman	705
Colonel in the army	413
Commerical artist	807
Computer programmer	218
Construction foreman	306
Construction labourer	105
Cook in a restaurant	1014
County court judge	213
Custom seamstress	107
Dairy farmer	310
Department head in city government	718
Diamond driller	416
Disc jockey	605
Draughtsman	707
Driving instructor	319
Economist	916
Electrician	607

Table 3.2 (continued)

2005 Titles That Were Retained Unchanged from 1965 (N = 153)	Identifying Code
Farm owner and operator	214
Farm labourer	912
File clerk	514
Filling station attendant	1020
Firefighter	1018
Fruit packer in a cannery	104
Funeral director	114
Garbage collector	1008
General manager of a manufacturing plant	101
High school teacher	1003
Hospital attendant	820
House carpenter	803
House painter	608
Housekeeper in a private home	313
Insurance claims investigator	211
Insurance agent	701
Janitor	518
Jazz musician	805
Job counsellor	208
Journalist	511
Lawyer	606
Livestock buyer	221
Locomotive engineer	407
Logger	1010
Longshoreman	906
Loom operator	621
Lunchroom operator	711
Machinist	714
Manager of a real estate office	907
Manager of a supermarket	1012
Manufacturer's representative	204
Mathematician	914
Mayor of a large city	414
Member of a city council	201
Member of Canadian House of Commons	318
Member of Canadian Senate	502
Merchandise buyer for a department store	521
Mining engineer	703
Motel owner	120
Mucking machine operator	814
Museum attendant	610
Musician in a symphony orchestra	412
Newspaper pressman	1019
Occupation of my family's main wage earner*	1021
Oil field worker	209
Oiler in a ship	720
Physician	411

Table 3.2 (continued)

2005 Titles That Were Retained Unchanged from 1965 (N = 153)	*Identifying Code*
Physicist	121
Physiotherapist	119
Playground director	710
Plumber	515
Post office clerk	716
Power lineman	903
Power crane operator	811
Private in the army	708
Production worker in the electronics industry	507
Professional athlete	920
Professionally trained librarian	317
Protestant minister	112
Psychologist	1009
Pumphouse engineer	917
Quarry worker	612
Railroad ticket agent	217
Railroad sectionhand	713
Railroad conductor	709
Real estate agent	611
Receptionist	401
Registered nurse	504
Sales clerk in a store	513
Saw sharpener	905
Sawmill operator	408
Sculptor	116
Service station manager	202
Sewing machine operator	1011
Sheet metal worker	421
Ship's pilot	316
Shipping clerk	816
Social worker	902
Someone who lives off inherited wealth*	908
Steam roller operator	216
Steel mill worker	817
Stockroom attendant	205
Superintendent of a construction job	405
Taxicab driver	510
Telephone operator	719
Timber cruiser	819
Tool and die maker	108
Trade union business agent	910
Trailer truck driver	106
Travel agent	110
Truck dispatcher	210
TV director	721
TV repairman	918
TV announcer	415

Table 3.2 (continued)

2005 Titles That Were Retained Unchanged from 1965 (N = 153)	*Identifying Code*
TV camerman	517
Typesetter	503
Typist	102
University professor	818
Used car salesman	1013
Veterinarian	320
Waitress in a restaurant	616
Warehouse hand	302
Welder	516
Wholesale distributor	519
Worker in a dry cleaning or laundry plant	801
Worker in a meat packing plant	706
YMCA director	314

2005 Titles That Were Slightly Altered from 1965 (1965 wording in brackets) (N = 21)		*Identifying Code*
Aircraft mechanic	(Airplane mechanic)	609
Automobile mechanic	(Automobile repairman)	505
Child-care provider in a private home	(Professional babysitter)	406
Elementary school teacher	(Public grade school teacher)	118
Flight attendant	(Air hostess)	307
Land surveyor	(Surveyor)	520
Librarian	(Professionally trained librarian – note: 1965 wording also carried, see #317	419
Mail carrier	(Mailman)	809
Mine safety inspector	(Mine safety analyst)	508
Newspaper press operator	(Newspaper pressman – note: 1965 wording also carried, see #1019)	212
Paper making machine operator	(Paper making machine tender)	410
Pharmacist	(Druggist)	207
Police officer	(Policeman)	921
Professional forester	(Professionally trained forester)	311
Public relations officer	(Public relations man)	215
Pumphouse operator	(Pumphouse engineer – note: 1965 wording also carried, see #917)	103
Roller operator	(Steam roller operator – note 1965 wording also carried, see #216)	815
Sales associate – retail	(Sales clerk in a store – note: 1965 wording also carried, see #513)	802
Someone who lives on social assistance*	(Someone who lives on relief)	813
Steam plant operator	(Steam boiler fireman)	301
Tractor-trailer driver	(Trailer truck driver – note: 1965 wording also carried, see #106)	418

Table 3.2 (continued)

2005 Titles That Were More Substantially Altered from 1965 (1965 wording in brackets) (N = 13)		*Identifying Code*
Apprentice bricklayer	(Apprentice to a master craftsman)	219
Automobile assembly worker	(Automobile worker)	712
Beauty salon operator	(Beauty operator)	808
Data entry operator	(IBM keypunch operator)	1005
Doorkeeper, hotel	(Elevator operator in a building)	304
Foreman of workers in a papermill	(Foreman in a factory)	308
Forensic laboratory technician	(Research technician)	220
Forging press operator	(Machine operator in a factory)	614
Medical laboratory technologist	(Medical or dental technician)	704
Owner of a coffee shop	(Owner of a food store)	919
Purchasing officer	(Government purchasing agent)	404
Textile dyer	(Textile mill worker)	305
Travelling salesperson, wholesale trade	(Travelling salesman)	915

Titles Added for the 2005 Study (N = 23)	*Identifying Code*
Accounts payable clerk	913
Administrative assistant	618
Chief of emergency medicine	203
Cleaning lady	909
Computer numerically controlled machining tool operator	506
Dental hygienist	604
Environmental science manager	111
Executive secretary	1015
Financial analyst	702
Flagperson on a road construction site	911
Gas field operations manager	501
Hospital information clerk	619
Manager, financial planning and analysis	1002
Manager of a coffee shop	717
Manager of a farm	620
Manager of a motel	821
Pollster	512
President of one of the large banks	613
Sociologist	715
Telemarketer	420
User support technician	403
Waste management director	615
Web site developer	617

Titles Asked of All Respondents (N = 4)	*Identifying Code*
Supervisor of survey interviewers	004
Survey interviewer	001
Survey research director	002
Survey statistician	003

Table 3.2 (continued)

Deleted Titles from 1965 (N = 23)	*Reasons for Deletion*
Aircraft worker	Too vague; has to match in NOC
Archaeopotrist*	A fictional title, used in 1965 to test whether respondents rated in ignorance
Assembly line worker	Too vague to code in NOC
Biologer*	A fictional title, used in 1965 to test whether respondents rated in ignorance
Commercial farmer	Reducing number of agricultural titles, in order to make room for newer occupations
Hog farmer	Cutting back agricultural titles
Laundress	Antiquated
Machine set-up man in a factory	"Man" would have had to be changed
Member of Canadian cabinet	As with provincial premier, it makes no sense to rate titles with so few incumbents
Musician	Excessively vague, there are more specific artistic titles in the list
Newspaper peddler	A nearly vanished occupation, not found in NOC
Occupation of my father when I was 16*	2005 study not attempting to examine occupational mobility, as 1965 study was
Owner of a food store	"Owner" concept not part of NOC. See discussion in text
Owner of a manufacturing plant	Cutting back on owners
Part time farmer	"Part-time" adds a second dimension; also wished to reduce the number of farm titles
Provincial premier	An occupation with only ten incumbents
Railroad brakeman	Antiquated
Someone who lives off property holdings*	Wanted to reduce the number of non-labour force occupations in 2005 study
Someone who lives off stocks and bonds*	Non-labour force (see above)
Stenographer	Obsolete
Troller	Wanted to diminish number of fishing titles, to make room for new-economy occupations
TV star	Too vague
Whistle punk	Logging occupation, to do with transporting newly felled trees, unlikely to be known to many in a 21st-century sample

* Non-labour force titles.

with no change whatsoever. Another 20 were modernized slightly, often in the interests of removing sexist language that might grate on twenty-first-century ears. "Mailman," for example, was changed to "mail carrier." Another cluster of 1965 titles was removed and replaced with new, only loosely matching, titles from 2005. Often the 1965 title replaced did not code easily into the

2001 National Occupational Classification (cf., Broom and Maynard 1969, 369–70). The 1965 title "foreman in a factory," for example, was too general to fit a NOC unit group. The title was changed in 2005 to "foreman of workers in a papermill." These loose fits are generally not included in the comparison tabulations between 1965 and 2005 that appear in later chapters. An attempt was made to steer the 2005 titles toward the contemporary labour force. As noted in an earlier chapter, the number of agricultural titles was reduced from 7 to 4. Some occupations, such as "laundress" and "stenographer," seemed decidedly obsolete by 2005. Reluctantly, I concluded that the colourful "whistle punk" title from the logging industry would have little recognition in a 2005 sample of Canadians. "Cod fisherman" was initially slated for deletion, but then was reprieved. When in doubt I would conduct a Google search to assess the visibility of a title, and cod fisherman generated tens of thousands of hits. Google, along with various consultants noted in the preface, was also the arbitrator for some of the title adjustments between 1965 and 2005. "Auto mechanic," for example, has far more presence on the Internet than "auto repairman," the term used in the 1965 study. The two fictitious titles from 1965, "biologer" and "archaeopotrist," were deleted since the point about many respondents rating an unknown title from its sound alone was established by Pineo and Porter and I did not wish to antagonize the respondents recruited with such great effort for 2005. Owing to interest in comparing prestige in 1965 and 2005 against census profiles for occupations, some of the non-labour force titles from 1965 (e.g., "someone who lives off property holdings") had low priority for 2005 and were dropped.

Fieldwork for the 2005 national survey was conducted by Jolicoeur et associés, a Montreal-based firm specializing in high-quality survey fieldwork. The sampling frame for the telephone calls was randomly selected telephone numbers, and the studied population consisted of anglophones and francophones eighteen years of age and older, living in Canada. The sample was compiled by ASDE Survey Samplers. The proportion of working numbers from the ASDE sample was 74.2 percent. The sample was stratified by region (Atlantic, Quebec, Ontario, Prairie, British Columbia), with 400 completions targeted for each stratum. Within the household, the respondent was randomly selected using the next-birthday method, from all those aged eighteen years and over. Calls took

Table 3.3
Fieldwork Results, 2005 National Survey

Region	Sample Size	Weighted Sample Size	Response Rate (%)
Atlantic	411	152	52.5
Quebec	409	497	51.2
Ontario	417	795	51.4
Prairie	414	335	53.0
British Columbia	402	274	44.2
Totals	2,053	2,053	50.3 (51.0 weighted)

place between 12 January and 24 March 2005. The response rate on the survey was 50.3 percent, averaged across all five strata. The interviews took most people between ten and twenty minutes. As the break-down in table 3.3 reveals, responses were especially hard to secure in British Columbia. Jolicoeur advised that the high incidence of non-English-speaking Chinese in the province was the main obstacle. Weighting the regional strata back to their correct proportions in the Canadian population edges the response rate up to 51.0 percent . In the context of telephone survey research in the first decade of the twenty-first century, the response rate is not too bad. The 2004 national election survey by the York University ISR, for example, with a much higher salience topic than occupational prestige, achieved a 53 percent response. A considerable effort was made by Jolicoeur to exceed a 50 percent response rate in each stratum. Thus, even though a ceiling of 14 call attempts was originally planned, 1,120 telephone numbers were called more than 14 times. As many as 25 callbacks were made in one case. Among households where an initial refusal was encountered, up to 3 refusal reversion attempts were made.

For the introduction defining the rating task of occupations, question wordings from earlier studies were followed word-for-word, when possible. A preamble with lineage back to Guppy and Siltanen (1975), Pineo and Porter (1967), and Siegel (1971) begins with the phrase "now we're going to talk about jobs." Our interviewers then added:

Imagine a ladder with nine rungs on it. We'll call the top rung number 9, the next number 8, and so on down to the bottom rung, number 1. For 25 occupations, I'll give you the name of the occupation and ask you to say "nine," meaning the top of the ladder, if you think that occupation has the highest possible social standing. Say "one" if you think the occupation has the lowest possible social standing. If it belongs somewhere in between, just say the number corresponding to the social standing of the occupation. An occupation right in the middle is a five. You can enter numbers with a decimal place if you wish.

Thus we were asking respondents to substitute a mental image for the cardboard ladder from earlier years. It may attract note among readers not steeped in the traditions of research on occupational prestige that this wording refers not to "occupation prestige" – the term in fact used by sociologists to refer to this field of study – but to "social standing." The viability of social standing as a meaningful phrase became an issue as the 2000 and 2005 surveys were being designed. The University of Waterloo research ethics committee queried the term, as did some pretest respondents. The phrasing traces back to earlier studies. The trail begins with George Counts's (1925, 17) statement to respondents: "In the following list are forty-five occupations which you are to arrange in order of their *social standing*" (my emphasis). Counts, however, had preceded that phrase with a preamble reading "[i]n most communities certain occupations are accorded a higher rating than others. There is a tendency for us to 'look up to' persons engaged in some occupations and 'down on' those engaged in others. We may even be ashamed or proud of our relatives because of their occupations." That gave much more priming and definition of "social standing" than later studies offered.

Two later studies steered away from "social standing," Smith (1943) opting for "prestige status" and Hall and Jones (1950) referring to "social prestige" in their first study in Britain. The latter, however, then switched to Counts's "social standing" in their later samples. Around the same time, the first (1947) NORC study had made reference to "general standing," presenting their national quota sample of Americans with the wording, "Now I am going to ask you how you would judge a number of occupations. For example, a railroad brakeman – which statement on this card best gives your own personal opinion of the general standing of a railroad brakeman? What number on that card would you pick out for him?" Reiss (1961, 4) observes that general standing was a substitution for Counts's social standing, which latter term NORC had

Table 3.4
Results of Word Search for "Social Standing" Using Hansard

Word or Phrase	Frequency of Occurrence in Hansard				
	2000	1999	1998	1997	Total
Anomie	0	0	0	0	0
Social class	0	0	0	0	0
Social standing	0	0	0	0	0
Social status	1	0	0	0	0
Socialization	2	4	1	0	7
Prestige	2		12	1	24
Self-esteem	6	21	15	7	49
Deskilling	92	0	0	0	92
Alienation	11	126	11	5	153
Identity	86	236	130	83	535

pretested with two urban samples in Ohio and apparently found problematic.

The second generation of NORC studies reverted to "social standing," also the choice of Bose in 1972 (Bose and Rossi 1983, 318). Pineo and Porter (1967, 28), concerned with accurate replication of the most recent NORC work, also used "social standing." Meanwhile, Powell and Jacobs (1984) in the United States and Coxon and Jones (1979b) in the United Kingdom had employed the NORC 1947 reference to "general standing." For accurate replication, the new Canadian work had to refer to "social standing," and that was my answer to the ethics committee. At the same time, sensing that "social standing" may have slipped out of active use in the language of today, I checked by performing a content analysis of Hansard, the record of House of Commons debates in Canada.

Since the late 1990s, Hansard has been available as electronic text, facilitating a word search. The debates among Canada's national legislators might reflect current cultural priorities and word usage. Table 3.4 summarizes the results of the search for ten sociological terms, including "social standing," that might have diffused into the main culture sufficiently to appear in House debates. It was a little sobering that no usage whatsoever of social standing occurred during the sessions reviewed between 1997 and spring 2000. "Prestige," in contrast, appeared 24 times in total, with at least one appearance in each of the years examined. It is easy to understand the frequent occurrence of terms such as "alienation" (153 mentions) or "identity" (535), because they have obvious political referents to regionalism (e.g., "Western alienation") and national unity (e.g., "Canadian identity"). "Deskilling," a term disseminated into public discourse via books such as Braverman's (1974) work on occupations, figured prominently in sessions of the House during 2000 but not in the earlier years examined. Perhaps a more striking example of diffusion of social science is the jargon-y term "self-esteem" with 49 appearances in the content analysis, well spread over the four reference years.

A broader sweep for social standing in everyday speech was undertaken with a search of literary fiction via the website www. searchbooks.com. The site found 116 matches to the keyword "social standing." A heavy Victorian-era over-representation in the entries is unmistakable. To refer to social standing may have already been a little archaic in the 1960s, although probably not in Counts's time in the twenties.[3] On the other hand, once one begins actively looking out for the term, it turns up even in the 2000s. The Toronto *Globe and Mail*, for example, wrote on 11 August 2001, in the context of an article on sexual abuse in an elite private school, that parents of the victims "were prepared to sacrifice their sons rather than risk their social standing" (A2). And from a *Globe* column of 26 June 2001 (A13) on a woman who worked as a rural school teacher in the 1930s: "[a]s for social standing, Margaret's was relatively high."

The Victorian and Edwardian literary passages make explicit the separation between social standing and wealth. The latter contributes to the former, but the concepts are separable. "Lady Otway," said Virginia Woolf in *Night and Day*, published in 1919, "was one of the people for whom the great make-believe game of English social life has been invented; she spent most of her time in pretending to herself and her neighbours that she was a dignified, important, much-occupied person, of considerable social standing and sufficient wealth." In a passage from a lesser-known writer from the late nineteenth century: "My mother, who was of higher social standing than my father – for he was a simple vicar and she was the Dean's daughter – had married him against the consent of her own people" (Linton 1885, 34). Characters from a 1911 novel stand "with prying eyes, ready to judge the social standing of the newcomers from their furniture" (Stone 1911, 120).

Owing to reservations about the currency of "social standing," a check-question was added into the year 2000 and 2005 prestige survey schedules. Before bringing up the first rating screen, inter-viewers, said "first, I should check that the words 'social standing' have meaning for you. If this is the case, we can go ahead." This question gave at least some acknowledgment to the problem that "the investigator" in prestige studies typically selects one or more dimensions for rating and "imposes it or them on the respondent" (Kraus et al. 1978, 900–1). Of the respondents from the Kitchener-Waterloo sample of 2000, 82.7 percent confirmed that they could rate occupations by social standing, echoed by 87.5 percent from the 2005 national Canadian survey. Respondents were not asked to define social standing, merely to indicate that the term had meaning to them. Following the interviewer specifications of the NORC tradi-tion, the fieldworkers in 2000 and 2005 were explicitly instructed *not* to define social standing for respondents. The only assistance allowed was, following the earlier studies, a note to interviewers advising: "Social standing: do not offer synonyms, but do say some-thing such as – 'well, you probably think some jobs have higher standing than others. Put the jobs with higher standing near the top of the ladder.'"

How much assistance to provide the respondent is a recurrent methodological issue in occupational-prestige research. Burshtyn (1968, 157), in a 1963 survey of occupational-prestige ratings among 175 Ottawa residents, noted that he opted to allow greater discretion to interviewers than was the NORC norm but still tried "to avoid cueing the respondent to use a single variable such as income, education, or authority, since one of the tasks of the analy-sis was to see to what extent these variables underlay the perception of the 'general standing' of occupations."

For the 2000 and 2005 survey respondents for whom "social standing" did *not* have meaning, the interviewer proceeded to a new screen reading: "Here are some other words describing how we might classify occupations. Could you choose the one that makes the most sense to you, and we'll go through the list of occupations according to that criterion."

These alternative criteria for rating, drawn largely from British work reviewed in chapter 1 but also from other sources such as Tiryakian (1958), are shown in table 3.5. They were offered to respondents in an order re-randomized with each administration of the survey. The 256 responses from 2005 ranged throughout the list of choices: 26 percent selected value to society, 24 percent standard

Table 3.5
Percentage of Respondents Choosing Various Criteria for Classifying Occupations

	Percentage of Sample Choosing Criterion	
Criterion	*KWMAS 2000*	*National 2005*
The standard of living an occupation provides	17.3	23.5
The power and influence over other people given by an occupation	18.4	9.0
The qualifications required to perform the occupation	27.4	16.9
The value to society	23.5	26.4
The general desirability of the occupation	10.4	7.3
How difficult it is to find a replacement worker in that occupation	not asked	7.3
None of these (with write-in probe screen)	3.1	9.5

Note: Order of choices randomized for each respondent; question asked only of those saying the words "social standing" have no meaning for them, before the interviewer began reading names of occupations. N = 61 in 2000; 256 in 2005.

of living, 17 percent qualifications. Among the choices accounting for less than 10 percent of the distribution, just 7 percent chose general desirability, the defining criterion sometimes attributed to occupation ratings tasks. Nine percent opted for power and influence, and 7 percent for how difficult it is to find a replacement worker, a label included in deference to the functional theory of occupational stratification. Just under 10 percent of cases rejected all the labels offered and constructed their own. So in 2005, we have just 24 of a total 2,053 cases both balking at the social-standing stimulus and not finding a choice they could identify with on the checklist of alternatives. And a mere 7 of these gave additional explanation. When probed in this way for rating criteria, some of the people simply said they find the whole exercise unfathomable. "None, I don't know what any of them means," one person told the interviewer. The table includes the distribution for the smaller data set from 2000, which shows a similar picture. Value to society was again important, and here the Canadians from 2000 and 2005 resemble British "upside downers" from 1953 (Young and Willmott 1956, 342).

In the instructions to interviewers, a stern warning used on earlier studies was repeated: "Under no circumstances are you to explain what a particular occupation is to the respondent. If he/she does not know what an occupation involves, just let him/her assign it the

Table 3.6
Answers of Respondents to the Question Whether Other People Would Give the
Occupations the Same Ratings As They Did?

	2000 KWMAS (%)	2005 National (%)
Yes	27.1	27.0
Yes, with some qualifications	27.8	6.1
No	43.1	45.4
No answer	2.0	21.4
N of cases	351	2,053

Note: "Don't know" and "no opinion" were offered as part of the closed-response checklist in
2005, but not in 2000. That accounts for the much higher "no answer" count in 2005.

'11' (don't know) code for now. He/she might also not know where to place an occupation in the ladder. Encourage the respondent to set aside any title he or she does not understand or cannot rate, but at the end ask him/her if he/she can now rate any he/she couldn't rate before."

An issue of whether the researcher wants a respondent's personal opinion or his/her report of perceived community opinion about the prestige of occupations recurs throughout discussions on question design in occupational-prestige studies. Tuckman (1947, 72), in his early Canadian study, had noted the problem in Counts's work. Anticipating similar arguments appearing later in the better-known analysis by Albert Reiss (1961, 22), Tuckman reported that pre-test respondents in Montreal were confused over the personal/community ambiguity to such an extent that an experiment with wording was used for the main fieldwork. One-half of the sample answered the same question Counts (1925) had posed, while those in the other half were more expressly asked about occupations "which *you* 'look up to'" (my italics). The "let's talk about jobs" wording from the second-generation NORC studies, with its "if you think" format, was supposed to have clarified the question toward the personal focus, but Pineo and Porter (1967, 28) felt that for some respondents "the question still does not make the path completely clear."

To more explicitly address this personal versus community issue, respondents in the 2000 and 2005 studies were asked, "Do you think most other people would give our list of occupations the same ratings you just did?" Answer choices and the frequencies of choosing them appear in table 3.6. The large number answering "no," between 40 and 45 percent in both surveys, suggests that the personal opinion versus community opinion ambiguity has not disappeared with the years. Indeed, it would be congruent with literature on the more free-wheeling self of the latter twentieth century (discussed in chapter 2) to suspect such division to be on the rise. I shall get to issues of consensus and dissensus, making use of the question just reported, in a later chapter.

Card and ladder methodology limited respondents to the nine choices pasted into the cardboard ladder, since people were asked physically to place each card into a slot. In a sense, the method imposes a theoretical model by presupposing that the occupational-status distinctions people make are covered with nine levels. In the early days of limited memory-capacity computing there were, of course, advantages to single-column codes on an IBM punch card. As seen in chapter 1, precisely such assumptions about the cognition of occupational differences have been contentious in occupational-prestige work postdating the NORC design (e.g., Coxon and Jones 1978, 120). The computer-assisted mode frees the researcher from the nine-integer scale, since cards are no longer being placed into slots. Allowing finer distinctions beyond the standard nine digits could, however, have jeopardized close replication of NORC design studies. The number of digits issue was therefore turned into an experiment involving random half samples of the KWMAS data for 2000. One random half of the respondents were offered an additional instruction reading, "You can enter numbers with a decimal place if you wish." Within the experimental group, only just over 1 percent of all key entries for the prestige-rating sort used a decimal place, and so the fineness of distinction provided by nine levels seems to be adequate. The entry field for the 2005 fieldwork allowed a decimal place, as the question wording reproduced above shows. Only a percentage point or so of the ratings carry a decimal place. Usually such a score is the midpoint between rungs of the imaginary ladder.

At the conclusion of the rating of occupations, once the entire set of titles had been processed, the following question was posed: "These questions have asked you about many different occupations. Can you tell us what factors you had in mind as you performed these ratings of occupations. For example, were any of the following important when doing the ratings? Let's use choices of very important, somewhat important, somewhat unimportant, very unimportant."

Response options were, again, presented in randomized order, which the computer-assisted format easily permitted. Options were the same as for the question about social standing as usable criterion, discussed above. There was a slight variation on both questions, across the 2000 and 2005 surveys. The former included the choice "whether the occupation is usually done by a man or a woman," in service of the gender theme in that research. Given the minimal gender factor in the 2000 ratings (Goyder et al. 2003), the perceived importance of gender was dropped in 2005, but a new choice added, "how difficult it is to find a replacement worker in that occupation," the option also offered in the probe for people not understanding social standing.

Responses appear in table 3.7, tabulated for both the 2000 and 2005 surveys. The response checklist was modified in 2005, mainly because a phrase used in 2000, the admittedly grammatically clumsy "very un-important," did not translate well into French. Qualifications required for an occupation and value to society lead the respondents' choices in both surveys, despite the different population coverage, mode of contact, and checklist wording across the two. Standard of living comes third in both data sets, and then the more minor factors. The general desirability of the occupation again does not particularly resonate with either of these two sets of respondents, even though this notion of desirability has been advanced in British research (Goldthorpe and Hope 1974) as the key to the meaning of occupational prestige, an idea deeply absorbed into the social-stratification literature (e.g., Featherman and Hauser 1976, 405; Boyd 1982, 4). The hierarchy of importance from table 3.7 reproduces in all essential respects the earlier question put to respondents uneasy with the social-standing criterion (see discussion above). There seems to be some good stability and robustness to these various probes into criteria respondents report using when faced with the occupation rating task.

Broken down by level of respondent's education, those with less formal schooling gave comparatively more weight to standard of living, general desirability, and ease of replacement. Qualifications were stressed in equal proportions, and value to society was attributed more importance by the more educated, as it was in the 1947 NORC study (Reiss 1961, 34).

Before leaving the occupation rating question, we asked: "Are there any other factors that, for you, determine the social standing

Table 3.7
Importance of Criteria for Ratings of Occupational Social Standing (percentages)

KWMAS 2000 (N = 351)	*Very Important*	*Somewhat Important*	*Somewhat Unimportant*	*Very Unimportant*	*No Answer*
The standard of living an occupation provides	36.4	46.4	11.9	4.5	0.9 (100%)
The power and influence over other people given by an occupation	32.5	43.0	11.7	12.2	0.6 (100)
The qualifications required to perform the occupation	75.6	18.1	4.1	2.1	0.0 (100)
The value to society	61.3	32.8	4.9	1.0	0.0 (100)
The general desirability of the occupation	24.6	51.5	14.9	7.6	1.4 (100)
Whether the occupation is usually done by a man or a woman*	7.6	14.3	16.1	62.0	0.0 (100)

Occupational Prestige in Canada: 2005 (N = 2,053)	*Very Important*	*Quite Important*	*Of little Importance*	*Not at all Important*	*No Answer*
The standard of living an occupation provides	34.4	39.6	14.9	10.1	1.0 (100%)
The power and influence over other people given by an occupation	24.1	39.6	22.9	12.3	1.2 (100)
The qualifications required to perform the occupation	57.7	32.6	6.3	2.9	0.4 (100)
The value to society	53.2	35.6	8.0	2.7	0.5 (100)
The general desirability of the occupation	25.1	43.1	21.3	8.5	2.0 (100)
How difficult it is to find a replacement worker in that occupation**	26.4	37.6	17.5	14.5	4.0 (100)

Note: Respondents were asked about the importance of rating criteria after the ratings had been performed.

*Asked only in 2000.   **Asked only in 2005.

of occupations?" In 2000, a non-trivial 40 percent answered yes, and many elaborated in the space for details provided on the question screen. Some of the write-in responses are merely underlining or re-phrasing choices already made from the closed-response question. Frequent mention is made, for example, of educational preparation, equivalent to the "qualifications" choice from the checklist. Others, however, introduce a variety of considerations into the assessment of occupational prestige. Respondents mentioned how well an occupation allows a balance with leisure time, the honesty of practitioners of an occupation, and the environmental implications of occupations, none of these being themes very reminiscent of functionalist-era interpretations of prestige. Service-sector or "people-oriented jobs" were seen as especially deserving of prestige for more than one respondent. It became apparent from inspection of these open-ended comments that occupations were often evaluated in terms of an incumbent of that occupation known to the respondent, as Glick et al. (1995) suggest, even though the question design of the NORC prestige studies works so hard to minimize that factor (Siegel 1971, 31). More than one respondent reminded us of "terminology," how "the words used by the survey to define the job can influence how we perceive the social standing." Relevant to the social-change focus of the present volume was one respondent's observation about "[t]ime in history, for example teachers do not have the same social standing they used to due to bad publicity from cases where teachers have abused children at school." Some respondents were genuine egalitarians, for example the one who told us "every job is just as important as any other job, i.e., if there's no janitor in the hospital there's no point in having doctors or nurses" (all the above, respondents on 2000 KWMAS). This was not the first time egalitarians have turned up on prestige surveys. There are examples from England (Young and Willmott 1956) and from Denmark (Svalastoga 1959, 58–9), although not from the United States, that I have encountered in the research reports. As later chapters shall document, the egalitarian streak in the twenty-first-century Canadian data has become sufficiently strong to have a noticeable impact on scores.

Over a quarter of the 2005 respondents offered further explanation beyond the checklist closed questions described in table 3.7. Some respondents were sociologically astute. "The way society and media present and perceive these occupations," one said. "Supply and demand," mentioned another. The power of labour unions to enhance status was noted. Resolute egalitarians turned up in 2005, as in 2000. "All jobs are equal in front of God. That's why I gave so many 5," said one person. "Everybody contributes to society," said another in the same vein. Another: "le statut social n'existe pas pour moi" (for me, social status does not exist). A few in 2005, as in 2000, drew the environmental impact of occupations into the equation. One person revealed frankly what sociologists interested in occupational prestige have often suspected, that the sound of an occupation title conveys status cues: "more upper-class jobs. [L]ike I rated jobs that to me sounded like they were more upper-class." It is a nice example of the stereotyping theme discussed by Coxon and Jones (1978, 2–9; see also Thielbar and Feldman 1969). Another respondent drew attention to a high proportion of immigrants in an occupation as a marker of low prestige. "L'attrait scientifique" (scientific image), one said, congruent with the analysis by Zhou (2005). Danger and risk were mentioned, as were skills separate from formal education. Some people said that it is not the job but how well the job is performed that determines prestige, echoing the prestige vs esteem distinction from chapter 1. A variant of that theme came from the several respondents who referred to the typical "integrity" or "honesty" of incumbents as being a key determinant of the prestige of the job itself. Some favoured sectors of the labour force, such as "producing" rather than "shuffling papers." A surprisingly frequent theme was the notion that a person who is conscientious at and content with his or her job has high prestige. Here again, respondents resist the sociologist's insistence on role over person.

There is a nuance within the occupational-prestige literature of good respondents who know how the society works and bad ones who have cognitive gaps and are not very useful to have on a survey. Such a division does not come through as one reads through the textual responses to the open-ended probes in the 2000 and 2005 surveys. Many times, people are giving views that fall off the main path for discussions of occupational prestige, but these are well-articulated thoughts that convey conviction and consideration. This material cautions against any strategy of trimming out respondents deemed to be insufficiently expert or knowledgable about occupations.

TIMER VARIABLES

Computerized survey administration programs allow recording of the time taken by each respondent to answer each question. Such variables add a behavioural dimension to the traditional attitude-opinion bias of survey research. In both the year 2000 pilot KWMAS survey and the national survey of 2005, timers were inserted for every one of the occupation titles. A data set to express the times was constructed by treating each time for each occupation as one observation in a long column. In the 2005 data, there were the four titles common across the entire sample, giving 2,053 times 4 = 8,212 lines of observations, plus the 21 titles rated within each sub-sample, sub-samples comprising around 200 cases each. The over-all cumulative file has 51,325 lines. The modal time for each rating was 5 seconds, the median 6 seconds, and, with the right-skewed distribution by which just small proportions puzzled for many seconds over a title and most moved along quickly, the mean number of seconds is 7.5. A plot in figure 3.1 shows the shape of the distribution for 2005. Ninety percent of all key strokes for the occupation rating were completed by the thirteenth second. In these calculations, times of less than 1 second have been excluded, since they are the result of cases where respondents went back to change a rating. Times over 1 minute have also been excluded, since they would most likely arise in cases where interviews were broken off and resumed on another occasion. There is the appearance of a natural breaking point in the distribution at around the sixty-second mark. The timer data are not perfect but do give a rough notion of how quickly respondents moved through the rating task.

COVERAGE OF THE LABOUR FORCE

Of 520 occupation unit groups in the NOC-S, 207, or 40 percent, were represented within the 210 labour force titles rated in the 2005 survey. Since there are dozens of separate names of occupations within many of the unit groups, a prestige study can capture only a fraction of the total labour force. Unit groups are, however, the finest calibration available with the Canada census and the basis upon which income and educational data are tabulated for each occupation. Of some 8.6 million full-year, full-time workers in the 2001 census, 60 percent were represented within the 210 labour

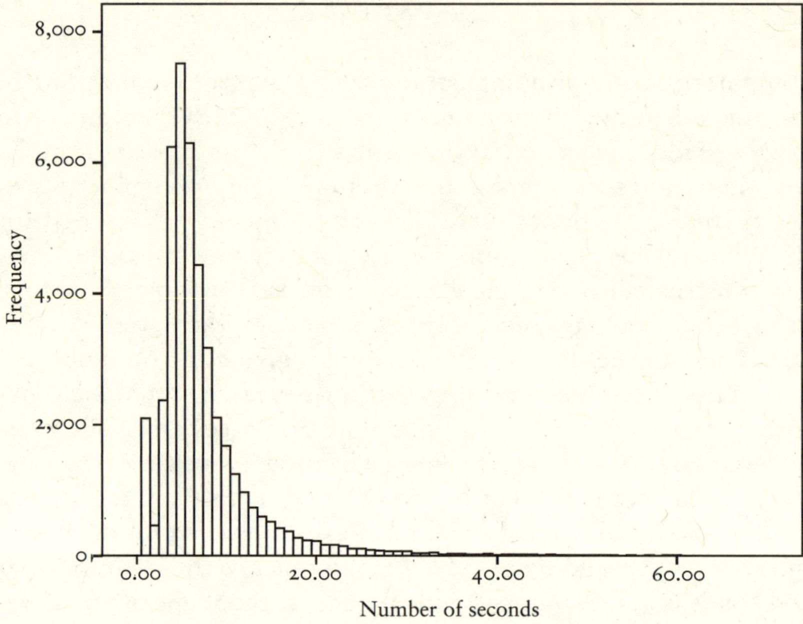

Fig. 3.1   Distribution times for ratings, 2005 survey. Cumulative over all respondents and all occupations, and excluding < 1 second and > 60

force titles examined in the 2005 survey. All 26 major groups within the Human Resources and Skills Development Canada (HRSDC) National Occupational Classification are represented, although two have just one title each.

Percentage coverage of the labour force was not a high priority with the present work. In contrast to the later NORC studies (Siegel 1971; Nakao and Treas 1994), and more like the British work of Goldthorpe and Hope (1974, 27), my concern was a theoretically informative sampling of occupations, rather than saturation coverage. Complete coverage of the Canadian labour force would have required fieldwork three times the size of that conducted in 2005. The increase in cost would not have justified the return.

SAMPLE REPRESENTATIVENESS

Comparisons between the 1965 and 2005 samples and the nearest decennial census appear in table 3.8. The analysis is modelled after work by Pineo (1967), in which the key socio-demographic infor-

Table 3.8
Sample-Census Comparisons, for 2005 and 1965 National Canadian Surveys (for Age 21 and Over, Unless Specified Otherwise)

Characteristics of Participants	2005 Sample (%)	2001 Census (%)	1965 Sample (%)	1961 Census (%)
Labour Force Status				
In labour force	68.9	67.8	52.5	55.8
Not in labour force	31.1	32.2	47.5	44.2
Significance test, sample sample vs. census		p > 0.5		p > .05
Sex				
Male	42.8	48.3	46.5	50.2
Female	57.2	51.7	53.5	49.8
Significance test, sample vs. census		p < .001		p > .05
Birthplace				
Canada	83.9	76.5	81.7	76.5
UK	2.1	2.8	6.7	8.3
USA	1.5	1.1	2.3	2.4
Europe	5.9	7.5	8.8	11.8
Other	6.7	12.1	0.5	1.0
Significance test, sample vs. census		p < .001		p < .02
Age				
21–24	6.8	7.2	8.3	10.0
25–29	7.5	8.8	10.9	10.8
30–34	8.8	9.7	15.2	11.1
35–39	10.4	11.7	12.2	11.6
40–44	12.2	12.0	13.7	11.3
45–49	11.8	10.9	10.1	9.8
50–64	28.9	22.9	20.4	21.9
65 or more	13.6	16.9	9.1	13.6
Significance test, sample vs. census		p < .001		p < .001
Education				
Less than bachelor's degree	69.7	82.8	93.2	96.8
BA or more	30.3	17.2	6.8	3.2
Significance test, sample vs. census		p < .001		p < .001
*Urban-rural**				
Census Metropolitan Area	53.6	78.2	45.4	47.9
Non-CMA	46.4	21.8	54.6	52.1
Significance test, sample vs. census		p < .001		p > .05

*Population 15 and over in 2001 census, 18 and over in 2005 sample. The city entries for the 2005 sample are open-ended names of cities, in which CMA's are greatly under-estimated. From Statistics Canada Community Profiles, the ratio of CMA to core city was calculated for each 2001 CMA. These were applied as correction factors to the 2005 sample estimates.

mation from the 1965 survey was compared with the 1961 census. Since these figures covered the population aged twenty-one and over, the 2005 data were computed the same way, even though the sample begins at age eighteen. As well, the categories used in the earlier comparison were duplicated as much as possible, for consistency, resulting in coding decisions (e.g., around country of birth) that might not be followed today if no historical comparison were being attempted. The 2005 survey figures are compared to the 2001 census. The 1965 sample was collected, as noted already, by personal interview, giving a 64 percent response rate, a much higher rate than the 51 percent from the 2005 telephone survey. Some survey non-response biasses consistent over the entire forty-year stretch will be observed below, while in other cases the challenges of modern fieldwork create unique problems for the data.

Often in both years, the samples did not match the census within the bounds of error allowed by a significance test at the .05 level. Only in the case of labour force status is the sample-census fit very close in both years. The rise in labour force participation between 1961 and 2001, from 55.8 percent to 67.8 percent, is the result, of course, mainly of the increase in the female work force. The 2005 survey under-enumerated males, to the quite noticeable degree of 5.5 percentage points (48.3 percent males in the 2001 census, 42.8 percent in the 2005 sample). The same over-representation of women was present in the 1965 data, but to a more muted degree. Both samples are biassed toward too many Canadian-born. The 2005 set has a sharp under-representation of non-European, UK or U.S. immigrants. As already noted, Jolicoeur reported particular problems in getting interviews from Chinese Canadians in British Columbia, and here is evidence of the consequence. The 2005 sample under-enumerated people aged under forty. In contrast, the 1965 interviewers fared poorly with the group aged fifty and over. Mode effect, in contrast, should see telephone contact succeeding particularly *well* among those under age forty-five, compared to the personal interview mode (Groves and Kahn 1979, 92). The present pattern thus points to a historical change whereby obtaining a survey response has become more difficult among the young middle aged. The categories for education are hard to equate over this forty-year comparison. In 1961, only 3.2 percent of the population had university completion. By 2001 there were many more non-university post-secondary options. Even with the massive rise in university education among the Canadian population, the characteristic "middle-class bias" is evident in both the 1965 and the 2005 samples. Proportionately, the degree of bias is surprisingly consistent (2005, 30.3, 17.2; 1965, 6.8, 3.2 – about two to one in each case). The 1965 sample under-estimated the urban (in Census Metropolitan Areas) population by just a trifle; by 2005 this bias had become massive, another casualty of the modern survey environment. The population in CMAs in 2001 was 78.2 percent from the census, with the 2005 sample estimate of 53.6 percent falling far short.

This review has detected several rather serious socio-demographic biasses in the 2005 sample data, perhaps most notably around education and residence in a CMA. It is fortunate that computer technology has advanced so much since 1965 that quite a different statistical approach can be taken to the data now, compared to then. In a later chapter scores at the level of the individual respondent will be examined across the core socio-demographic categories. It will be shown how easily prestige scores for each occupation can be corrected for systematic bias attributable to groups such as the less educated.

COGNITIVE EXPERIMENTS WITH OCCUPATION TITLES

In framing the list of occupations for the 2005 survey, issues of whether or not to modernize titles frequently arose. For six of the 1965 titles, both old and new title wordings were deliberately carried in 2005. Results from the six comparisons appear in table 3.9. These scores are all from the 2005 survey. Generally, it is reassuring that minor variations have little effect on scores. Consider, for example, "trailer-truck driver" from 1965, which struck some of the informants I consulted as a strange wording for 2005. The alternative wording "tractor-trailer driver," rated by sub-sample four, came in at 53.81 points, indistinguishably above the older wording, rated by sub-sample one. Adding the qualifier "professionally trained" to "librarian," the 1965 wording, made no discernable difference since plain "librarian" was scored minutely higher (63.24 vs 62.34). In contrast, the noun "operator" seems to depress scores when it appears in an occupation title. "Pumphouse engineer" from 1965 was rated some 13 points higher than "pumphouse operator,"

Table 3.9
Results from Wording Experiments

1965 Wording of Title [Occupation Number]	Mean Score (s.d.) [Median Time]	2005 Wording of Title [Occupation Number]	Mean Score (s.d.) [Median Time]
Professionally trained librarian [317]	62.34 (22.83) [6]	Librarian [419]	63.24 (22.43) [4]
Newspaper pressman* [1019]	55.25 (22.22) [5]	Newspaper press operator [212]	50.91 (21.23) [5]
Pumphouse engineer* [917]	63.49 (21.90) [6]	Pumphouse operator [103]	50.27 (23.42) [7]
Steam roller operator* [216]	44.59 (22.24) [5]	Roller operator [815]	48.64 (21.04) [6]
Sales clerk in a store* [513]	47.57 (22.68) [5]	Sales associate – retail [802]	49.00 (19.79) [6]
Trailer-truck driver [106]	53.31 (25.48) [5]	Tractor-trailer driver [418]	53.81 (23.54) [5]

*Difference of means test has $p < .05$ across row.

a statistically significant difference. Similarly, "newspaper pressmen" had a score of 55.25, noticeably above "newspaper press operator," at 50.91. The loftier phrasing "sales associate" in place of "sales clerk" raised the prestige of this occupation, but by only a trivial, albeit statistically significant, amount.

Table 3.9 includes time to rate each title. Owing to the skew typical of the timer variables, it is the median rather than the mean that is entered. Only in one comparison, "librarian" when substituted for "professionally trained librarian," did the modernized wording result in quicker decisions for respondents. All-in-all, these experiments suggested that small wording variations are not an issue in occupational prestige ratings except for a few key qualifiers such as "engineer," which today more than in 1965 implies a university-trained professional engineer, and the status-detracting "operator."

With this description of the main features of the data, we may proceed in the next chapter to substantive results.

ZERO-TO-ONE-HUNDRED SCALE

I followed the long-standing tradition in occupational-prestige research of transforming the nine categories presented to respondents into a 0-to-100 scale. The transformation is as follows: multiply raw scores (1 to 9) by 12.5, and then subtract 12.5 from that product (Nakao and Treas 1994, 8). The notion is that the transformed scores are a little easier to read and interpret. I tend to report transformed scores when talking about occupations (as in chapter 4) and raw scores when talking about respondents (as in chapter 5, for example).

METHODOLOGICAL SUMMARY

Trade-offs permeate research on occupational prestige, as in many areas of social research. The NORC rating question design is simple, and methodologically skilled critics could easily raise that to "simple-minded." In this study I am playing the replication card, stressing value in repeating, as closely as possible, a study from 1965 in 2005, nearly two generations later. As shown in later chapters, some of the longitudinal differences are striking. For the main findings, the precise statistical specification does not matter. Readers seeking the greatest statistical rigour will say that the NORC one-to-nine scale is ordinal, not interval, and they may want to see ordinal regression results, which Zhou (2005) introduced. My reply is that ordinal regression, which I did experiment with, simply substitutes a scoring that shifts with each re-specification of the model and that is not a solution to interpreting what people mean when they select a score for an occupation. Appendix A provides a table comparing OLS results against ordinal regression. Bates et al. (1986) present evidence that prestige scores are methodologically robust. Another critic could point to the innovative methodological work done over the years on design of the rating task, and some of the main developments were sketched in chapter 1. My reply here is that the richest designs involve far more response burden than we can ask of the twenty-first-century survey respondent sampled from the general public. Many of the more complex measures have involved university student samples, who are semi-captive and well accustomed to performing cognitive tasks (e.g., Villemez 1974). A magnitude-scaling (Kuennapas and Wikstroem 1963; Lodge 1981) approach to occupational prestige, for example, simply would not work with a general-public sample, and yet it is what the general public thinks about occupations that makes this research tradition worthwhile.

magnitude-scaling (Kuennapas and Wikstroem 1963; Lodge 1981)

4

High Scores and Low Scores

The examination of occupational-prestige ratings will begin with the individual scores and then shift to modeling the entire set. Table 4.1 shows the scores for all 214 titles rated in the 2005 survey. This includes some non-labour force titles and the deliberately overlapped ones noted in chapter 3. Later tables will reduce down to labour force occupational titles rated in both 1965 and 2005, but, to start with, occupational prestige 2005 version, the first such scale at the national level in Canada in forty years.

"Physician" led the scale in 2005, with a score of 90. In 1965 physician was second-ranked, after "provincial premier," a title not rated in 2005. Other professions such as "university professor" and "biologist" appear among the top ten scores, but so, more surprisingly, does "firefighter," with a score of 82. One of the most spectacular gainers in prestige over forty years, firefighting received favourable mass media coverage during the 9/11 tragedy. For example, from a column reviewing several books on 9/11: "Oligarchs, politicians and celebrities, their wealth, power or fame suddenly meaningless, stood shoulder to shoulder with the firefighters, police, paramedics and public from far and near, the whole great, warm tide of humanity suddenly united and made equal by a pitiless storm and the thunderclouds of death" (*Globe and Mail*, 7 September 2002, D2).

People living in the risk-averse (Giddens 1991, chap. 4) social climate of global information-age society were reminded that, when the veneer of civilization and normality breaks down, no

Table 4.1
Scores for all Occupation Titles Rated in 2005, in Descending Order

Identifier in 2005 Dataset	Title Rated	Score (0–100 Format)	Standard Deviation
OC411	Physician	90.5	13.8
OC203	Chief of emergency medicine	88.3	18.7
OC818	University professor	84.3	18.4
O1018	Firefighter	82.3	17.7
OC117	Biologist	82.3	17.4
OC602	Airline pilot	82.2	17.6
OC504	Registered nurse	81.6	15.3
OC207	Pharmacist	81.5	18.2
OC121	Physicist	80.6	20.5
OC213	County court judge	80.6	23.7
OC414	Mayor of a large city	80.4	21.1
O1003	High school teacher	80.3	17.4
OC921	Police officer	78.6	22.5
OC320	Veterinarian	78.1	17.4
OC613	President of one of the large banks	77.8	26.1
OC220	Forensic laboratory technician	77.7	18.5
OC806	Chemist	77.7	20.4
OC118	Elementary school teacher	77.5	17.8
O1021	Occupation of my family's main wage earner	77.3	18.5
O1004	Architect	77.3	17.4
OC402	Civil engineer	77.3	17.8
O1009	Psychologist	76.7	20.6
OC704	Medical laboratory technologist	75.7	19.9
OC111	Environmental science manager	75.6	19.3
OC119	Physiotherapist	75.4	18.1
OC609	Aircraft mechanic	75.1	19.8
OC914	Mathematician	74.8	20.6
OC703	Mining engineer	74.6	19.6
OC413	Colonel in the army	74.1	21.8
OC101	General manager of a manufacturing plant	73.4	19.7
OC316	Ship's pilot	73.2	20.3
OC606	Lawyer	73.1	27.4
OC715	Sociologist	73.0	19.2
OC902	Social worker	71.4	21.2
OC214	Farm owner and operator	70.5	22.4
O1016	Chiropractor	70.3	22.2
O1002	Manager, financial planning and analysis	70.1	20.9
OC702	Financial analyst	69.3	21.0
OC620	Manager of a farm	69.2	20.4
OC904	Author	69.0	23.5
OC804	Bank manager	69.0	22.2
OC812	Accountant	68.9	22.7
OC412	Musician in a symphony orchestra	68.5	22.8
OC916	Economist	68.4	19.2
OC511	Journalist	68.0	20.8

Table 4.1 (continued)

Identifier in 2005 Dataset	Title Rated	Score (0–100 Format)	Standard Deviation
OC607	Electrician	67.9	21.9
OC405	Superintendent of a construction job	67.8	20.8
OC721	TV director	67.7	21.8
OC718	Department head in city government	67.2	24.7
OC309	Building contractor	67.2	18.4
OC508	Mine safety inspector	67.1	23.4
OC407	Locomotive engineer	67.0	22.0
OC218	Computer programmer	66.5	21.3
OC604	Dental hygienist	66.4	22.1
OC501	Gas field operations manager	65.9	21.5
OC406	Child-care provider in a private home	65.1	26.1
OC113	Bookkeeper	65.0	20.3
O1015	Executive secretary	64.3	20.0
OC520	Land surveyor	64.1	21.1
OC615	Waste management director	64.1	21.2
OC311	Professional forester	64.1	21.9
OC707	Draughtsman	64 0	18.5
OC917	Pumphouse engineer	63.5	21.9
OC502	Member of Canadian Senate	63.5	31.2
OC318	Member of Canadian House of Commons	63.3	29.1
OC419	Librarian	63.2	22.4
OC920	Professional athlete	63.1	27.8
OC415	TV announcer	63.1	21.7
OC515	Plumber	62.9	20.6
O1012	Manager of a supermarket	62.8	19.7
OC903	Power lineman	62.7	24.6
OC310	Dairy farmer	62.5	23.3
OC317	Professionally trained librarian	62.3	22.8
OC208	Job counsellor	62.2	22.7
OC820	Hospital attendant	62.1	24.5
OC314	YMCA director	61.8	22.8
OC919	Owner of a coffee shop	61.4	22.6
OC306	Construction foreman	61.3	17.5
OC803	House carpenter	61.1	20.2
OC506	Computer numerically controlled machining tool operator	60.9	24.6
OC114	Funeral director	60.9	23.1
OC907	Manager of a real estate office	60.8	21.6
OC108	Tool and die maker	60.3	21.2
OC603	Advertising executive	60.3	24.3
OC516	Welder	60.2	22.3
OC112	Protestant minister	60.1	29.9
OC201	Member of a city council	60.1	25.0
OC714	Machinist	59.9	24.2
OC517	TV cameraman	59.8	21.8
OC505	Automobile mechanic	59.8	20.7

Table 4.1 (continued)

Identifier in 2005 Dataset	Title Rated	Score (0–100 Format)	Standard Deviation
OC303	Administrative officer in federal civil service	59.7	24.5
OC215	Public relations officer	59.1	22.8
OC709	Railroad conductor	58.9	23.8
O1006	Bus driver	58.9	25.1
OC403	User support technician	58.9	21.1
OC507	Production worker in the electronics industry	58.9	21.5
OC307	Flight attendant	58.7	22.3
O1014	Cook in a restaurant	58.6	22.6
OC617	Web site developer	58.5	24.6
OC2	Survey research director	58.4	22.3
OC120	Motel owner	58.2	22.3
OC521	Merchandise buyer for a department store	58.0	18.7
OC811	Power crane operator	57.6	22.2
OC209	Oil field worker	57.5	22.6
OC619	Hospital information clerk	57.5	24.3
OC708	Private in the army	57.5	28.1
OC105	Construction labourer	57.4	25.1
OC618	Administrative assistant	57.3	21.9
O1007	Advertising copy writer	57.3	20.6
OC807	Commercial artist	57.0	22.3
OC211	Insurance claims investigator	56.9	23.3
OC912	Farm labourer	56.9	25.9
OC805	Jazz musician	56.9	23.0
OC519	Wholesale distributor	56.8	18.7
OC809	Mail carrier	56.7	21.4
O1001	Bricklayer	56.2	21.7
OC503	Typesetter	56.1	22.6
OC321	Catholic priest	56.1	29.6
OC116	Sculptor	55.9	25.6
OC416	Diamond driller	55.8	23.5
OC913	Accounts payable clerk	55.5	22.1
O1019	Newspaper pressman	55.2	22.2
OC308	Foreman of workers in a papermill	55.2	19.9
OC611	Real estate agent	55.1	22.1
OC710	Playground director	55.0	25.0
OC821	Manager of a motel	54.7	22.9
OC204	Manufacturer's representative	54.6	19.7
OC910	Trade union business agent	54.2	23.7
OC301	Steam plant operator	54.0	22.7
OC901	Clerk in an office	54.0	20.2
OC418	Tractor-trailer driver	53.8	23.5
OC110	Travel agent	53.8	21.7
OC817	Steel mill worker	53.7	22.9
OC3	Survey statistician	53.6	22.5
OC601	Ballet dancer	53.4	28.3
OC404	Purchasing officer	53.3	19.3

Table 4.1 (continued)

Identifier in 2005 Dataset	Title Rated	Score (0–100 Format)	Standard Deviation
OC106	Trailer truck driver	53.3	25.5
OC401	Receptionist	53.2	23.6
OC221	Livestock buyer	53.1	22.9
OC315	Baker	53.1	22.9
OC312	Bank teller	53.0	23.6
OC612	Quarry worker	53.0	23.6
OC701	Insurance agent	53.0	22.6
OC421	Sheet metal worker	52.9	22.3
OC712	Automobile assembly worker	52.9	25.2
OC107	Custom seamstress	52.8	22.8
OC720	Oiler in a ship	52.8	24.4
OC409	Butcher in a store	52.7	23.5
OC319	Driving instructor	52.6	22.6
OC713	Railroad sectionhand	52.6	24.2
OC4	Supervisor of survey interviewers	52.4	22.4
OC906	Longshoreman	52.2	20.6
OC716	Post office clerk	52.1	24.3
OC608	House painter	51.6	21.7
OC717	Manager of a coffee shop	51.5	22.5
O1010	Logger	51.2	25.4
OC408	Sawmill operator	51.2	21.1
OC212	Newspaper press operator	50.9	21.4
OC509	Coal miner	50.7	25.7
OC512	Pollster	50.4	25.6
OC814	Mucking machine operator	50.4	22.5
OC103	Pumphouse operator	50.3	23.4
OC915	Travelling salesperson, wholesale trade	50.3	22.4
OC115	Barber	49.8	24.3
O1005	Data entry operator	49.4	21.1
OC808	Beauty salon operator	49.0	22.9
OC802	Sales associate – retail	49.0	19.8
OC911	Flagperson on a road construction site	48.8	27.6
OC719	Telephone operator	48.8	24.7
OC815	Roller operator	48.6	21.0
OC918	TV repairman	48.6	24.0
OC621	Loom operator	48.4	21.6
OC219	Apprentice bricklayer	48.4	22.6
OC616	Waitress in a restaurant	48.3	24.1
OC614	Forging press operator	48.4	20.3
OC81	Timber cruiser	48.2	23.0
OC1	Survey interviewer	48.1	24.5
OC410	Paper making machine operator	47.9	25.0
O1008	Garbage collector	47.9	28.2
OC305	Textile dyer	47.8	20.6
OC102	Typist	47.6	23.3
OC513	Sales clerk in a store	47.6	22.7

Table 4.1 (continued)

Identifier in 2005 Dataset	Title Rated	Score (0–100 Format)	Standard Deviation
OC705	Cod fisherman	47.6	25.3
OC202	Service station manager	47.5	23.2
OC909	Cleaning lady	47.4	25.5
OC313	Housekeeper in a private home	46.9	25.6
OC908	Someone who lives off inherited wealth	46.3	30.4
OC610	Museum attendant	46.1	23.0
OC514	File clerk	45.9	21.4
OC109	Cashier in a supermarket	46.0	26.8
OC810	Carpenter's helper	45.8	21.4
OC101	Sewing machine operator	45.3	23.3
OC210	Truck dispatcher	44.8	23.4
OC518	Janitor	44.8	25.4
OC216	Steam roller operator	44.6	22.2
OC816	Shipping clerk	43.7	21.7
OC706	Worker in a meat packing plant	43.6	26.2
OC711	Lunchroom operator	43.3	27.1
OC206	Book binder	43.3	22.9
OC417	Bartender	43.1	23.6
OC510	Taxicab driver	41.5	25.0
OC217	Railroad ticket agent	41.5	22.9
O1020	Filling station attendant	41.2	26.6
OC905	Saw sharpener	41.1	24.3
OC205	Stockroom attendant	40.4	24.7
OC104	Fruit packer in a cannery	40.1	24.5
OC302	Warehouse hand	39.5	22.3
OC801	Worker in a dry cleaning or laundry plant	38.3	21.0
O1017	Bill collector	38.1	25.9
OC605	Disc jockey	37.8	27.0
O1013	Used car salesman	37.1	24.2
OC304	Doorkeeper	36.1	23.5
OC420	Telemarketer	32.8	29.3
OC813	Someone who lives on social assistance	22.1	22.6

Note: Computed from the survey Occupational Prestige in Canada: 2005. 214 titles rated.

occupational function exceeds in importance the rescue and care of victims. Even before September 2001, occupations such as firefighter and nurse had been ascending in prestige. In the year 2000 pilot study for Kitchener-Waterloo, firefighters had 75 points (up from 52 in 1975), while nurses scored 77 (up from 67). The high profile of terror between 2000 and 2005 seems to have accelerated that upward momentum. It is much the same for police officer and for several of the other vital services. A column from the *Globe and Mail* of 16 July 2004 (A13) commented on a power cut with the words "despite the glam of IT and the cultural industries, we all remain dependent on those who have the ability to grow a crop, sew a garment, fix a car or repair a power line." In the Leger Marketing survey of occupations most trusted for 2006, nurses came second (95 percent trust) behind firefighters (96 percent trust), well ahead of judges (78 percent) not to mention lawyers (48 percent). In the United States, although an academic survey on occupational prestige has not been conducted since 1989, a Harris Poll from 2005 agreed that "firemen, doctors, scientists, nurses and teachers are all seen as prestigious occupations by U.S. adults."[1]

George Counts (1925) might have noted the high prestige of school teaching in table 4.1, some eighty years after his explorations on the prestige of this calling just after World War One. As in the 1920s data from the United States, respondents in the 2005 Canadian sample allowed a little more prestige to teachers at the high school (80) than to those of elementary (78) levels. Both finished among the 20 highest-rated occupations.

Corporate leaders, despite their high earnings over the past two decades, do not dominate the top of the prestige ratings. The highest-scoring corporate occupation is "president of one of the large banks" in fifteenth place in the rank-order, scoring 78, despite the big salary drawn by the CEO of any of the major Canadian banks. Here is one of many indicators that earnings are only part of what determines prestige. Just as press commentary over the past half dozen years praises the essential service occupations such as firefighter, it has, as noted in chapter 2, attacked the inflation of salaries for company CEOs, both in Canada and the United States. The mortgage crisis in the United States in 2008, occurring well after the 2005 survey was collected, can only have deepened the reservations members of the public hold about corporate leaders.

With the score for "occupation of my family's main wage earner" at 77, or the 91st percentile, we have first evidence of prestige maximization of self or near-self. The same cue scored much closer to the middle, its logical location, in 1965 (62nd percentile). As suggested earlier, part of twenty-first-century culture seems to be a nurturing of the self-concept, less common a generation ago. A 22 August 2007 (C2) *Globe and Mail* report on its "weekly web poll," interesting if utterly unrepresentative by scientific survey standards, expresses the modern way of self-evaluation. Asked "where do you think you rank as a performer at your company?" an incredible 51 percent of respondents placed themselves in the top 10 percent. Only ratings of graduate students by their professors writing reference letters are more inflated.

Among the academic professions, the general role of "university professor" outscores each of the specific disciplines rated, a well-established pattern in prestige surveys (Collins 2000, 18). Natural scientists (biologist, physicist, chemist) rank above social scientists, who have their own pecking order of psychologist, sociologist, economist. I hope reporting these findings does not create faculty club disharmony across Canadian campuses.

The first clearly blue-collar title is "aircraft mechanic," at 75, in the 88th percentile in the 2005 list, up from 61st in 1965. "Farm owner and operator" rose in relative prestige from the 50th percentile in 1965 to the 84th in 2005, scoring 71 in the latter year. That, of course, is contrary to what seemed likely (chapter 2) before examining the data, but it is part of the renewed appreciation of the basic occupational functions that seems to be taking place. Arts occupations make their first appearance with "author" at the 81st percentile (83rd percentile in 1965). "Musician in a symphony orchestra," with a score rounding up to 69 in 2005, falls within a point of "author" in this more recent survey, compared to a little lower, relatively, in 1965.

The curiously named "professional babysitter" title from 1965, near the bottom at the 11th percentile in this earlier survey, leaped to the 74th percentile (65 points) in 2005 after being renamed "child-care provider in a private home." The comparison is inexact, given the radical title rewording, but it is hard to dispel the impression that in the era of dual-career couples, finding competent child care is an issue of far different priority than in the 1960s environment of only 33 percent of women in the paid labour force. Amazingly, "child-care provider" scores slightly above occupations such as "member of the Canadian Senate" or "member of the Canadian House of Commons." These inversions are something readers of late-twentieth-century and early-twenty-first-century occupational prestige scales must get used to. Sawinski and Domanski (1991a, 232), for example, drew attention in their data to the "astonishing" ascent of the title "miner," to 2d rank out of 29 in 1989. Even with the "crucial role of mining for the recovery of the Polish economy," there must have been a strong dimension of approval/disapproval at work for turn-of-century raters of occupational prestige. As noted in the last chapter, this comes out in open-ended comments by the Canadian survey respondents. Among people feeling that standard of living is "not at all important" for deciding on the prestige of an occupation, the child-care score jumped to 75. Among people believing "most other people would give occupations the same ratings you just did," the score for child-care provider was lower than for those who thought they were separated from general opinion. Other evidence on this contrarian streak comes from a letter to the editor of a newspaper from 2004 (*Globe and Mail*, 13 November, A26). A reader from Vancouver wrote, "We should not only pay child-care workers more than gas-station attendants, we should pay them more than university professors." Some sociologists might want to dismiss the high score being attributed to child-care workers in Canada or miners in Poland as reflecting ignorance or flippancy among the public, but it is more within the sociological tradition to think about what motivates people to make ratings so out of line with educational prerequisites and income rewards for occupations.

As a colleague remarked, it is as though the survey respondents are by-passing "common understandings of class or status among sociologists," in at least some of their ratings, and thinking in terms of "the discredited concept"of functional importance (Anonymous 2008). I think the essential shift is that the functional importance of an occupation has become decoupled from the replaceability of an individual worker in that occupation. Davis and Moore (1945, 242–4), in their foundational article on this topic, began with the declaration that "the main functional necessity explaining the universal presence of stratification is precisely the requirement faced by any society of placing and motivating individuals in the social structure." This placing and motivating of individuals was accomplished through pay ("the things that contribute to sustenance and comfort"), good working conditions ("things that contribute to humor and diversion"), and prestige ("things that contribute to self respect and ego expansion"). In a section on "the two determinants of positional rank," they refer to "differential functional importance" of the occupation as one factor and scarcity of personnel as the other. The issue of replaceability enters here, since Davis and Moore understand scarcity as derived mainly from length and difficulty of training required. The "two determinants" used to overlap, but perhaps not so much now. Therefore the notion of each occupation having a final, unambiguous rank erodes, and we have the sociologically puzzling finding of occupations that do not have especially high training prerequisites or very high incomes holding high prestige.

Respondents on surveys of occupations most trusted have been expressing their distrust of politicians for years (e.g., Ekos results reported in the *Globe and Mail* of 6 May 1996, A3, showing "politicians" trusted by only 15 percent of Canadians, against 80 percent trusting farmers). The 2005 prestige scores tally with these other studies. Once more, and true to the post-modernist theme noted in chapter 2, the twenty-first-century respondents seem less likely than their counterparts in 1965 to recite back scores for the prestige of occupations based on external markers such as educational prerequisites, income and mid-twentieth-century assessments of functional importance. I shall investigate this more formally below.

The middle of the 2005 range brings together an assortment of occupations as varied as "bus driver" (old economy), "user support technician" (new economy), "flight attendant" (service economy), "motel owner" (self-employed sector). As noted in chapter 3, owner-titles were minimized in 2005, since ownership is not conceptually part of the NOC code, as it was with the classification for occupations that Pineo and Porter (1967) were working with. I did, however, embed one experiment comparing owners and managers, using motels as the case study. Pineo and Porter examined "motel owner," and for 2005, along with that title, "motel manager" was added. As the middle portion of table 4.1 shows, the ownership specification added some 3.5 prestige points to the motel score.

The clergy were treated harshly by the 2005 respondents (e.g., "Catholic priest," 118th of the 214 titles). Priests only make the middle of the trust lists generated by commercial survey firms such as Leger and in recent years have received adverse press coverage (e.g., "Priest Says Boy Sexually Assaulted Once," *Cape Breton Post*, 6 September 2007, front page).

The bottom half of table 4.1 mixes lower white-collar with lower service and unskilled blue collar occupations. There is little new economy premium apparent. For example, "data entry operator" 165th of the 214, falls immediately after such an ancient service occupation as "barber," closely followed by "flagperson on a road construction site." "Telephone operator," a favourite example for

Menzies (1996) of a once-important occupation de-skilled by technology, is in the lowest quarter of the ratings in 2005.

The notion of moral disapproval driving down some ratings reappears when the score for "telemarketer" (33 points, second lowest, followed only by "someone who lives on social assistance") is compared with "survey interviewer" at 48 points, a much higher score for a skill set similar to a telemarketer's.

Occupational prestige ratings for 2005, then, clearly involve more than the respondent's knowledge of educational preparation and income rewards for occupations. By regressing prestige scores onto, first, mean educational level for each title recorded in the census and then income, we can identify for which occupations the prestige score departs most greatly from the straightforward socioeconomic expectations. To do this, the occupation titles rated had to be translated into National Occupation Classification (NOC) unit groups (2001 edition), the four-digit detailed classification used in the census. Danger of slippage arises in making these matches. Professions such as "lawyer" are unambiguous, but not a title such as "jazz musician," falling into NOC 5133 unit group "musicians and singers." That category combines jazz musicians with rock singers, opera singers, private music teachers, and others. The earnings would fluctuate greatly within the unit group, and so the information gained about jazz musicians is only approximate. A title such as "TV announcer," NOC 5231 ("announcers and other broadcasters") cannot distinguish between a local-station announcer and those appearing on the national networks. Despite these complications, there is much to be learned from the census data.

Figure 4.1 plots prestige for the labour force titles rated in 2005 (excluding, for example, "someone who lives on social assistance" or "occupation of my family's main wage earner") by education. The education code here is the proportion with university as of the 2001 census less the proportion with elementary only, used partly to facilitate jumping across census years (as done later in this chapter), but also to remain close to the practice used in work on socioeconomic indexes for occupations (Blishen et al. 1987). The graph has been swept for outliers of 15 prestige points or more. These are labeled on the plot and show some of the most extreme cases of prestige either above or below what would be predicted from education.

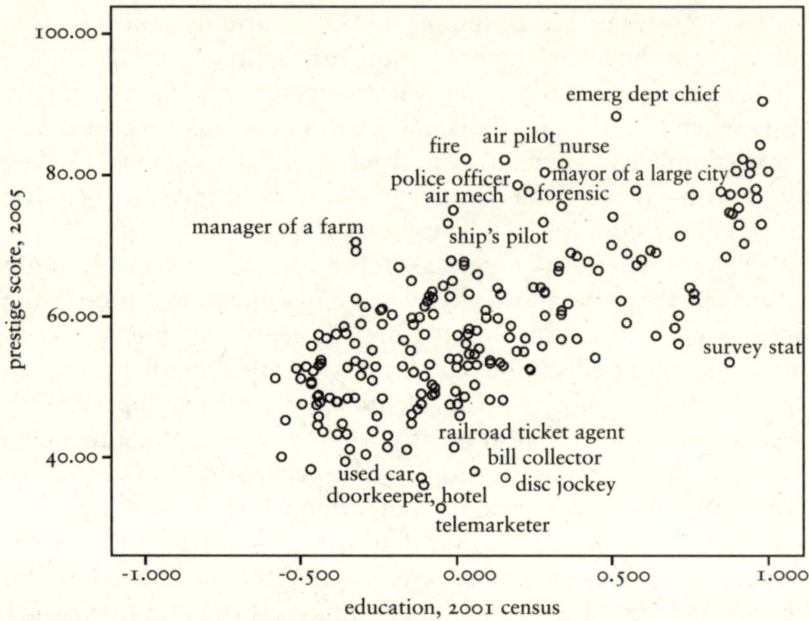

Fig. 4.1   Prestige scores for 2005 regressed onto mean education for the matching NOC unit group. *Note*: Titles labeled are outliers of 15 points or more, from actual prestige minus predicted prestige based on education, where predicted = 18.611 * education + 57.190 (R = .681). Education coded as proportion with university minus proportion with elementary only

The prestige premium for "chief of emergency medicine" rides on the high prestige enjoyed by health professions generally. This new title for the 2005 survey comes directly from the NOC manual, being one of the entries for "managers in health care," NOC 0311. The proportion with university less the proportion with elementary education only is .51, compared with .98 for physicians. The .51 figure (55 percent with university education minus 4 percent with only elementary) may seem low, but these workers are managers, not physicians. Moreover NOC 0311 includes a variety of other health care managers alongside chiefs of emergency medicine. The premium prestige for farming is detectable once again from the figure 4.1 graph, and also for protective service occupations such as firefighter. Pilots, whether of aircraft or ships, fare well, perhaps again reflecting Giddens's theme of aversion to risk in late modern society. Most of the underperforming occupations in terms of prestige relative to education make intuitive sense, e.g., "bill collector,"

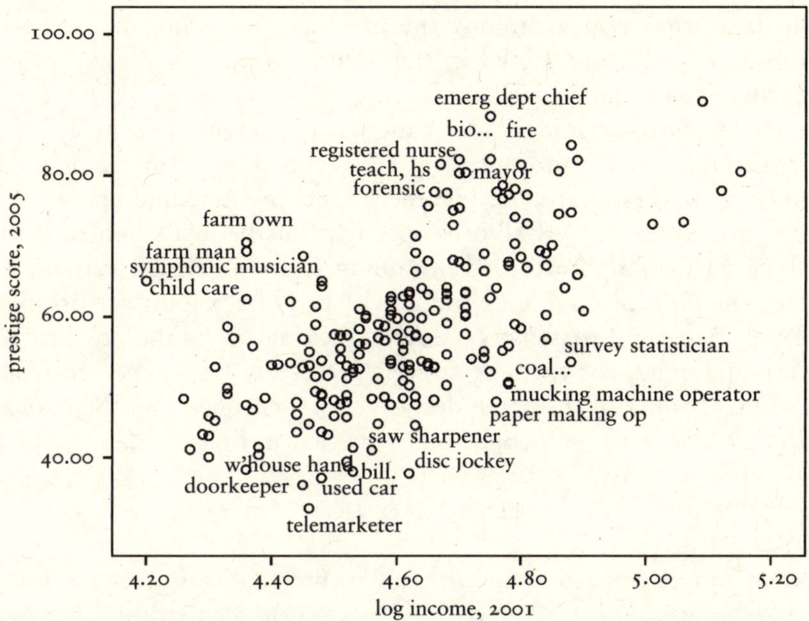

Fig. 4.2 Prestige scores for 2005 regressed onto mean log income for the matching NOC unit groups. *Note*: Titles labeled are outliers of 15 points or more, from actual prestige minus predicted prestige based on log mean income, where predicted = 42.403 * income − 136.813 (R = .62). Education and income date from Statistics Canada file labeled 97F0019XCB2001050

but the low prestige in relation to education for "railroad ticket agent" attracts notice. This is not simply an old economy prestige mark-down, because "locomotive engineer" has 13 more prestige points than predicted from education. Possibly the long arm of the Internet is at work here, with many respondents reasoning that they can book their VIA tickets on-line. Railroad ticket agent lost standing between 1965 and 2005, as documented below in table 4.2.

The same comparison as above was repeated for income, with figure 4.2 plotting prestige against log mean income for the NOC unit group best corresponding to the title rated. Income is logged owing to the skew in the distribution. Rainwater (1974, 143) shows that without the transformation the relationship between income and prestige is curvilinear. The logarithm produces a statistic much like the median. Fifteen points or more between actual and predicted prestige is again used to mark notable outliers. Some by now old favourites appear among the prestige over-achieving occupations, but these are joined in the income graph by "high school teacher" and "musician in a symphony orchestra." The prestige flowing to seemingly all medical occupations is seen for both "registered nurse" and "medical lab technician." Among prestige under-achievers relative to income, "mucking machine operators" out-earn 85 percent of all other occupations being examined here. Mucking machines are used in mining to load debris for removal from the pit face. Reference to "muck" can't be helping the prestige score. "Survey statisticians" may be picking up public hostility to over-surveying, for their prestige is far below that expected from earnings. Some of the same despised occupations from the education plot, such as "bill collector," reappear in figure 4.2.

GAINS AND LOSSES

Focus moves now to the main issue of prestige shift over the forty years between the 1965 and 2005 surveys of occupational prestige in Canada. Table 4.2 records the title-by-title results for 179 matching labour force titles, arranged in descending order from the greatest gain to the greatest loss. Where dual wordings for 1965 titles were carried in 2005 (see chapter 3, table 3.9), the exact duplicate title from 1965 is the one used. The average score for the 179 increased by 12 points between surveys, and this marker is inserted into the table to identify titles that gained prestige, but to a below average extent.

Naturally, some regression to the mean effect appears in these change-scores, since titles with low 1965 scores have the greatest room for increase, and vice versa. Nevertheless, it is striking how large some of the gains are. Child-care provider, with the wording change between surveys, has already been discussed, along with the rise in prestige by firefighters. Consider, however, a title like "garbage collector," a quintessential example of a humble calling. Rising from 15 points in 1965 to 48 in 2005, the gain is huge, far exceeding the 12 points increase across the board. There are many more examples among the top gainers in table 4.2, cutting across the service and manufacturing sectors: "construction labourer," "cook in a restaurant," "waitress," "janitor," etc. The twenty-first-century premium on health-related occupations resurfaces with the 27-point gain by "hospital attendant." What is going on? The

Table 4.2
Scores for 2005 and 1965, for Occupation Titles Rated in Both Years

Title	1965 Score	2005 Score	Gain or Loss
Child-care provider in a private home	25.9	65.0	39.1
Firefighter	43.5	82.3	38.8
Farm labourer	21.5	56.9	35.4
Garbage collector	14.8	47.9	33.1
Construction labourer	26.5	57.4	30.9
Private in the army	28.4	57.5	29.1
Cook in a restaurant	29.7	58.6	28.9
Waitress in a restaurant	19.9	48.4	28.5
Janitor	17.3	44.8	27.5
Hospital attendant	34.9	62.1	27.2
Police officer	51.6	78.6	27.0
Farm owner and operator	44.1	70.5	26.4
Logger	24.9	51.2	26.3
Quarry worker	26.7	53.0	26.3
Longshoreman	26.1	52.2	26.1
Railroad sectionhand	27.3	52.6	25.3
Oiler in a ship	27.6	52.7	25.1
Aircraft mechanic	50.3	75.1	24.8
Pumphouse engineer	38.9	63.5	24.6
Cod fisherman	23.4	47.6	24.2
Coal miner	27.6	50.7	23.1
Bus driver	35.9	58.9	23.0
Bartender	20.2	43.1	22.9
Carpenter's helper	23.1	45.8	22.7
Oil field worker	35.3	57.5	22.2
House carpenter	38.9	61.1	22.2
Power lineman	40.9	62.6	21.7
House painter	29.9	51.6	21.7
Automobile mechanic	38.1	59.8	21.7
Steam plant operator	32.8	54.0	21.2
Sales clerk in a store	26.5	47.6	21.1
Mail carrier	36.1	56.7	20.6
Trailer truck driver	32.8	53.3	20.5
Saw sharpener	20.7	41.1	20.4
Plumber	42.6	62.9	20.3
Bricklayer	36.2	56.2	20.0
Custom seamstress	33.4	52.8	19.4
Steel mill worker	34.3	53.7	19.4
Textile dyer	28.8	47.8	19.0
Mucking machine operator	31.5	50.4	18.9
Worker in a meat packing plant	25.2	43.6	18.4
Welder	41.8	60.2	18.4
Clerk in an office	35.6	54.0	18.4
Dairy farmer	44.2	62.5	18.3
Warehouse hand	21.3	39.4	18.1
Housekeeper in a private home	28.8	46.8	18.0
Locomotive engineer	48.9	66.9	18.0

Table 4.2 (continued)

Title	1965 Score	2005 Score	Gain or Loss
Elementary school teacher	59.6	77.5	17.9
Butcher in a store	34.8	52.7	17.9
Filling station attendant	23.3	41.2	17.9
Tool and die maker	42.5	60.3	17.8
Electrician	50.2	67.9	17.7
Worker in a dry cleaning or laundry plant	20.8	38.3	17.5
Power crane operator	40.2	57.6	17.4
Sewing machine operator	28.2	45.3	17.1
Sheet metal worker	35.9	52.9	17.0
Automobile assembly worker	35.9	52.9	17.0
Fruit packer in a cannery	23.2	40.1	16.9
Registered nurse	64.7	81.6	16.9
Taxicab driver	25.1	41.5	16.4
Paper making machine operator	31.6	47.9	16.3
Social worker	55.1	71.4	16.3
Airline pilot	66.1	82.2	16.1
Doorkeeper, hotel	20.1	36.1	16.0
Jazz musician	40.9	56.8	15.9
Museum attendant	30.4	46.1	15.7
Machinist	44.2	59.9	15.7
Bookkeeper	49.4	65.0	15.6
Loom operator	33.3	48.4	15.1
Post office clerk	37.2	52.1	14.9
Cashier in a supermarket	31.1	45.9	14.8
Stockroom attendant	25.8	40.4	14.6
Apprentice bricklayer	33.9	48.4	14.5
Receptionist	38.7	53.2	14.5
Baker	38.9	53.1	14.2
High school teacher	66.1	80.3	14.2
Sawmill operator	37.0	51.1	14.1
Typesetter	42.2	56.1	13.9
Superintendent of a construction job	53.9	67.7	13.8
Beauty salon operator	35.2	49.0	13.8
Owner of a coffee shop	47.8	61.4	13.6
Railroad conductor	45.3	58.9	13.6
Ship's pilot	59.6	73.2	13.6
Livestock buyer	39.6	53.1	13.5
Forging press operator	34.9	48.4	13.5
File clerk	32.7	45.9	13.2
Shipping clerk	30.9	43.7	12.8
Computer programmer	53.8	66.4	12.6
Truck dispatcher	32.2	44.8	12.6
Musician in a symphony orchestra	56.0	68.5	12.5
Steam roller operator	32.2	44.6	12.4
Newspaper pressman	43.0	55.2	12.2
Playground director	42.8	55.0	12.2
Pharmacist	69.3	81.5	12.2

Table 4.2 (continued)

Title	1965 Score	2005 Score	Gain or Loss
	Point of mean increase (12.0 points)		
Lunchroom operator	31.6	43.3	11.7
TV camerman	48.3	59.8	11.5
TV repairman	37.2	48.6	11.4
Veterinarian	66.7	78.1	11.4
Diamond driller	44.5	55.8	11.3
Driving instructor	41.6	52.6	11.0
Forensic laboratory technician	66.9	77.7	10.8
Building contractor	56.5	67.2	10.7
Telephone operator	38.1	48.8	10.7
Bank teller	42.3	53.0	10.7
Barber	39.3	49.8	10.5
Manager of a supermarket	52.5	62.8	10.3
Construction foreman	51.1	61.3	10.2
Travelling salesperson, wholesale trade	40.2	50.3	10.1
Mine safefy inspector	57.1	67.1	10.0
Biologist	72.6	82.3	9.7
Professional athlete	54.1	63.1	9.0
Wholesale distributor	47.9	56.8	8.9
Bill collector	29.4	38.1	8.7
Advertising copy writer	48.9	57.2	8.3
Medical laboratory technologist	67.5	75.7	8.2
Book binder	35.2	43.3	8.1
Production worker in the electronics industry	50.8	58.9	8.1
Real estate agent	47.1	55.1	8.0
Timber cruiser	40.3	48.2	7.9
Travel agent	46.6	53.8	7.2
Journalist	60.9	68.0	7.1
Merchandise buyer for a department store	51.1	58.0	6.9
Motel owner	51.6	58.2	6.6
Economist	62.2	68.4	6.2
Telemarketer	26.7	32.8	6.1
Service station manager	41.5	47.5	6.0
Funeral director	54.9	60.9	6.0
Used car salesman	31.2	37.1	5.9
Insurance claims investigator	51.1	56.9	5.8
Railroad ticket agent	35.7	41.5	5.8
Mining engineer	68.8	74.6	5.8
Typist	41.9	47.6	5.7
Insurance agent	47.3	53.0	5.7
TV director	62.1	67.7	5.6
TV announcer	57.6	63.1	5.5
Accountant	63.4	68.9	5.5
Trade union business agent	49.2	54.1	4.9
Ballet dancer	49.1	53.4	4.3

Table 4.2 (continued)

Title	1965 Score	2005 Score	Gain or Loss
Foreman of workers in a papermill	50.9	55.2	4.3
General manager of a manufacturing plant	69.1	73.4	4.3
Professionally trained librarian	58.1	62.3	4.2
Author	64.8	69.0	4.2
Chemist	73.5	77.7	4.2
Civil engineer	73.1	77.3	4.2
Professional forester	60.0	64.0	4.0
Draughtsman	60.0	64.0	4.0
Job counsellor	58.3	62.2	3.9
Advertising executive	56.5	60.2	3.7
YMCA director	58.2	61.8	3.6
Physiotherapist	72.1	75.4	3.3
Colonel in the army	70.8	74.1	3.3
Physician	87.2	90.5	3.3
Physicist	77.6	80.6	3.0
Manufacturer's representative	52.1	54.6	2.5
Manager of a real estate office	58.3	60.8	2.5
Land surveyor	62.0	64.1	2.1
Mathematician	72.7	74.8	2.1
Chiropractor	68.4	70.3	1.9
Psychologist	74.9	76.7	1.8
Data entry operator	47.7	49.4	1.7
Flight attendant	58.6	57.0	1.6
Mayor of a large city	79.9	80.4	.5
Commerical artist	57.2	57.0	–.2
Disc jockey	38.0	37.8	–.2
University professor	84.6	84.3	–.3
Architect	78.1	77.3	–.8
Sculptor	56.9	55.8	–1.1
Public relations officer	60.5	59.1	–1.4
Bank manager	70.9	69.0	–1.9
County court judge	82.5	80.5	–2.0
Member of a city council	62.9	60.1	–2.8
Purchasing officer	56.8	53.3	–3.5
Department head in city government	71.3	67.2	–4.1
Protestant minister	67.8	60.1	–7.7
Administrative officer in federal civil service	68.8	59.7	–9.1
Lawyer	82.3	73.1	–9.2
Catholic priest	72.8	56.1	–16.7
Member of Canadian House of Commons	84.8	63.3	–21.5
Member of Canadian Senate	86.1	63.5	–22.6

Note: 179 matching titles between 1965 and 2005. The titles listed are as worded for the 2005 fieldwork.

surveys are not equipped to give a full answer, because reasons for ratings were not investigated in 1965. But the responses of participants in the 2005 survey to open-ended questions about the criteria used in making the ratings of social standing and how their ratings might differ from other peoples' give some clues. Chapter 3 gave the question wordings. The following answers are chosen selectively, admittedly, from the hundreds of statements volunteered. To be sure, many respondents named the standard structural-functionalist criteria, such as level of formal education and pay. Nevertheless, the quotations indicate that more than the occasional respondent sees a prestige-claim for skilled blue-collar work:

> We're missing a lot of trades, there's not enough respect for the trades. People judge according to education.
> The importance of trades.
> Certain skills are important to me – miner – bricklayer.

Pertinent to the rise in scores for occupations such as garbage collector and janitor is the respondent who said, "No jobs are 'menial' or without signification in society. The 'menial' ones are those where there are too many generals and not enough soldiers."
The following respondents articulate why police and firefighters gained so much prestige:

> I think highly of those in search and rescue and those that protect us like police and firefighters.
> The intensity, risk, and stress in occupations like firefighter, nurses, doctors. Whereas plumbers, although they work hard don't have as much risk and stress.

Another also picks up the health care theme, citing "[t]he risk on the job, for example I'd rate police officer higher. Also an industry like healthcare where they're underpaid and have risks, I appreciate their hard work."
I have a file of some twenty newspaper clippings from the past few years noting the shortage of skilled tradespeople and extolling the satisfaction in such work. Some examples: from 2002, "we will face labour shortages, especially for skilled workers" (*Globe and Mail*, 11 October, A13); 2003, "postings for skilled workers increase" (*Globe and Mail*, 17 January, C1); 2004, "we may require fewer MBAs, but we most assuredly need far more trades" (*Globe and Mail*, 9 September, A2); 2005, "the blue collar is back in style" (*Globe and Mail*, 29 January, F1); 2006, "trades enjoy renaissance among job seekers" (*Globe and Mail*, 6 May, B11); 2007, "attitudes toward skilled labour must change" (*The Daily News*

(Halifax), 8 September, 23). From the academic literature, consider the respondent in Crysdale et al. (1999, 43) who says, "trades should have more prestige." Coming to the same conclusion from a different direction, Sennett (2008, 286) argues for the unity of all labour and writes "The working human animal can be enriched by the skills and dignified by the spirit of craftsmanship." Ours is not the first time in history that the dignity of manual labour has been asserted, as the following quotation from a Massachusetts labour leader dating back to 1832 illustrates: "[t]he laboring classes in our country, in consequence of the inroads and usurpations of the wealthy and powerful, have for years been gradually sinking in the scale of public estimation" (in Schlesinger 1950, 133). In the twenty-first century, however, assertions of the dignity of all labour make an especially striking counter-theme to the conventional celebration of the "sexier" knowledge-economy occupations.

Respondents in the 2005 survey knew they were departing from mid-twentieth-century assumptions in their down-grading of some occupations of traditionally high prestige. Consider these two examples:

[W]e look up to certain people like doctors but not to a degree that they once were."
I ... value the workers themselves more than the managers and bosses and the high-ranking occupations. If a worker knows how to do their job well they wouldn't need the bosses, right?

Respondents also showed awareness of departing personally from what they deemed the 2005 standard consensus to be. In the question described in chapter 3, asking, "do you think most other people would give the occupations the same ratings you just did," 45.4 percent replied "no" (33.1 percent "yes" or qualified yes, 21.4 percent "don't know"). An almost identical 44 percent said "no" in the year 2000 Kitchener-Waterloo survey. As some of the open responses from 2005 noted:

We all have different opinions.
Chacun a une perception différente.
Everybody has their own views... depending on the vision.
I am an ordinary Joe, so rich people or boss's answers won't be the same.

Because I'm a tradesman. I put people that work hard on a higher scale.
I think I'm biased towards the trades and blue-collar jobs.

Such responses are echoed in other cultural documents from the twenty-first century. "Dignity Is Not Negotiable," read the headline in the *Globe and Mail* careers section of 26 November 2003 (C1). "Rankism is the new bane of society. It's time to make it stop." The writer of a letter to the editor commented on 5 May 2006 that "my husband worked at Metro Toronto's main sewage-treatment plant ... [h]e considered this useful work and never hung his head in shame in front of our children" (*Globe and Mail*, A24).

Many of the greatest losses in prestige come from the administrative occupations. The plight of "member of a city council," for example, is not reducible simply to regression to the mean (starting from a high score and having nowhere to go but down). This occupation scored 63 in 1965, comfortably above the average of 46 for that year. The score of 60 in 2005 marked a drop of three points in the environment of average gains of 12 points. It was the same for "department head in city government" and "administrative officer in the federal civil service." Most severely punished of all in 2005 were "member of Canadian House of Commons" and "member of Canadian Senate." I have remarked on the sharp drop in prestige for Catholic priests already.

An interim step between title-by-title examinations of prestige shifts and a full-modeling approach appears in table 4.3. This is also the moment to consider alternative methods of assessing prestige change. So far the simple difference between 2005 and 1965 scores has been used. While this helps give a first look at the data, a method is needed that frees the analysis from constantly re-discovering that 2005 raters squeezed up the whole scale by compressing the 1965 bottom into the 2005 middle. Table 4.3 tracks prestige shift within the major groups of the NOC while using two sets of change scores. Within groups having five or more titles, as an arbitrary cut-off that excludes eight groups, simple change scores are entered along with regression-adjustment scores (in italics) underneath. The regression adjustment subtracts from each 2005 score the score for that year predicted from 1965. That removes the general upward drift in prestige scores. While it might seem logical merely to subtract from the simple difference a constant 12 points

Table 4.3
Two Types of Prestige Change Score, by NOC Major Groups, for Groups Represented by Five or More Titles

	Business, Finance, and Administrative	Natural and Applied Sciences, etc.	Health	Social Science, Education, Government Service, Religion	Art, Culture, Recreation, Sport	Sales and Service	Trades, Transport, and Equipment Operators	Primary Industry	Processing, Manufacturing, Utilities	All
Senior management										−19.9
										−7.0
Other management										−5.4
										−1.3
Skill A		−7.5	−4.0	−10.1	−6.2					
		2.6	7.0	0.6	−2.0					
Skill B	−10.0	−1.7			−5.9	3.9	6.4	8.4		
	−5.4	2.3			−4.3	2.3	3.5	3.7		
Skill C	0.2					4.0	8.2		3.6	
	−3.9					−1.3	0.5		−1.1	
Skill D						3.8	15.7			
						−5.5	5.7			

Note: Skill A – "occupations usually require university education; B – "usually require college education or apprenticeship training"; C – "usually require secondary school and /or occupation-specific training"; D –"on-the-job training is usually provided for occupations." Upper entry is 2005 prestige score less 1965 prestige score less 12.0 (mean increase); lower entry is prestige change from regression adjustment, where adjusted score = 2005 score − (.564 * 1965 score) + 32.308.

(the mean increase between 1965 and 2005), that is an average describing only the middle of the distribution. The average increase is only 1.7 points in the upper quintile of the 1965 scores, against 22 points in the bottom quintile. The regression adjustment fits a least-squares line to the actual scores for 1965 and 2005, rather than assuming a slope of 1.0 between the two as the simpler method does. As Cohen and Cohen (1975, 379–82) observe, the regression approach imagines some of the extreme low and high scores for the earlier period to be the result of measurement error, and it discounts on that basis.

These statistical points are reflected in table 4.3. For a mid-level major group such as skilled sales and service at skill level B, the simple difference and regression-adjustment are nearly the same. For a group such as trades, transport, and equipment operators at skill level D, which had a mean 1965 prestige score of only 24, the reading of upward shift to 2005 is far more conservative using the regression method (+5.7 points) than as a simple difference (+15.7 points). The payoff from the regression adjustment comes with comparisons such as skill A (jobs requiring university education) with managerial occupations. Neither section gained as much as lower-skill occupations, but the A skill level, largely composed of professional occupations, fared well in comparison to managers.

MODELING CHANGE IN SIZE OF SCORE

It has been seen that title-by-title examination suggests a "prestige squeeze" whereby some of the formerly high-power occupations have been humbled by the members of the public performing the 2005 ratings, while more modest occupations requiring less education, giving less income, and entailing less power have sharply raised scores. It is also true that education, income, and skill levels have been shuffling over the forty years, along with gender mix. We need to see how much of the 1965–2005 shift is attributable to such factors, in other words, to test the "issue 1" hypotheses outlined in chapter 2.

A first point is that the prestige as averaged across respondents making the ratings is, counter-intuitively, no more tied to educational prerequisites in 2005 than forty years previously. An ordinary least-squares (OLS) regression model for the 1965 and 2005 scores merged into one file outlines this. As seen in table 4.4,

Table 4.4
Effect of Education and Income on Prestige Score, 1965 and 2005

	Predicting Prestige Score, 1965 and 2005 Merged	
	B *(Unstandardized)*	*Beta* *(Standardized)*
Year (1965 = 0, 2005 = 1)	–5.979	–0.190
Income (log)	30.094***	1.056***
Income by year	–5.299	–0.777
Education	20.610***	0.701***
Education by year	–6.951**	–0.133**
Constant	–50.728	
R^2 (adj.)	.704	

Note: Based on 177 matching titles (excluding two farm occupations, which lack income data).
** p < .01.   *** p < .001

prestige is a close function of income rewards and educational preparation (coefficients in standardized form of 1.056 and .701 respectively). The negative signs for the interactions "income by year" and "education by year" mean a weaker association between prestige and the two census variables in the more recent data. With all the rhetoric about the need for formal education in the new economy, the opposite would have been more expected. "Government investment in basic and higher education, infrastructure, and scientific research is absolutely essential to a prosperous economy" ("Eat or Be Eaten," *The Walrus*, October 2007), but the 2005 survey respondents do not seem to translate that mantra into any enhanced linkage between educational preparation and their perceptions of prestige for occupations. Insofar as the 177 matching titles being examined here can be considered a sample from the larger universe (Nakao and Treas 1994, for example, collected ratings for 740 occupations), the significance test for the education interaction is easily (p < .01) significant, but the one for income is not. In other words, we should say that the predictability of prestige from income was essentially the same in 1965 and 2005, but the 2005 scores are indeed less tied to education, and that should hold for all possible scores. The educational difference is easily visible when plotted in graph form (figure 4.3). The education scale is, as noted, "proportion with university" less "proportion with elementary only"; thus, the possible range is –1 to +1. With educational upgrading during the latter twentieth century, the lowest x-axis

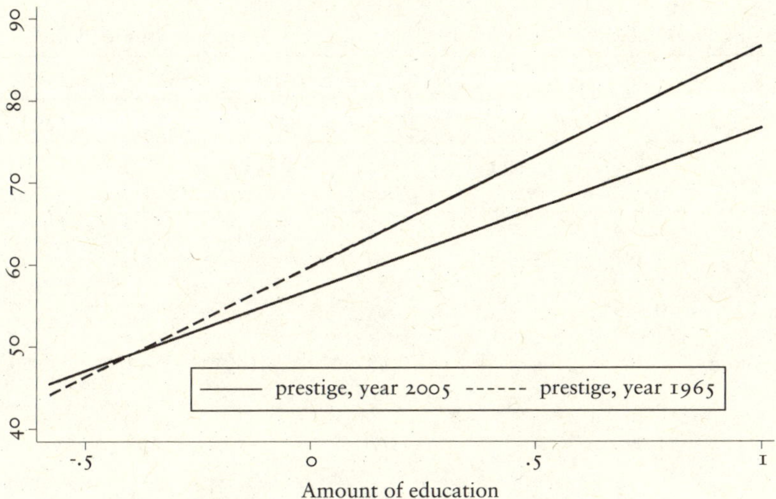

Fig. 4.3   Slope of education, predicting occupational prestige, 1965 and 2005

score for the titles examined is about –.5 in 2005. The changed importance of education is a statistical reflection of the patterns encountered in title-by-title examination, above, whereby people today seem to be attributing renewed prestige to manual and pro-tective service work.

In the modeling summarized in table 4.5, longitudinal changes in education and income as determinants of prestige change are ana-lyzed. The dependent variable in this OLS regression is 2005 pres-tige. Prestige for 1965 is entered as a predictor, which has the effect of re-defining the 2005 prestige into a change score. The same effect would be achieved by regressing 2005 prestige onto 1965 prestige, thus computing the prestige predicted for 2005 on the basis of 1965 information, residualizing this (subtract 2005 predicted from 2005 actual prestige), and making that the dependent variable (as in the lower rows of table 4.3). By including the 1965 prestige scores directly within the model, we have a way of tracking the level of explanation. Thus, the simple correlation between prestige for 1965 and 2005 for the 177 titles being examined here (those match-ing, and with complete education and income data for 1961 and 2001) is $r = .821$. This slips to .758 when expressed as a beta coeffi-cient in table 4.5, because change in income ("income residual") is accounting for some of the temporal change in prestige. That

Table 4.5
Effects of Education, Income, and Gender Composition on Change in Prestige Score

| | Predicting Change in Prestige Score | | | | | |
| | Model 1 | | Model 2 | | Model 3 | |
	B (Unstd)	Beta (Std)	B (Unstd)	Beta (Std)	B (Unstd)	Beta (Std)
1965 prestige score	.524***	.758***	.585***	.849***	.538***	0.780***
Education residual (1961–2001)	−.387	−.006				
Income residual (1961–2001)	20.589***	.206***			7.247***	0.173***
Gender composition residual (1961–2001)			−9.897***	−.149***	−4.082	−0.061
Constant	34.096		31.231		33.450	
R^2 (adj.)	.706		.690		.708	

** $p < .01$.   *** $p < .001$

Education residual, 1961/01: 2001 education − ((.779*1961 income) + .460) $R^2 = .813$.
Income residual, 1961/01: 2001 income − ((.581*1961 income) + 2.539)) $R^2 = .500$.
Gender residual, 1961/01: 2001 % female − ((.814*1961 % female) + .200) $R^2 = .614$.
177 titles.

supports hypothesis (b) from chapter 2, under "size of score." In contrast, hypothesis (a) in that section, suggesting the importance of education, is not viable. From table 4.4 results, it makes sense that change in income explains some of the change in prestige, 1965 to 2005, but change in educational preparation does not. We know that income has a stable, predictable effect on prestige in both years, while education's predictive importance for prestige has declined.

Changes in incomes for occupations as related to change in occupational prestige were tracked by twenty-year periods (table 4.6). The greatest effect occurs at the beginning of the period. As incomes for occupations shift over the decades, it seems to take time for these to be assimilated, perhaps legitimated, within the heads of survey respondents. It will be a topic for future research to examine whether the shifting prestige of occupations that is now going on translates into income changes in the censuses for future years. Certainly one of the policy implications of occupational-prestige research is the support occupational groups may gain for wage claims.

Table 4.6
Effect on Prestige Scores of Changes in Income over Two Decades

	B (Unstd)	Beta (Std)
1965 prestige score	.523***	.759***
Income, 1961–1981 residual	18.244***	.190***
Income, 1981–2001 residual	13.758*	.092*
Constant	34.263	
R^2 (adj.)		.709

* p < .05.   *** p < .001

Income residual, 1961/81: 1981 income – ((.849 *1961 income) + 1 .134) R^2 = .663.

Income residual 1981/01: 2001 income – ((.694*1981 income) + 1.732) R^2 = .776.

177 titles.

The three greatest income gainers between the 1961 and 2001 censuses for the 177 titles examined here are "general manager of a manufacturing plant," up .30 log dollars, "physician," up .33 log dollars, and "mucking machine operator," a title singled out for attention earlier, at .33 log dollars. Although the log units are awkward, they serve a function already noted and, expressed in their present residualized form, are constant dollar change scores. Returning to table 4.5, the model then "says" that mucking machine operators should have gained prestige owing to their income gains between 1961 and 2001 relative to other occupations in Canada. The predicted 2005 prestige for mucking machine operators is 57.6, composed of 34.096 baseline from the model constant, 16.506 from their 1965 prestige (coefficient of .524 times 1965 prestige of 31.5), 6.885 points owing to relative gain in income (coefficient of 20.589 times 0.3344), with a trivial 0.067 from the non-significant and tiny negative noise-coefficient for educational credentials (coefficient of –.387 times –.172). The actual 2005 prestige score was 50.4, so the model overstates the gain, not unexpectedly given the unexplained variance of 29 percent in the model.

Change in the proportion female in occupations between the censuses of 1961 and 2001 is mildly related to change in prestige score, 1965 to 2005 (beta of –.149 from model 2, table 4.5). The direction, consistent with hypothesis (c) from chapter 2 (size of score section), is that occupations gaining in their share of women were those losing prestige. The effect is tied up with changes in income over time, however. When proportion female was entered into a model (see table 4.5, model 3) alongside change in income, the gender effect slipped below the .05 level of statistical significance. The same occupations gaining in share of women also were those (to the extent of r = −.43) with losses in mean earnings relative to other occupations. The data file of occupation titles being used for this analysis also had income and gender change between each decade between 1961 and 2001. I wondered if the correlations between change in proportion female and change in mean income lagged across decades would establish whether it is women entering an occupation that drives down income or whether declining income in an occupation creates an opportunity for entry by women. Nothing clear emerges from such analysis. The changes are occurring within decades, not across, and the relationship between occupation, gender, and income clearly is complex. Femininization of an occupation could reduce earnings if, as in the example of law, women preferred to exchange some billable hours for more family time (McKenzie Leiper 2006). Frenette and Coulombe (2007, 22) note that the new generation of highly educated young Canadian women tended to concentrate their employment in the health and education fields, both public sector parts of the economy that "saw substantial wage freezes and rollbacks in the 1990s." This is not to evade the possibility that women's work is under-valued, but the relationship between gender change and income change is complex.

Chapter 2 (hypothesis (d)) made reference to the possible impact of changing skill sets on occupational prestige, and now that theme can be revisited. The 1971 census classification dictionary for occupations (CCDO) and the 2001 National Occupational Classification (NOC) coded for a set of what are termed aptitudes comprising "general learning ability," "verbal ability," "numerical ability," "spatial perception," "form perception," "clerical perception," "motor co-ordination," "finger dexterity," and "manual dexterity." These codes span much of the 1965 to 2005 period. As the manual for the 1971 census coding for occupations reads, "[o]ver the years it has been demonstrated that certain aptitudes are important in job success. For CCDO purposes APPTITUDES are defined as the specific capacity or potentiality required of an individual in order to facilitate the learning of the skills needed for a task or job duties" (Department of Manpower and Immigration 1971, xii). Each aptitude was coded onto a scale ranging from 1 (highest) to either 4 or 5. The Human Resources and Skills Development *Career*

Table 4.7
Pearsonian Correlations between Change in Aptitude Scores, 1971 and 2001, and
Change in Prestige, 1965–2005.

Change in prestige with change in	*Correlation*
General learning ability	.145
Verbal ability	.127
Numerical ability	.154*
Spatial perception	.125
Form perception	.284***
Clerical perception	–.049
Motor co-ordination	.089
Finger dexterity	.064
Manual dexterity	.195*

Note: 179 titles. Prestige variable is 2005 score less score predicted from 1965 score.

Handbook (HRSDC 2001) notes the continuity in "theoretical principles and level configuration" between the 1971 and 2001 codings. The aptitudes were transformed into change variables by the same regression method used above for variables such as change in income or gender distribution. Several of these aptitude change variables had no relation to change in occupational prestige, as seen in a set of simple correlation coefficients presented in table 4.7. Prestige here is a change score (score for 2005 less score predicted from 1965 score [same as in table 4.3, lower rows]). A diverse pair of aptitudes (numerical, manual) have just-significant association with change in prestige, along with the .127 correlation for verbal, which is 0.1 significant. Form ability has the strongest consequence for prestige shift, but spatial ability does not to even a 0.1 degree of statistical significance. Form perception is understood within the CCDO as "ability to perceive pertinent details in objects, or in pictorial or graphic material. To make visual comparisons and discriminations and see slight differences in shapes and shadings of figures and widths and lengths of lines" (Department of Manpower and Immigration 1971, xii–xiii). Some occupations gaining in level of form perception between 1971 and 2001 and prestige between 1965 and 2005 include "chemist," "medical laboratory technologist," and "superintendent of a construction job." Some occupations moving in the opposite direction on both counts are "data entry operator," "file clerk," and "shipping clerk." I wondered if computer graphics applications have raised the form perception skill requirements and hence prestige for some occupations.

Table 4.8
Summary Model, Analysis of Shift in Mean Scores for Titles

	B (Unstd)	Beta (Std)
Prestige score, 1965	.514***	.741***
Income residual, 1961 to 2001	16.556***	.166***
Change in gender, 1961 to 2001	−1.696	-.025
Residual, numerical ability	.953	.043
Residual, form perception	2.640*	.098*
Residual, manual dexterity	2.024†	.069†
Residual, newspaper coverage	3.515†	.082†
Constant	34.485	

Note: 177 titles, R^2 (adj.) = .737.
† p < .1.   * p < .05.   *** p < .001.

Occupations might gain prestige by improving their identification with the core institutional realm of values and beliefs that Zhou (2005) discussed. They might, for example, change the occupational title from "sales clerk" to "sales associate" (see table 3.9). They might advertise in the mass media in order to emphasize their level of professionalism or their access to a scientific knowledge base. They may receive press coverage as they strive to increase their professional identity (e.g., "Pharmacists Want Power to Prescribe Drugs," *National Post*, 11 July 2006). There are not the data within the present analysis to be definitive here, but I do have a reading on how favourably or unfavourably occupations were represented in a national Canadian newspaper for 1964 and 2004.[2] The hypothesis of course is that occupations receiving more favourable press in the later period will be those gaining prestige.

Coverage in 1964 corresponded at least to a modest degree with prestige scores for 1965 (r = .415), as did 2004 press coverage with 2005 prestige r = .457). And so, as we could expect, change in press coverage does coincide with change in prestige score. The political roles such as "mayor of a large city" both sustained unfavourable press coverage over the forty years and lost prestige. As a correlation over all titles, however, the relationship is a modest r = −.162 (p < .03), indicating only a small general effect.

In table 4.8, all the change variables already discussed are gathered into one model for predicting prestige shift. From the significance tests, essentially all the variance in prestige shift is carried by change in income and change in form perception scores. While it has already been seen that prestige-gaining occupations are those resisting femininization and avoiding unfavourable press coverage, these two variables are tied up with income shift.

CONCLUSION

The main point of this chapter is the upward prestige squeeze by formerly low-standing occupations from outside the new economy. Once that part of the change is acknowledged, it becomes hard to account for too much more of the variance in scores. The simple descriptive tabulation from table 4.3 explained some 26 percent of the variance in occupation shift, while models with change variables explain only some 17 percent.[3] Ratings in 2005 became more quirky, as signalled by the diminished strength of educational preparation for occupational prestige. Certainly, prestige shift is related to income shift, as was expected from first principles of occupational research outlined in chapters 1 and 2. It is plausible that members of the public, caring as most do about money, have good knowledge of occupational incomes. From material in chapter 3, income is one of the several criteria people use in gauging prestige. Femininization is harder to interpret. Occupations increasing in their proportion female indeed have tended to slip in prestige, but that coincides with income shift. Aptitude for form perception, having a good eye for non-verbal/numerical nuances of documents, is the only predictor of prestige shift strong enough to sit alongside income change in a model. Perhaps the rise of computer-generated graphics in many parts of the workforce has raised the importance of form perception. We come back to the opening point of this chapter, that the clearest aspect of prestige shift between 1965 and 2005 is the upward squeeze whereby formerly low-status occupations, often in the trades and protective service sectors, were granted spectacular gains by respondents in the 2005 sample.

Part of the difficulty in reducing prestige shift among the 179 occupations common to the 1965 and 2005 Canadian prestige studies to a simple formula is the variability between raters. They are not speaking with one voice, especially in the latter year, and a later chapter moves into that aspect of the data.

5

The Individual Rater

If all raters thought the same way, and that is the assumption implicit in chapter 4, analysis of scores would be simple. But that is far from so, and now the possibility of inter-respondent variations in scorings for occupations is examined, focusing on a set of socio-demographic variables common to both the 1965 and the 2005 data sets. The attention thus shifts from the characteristics of the occupations being rated to the characteristics of the people performing the ratings.

Some hypotheses about prestige-scoring at the level of individual respondents were sketched in chapter 2. It seemed most likely that young people and the highly educated would give lower scores, offset by a tendency for immigrants and those in the labour force to score prestige relatively highly. Since, as profiled in chapter 2, the socio-demographics of Canada, and indeed all late modern societies, have shifted so much over the past forty years, it may be possible to explain some of the changes in mean prestige scores in terms of population change.

Setting up the data for analysis at the level of the individual rater required several steps, described next.

ONE LONG FILE

The data were arranged with all the title scores in one long column, respondent socio-demographic data being repeated for each title. The 1 to 9 scale employed for data gathering was transformed into the 0–100 metric described at the end of chapter 3. For the 1965 Canada survey, the file for individuals has 141,947 lines of data

(179 titles, each one having ratings for respondents number 1 through to 793). Missing data among the ratings (about 6 percent) reduces the working N to 133,866. Each record gave identical core socio-demographic information for variables whose codes for 1965 and 2005 could be reconciled. These variables are region, respondent in the workforce, respondent's spouse in the workforce, Canadian vs foreign-born, age group, male vs female, Francophone vs other language, university-educated. The 1965 sample contains respondents aged twenty-one and up, and the small percentage of 2005 respondents under age twenty-one was trimmed out to maintain comparability. Table 5.1 lists this set of socio-demographics common to both samples, together with the coding system compatible across both data sets and frequency distributions. Points such as the aging of population over the past forty years (see chapter 3, table 3.8) are re-expressed in this long file. Region is included in models, in part to acknowledge the regionally stratified sampling plan for 2005 by which equal numbers were drawn from each of five parts of Canada.

The statistical power of the data thus arranged is not as large as might be expected, owing to the clustering by respondent. There are still only 793 respondents in the 1965 data set, even though there are over 100,000 person-title ratings of occupations. Standard errors in models below were therefore bootstrapped in STATA, with respondent identification entered as the cluster variable. The 2005 data were treated in the same way, giving 35,391 complete lines of data, although the clustering is less severe in these data owing to the allocation of titles to sub-samples.

A FIRST MODEL FOR INDIVIDUALS

The first model for individuals, using the entire stacked file for both years, appears in table 5.2 and shows that few of the socio-demographic categories are exercising a decisive global effect on the size of prestige score. Even the largest standardized beta coefficients, the −.042 for university-educated or .050 for Francophones, are dwarfed by the coefficient (.191 standardized coefficient, 13.1 in raw points) for upward shift in prestige ratings between 1965 and 2005. The model *does eliminate* the hypothesis that upward movement in scores is driven simply by socio-demographic change. If it were, the historical effect as estimated within the multivariate

Table 5.1
Index of Socio-Demographic Variables with Compatible Categories, 1965 and 2005

		Percentage Distributions	
Variable	*Codes*	*2005**	*1965*
Regions*			
Atlantic	= 1, else 0	20.3	10.0
Quebec	= 1, else 0	20.1	26.9
Ontario	= 1, else 0	20.2	34.4
Prairie	= 1, else 0	20.0	19.4
BC	= 1, else 0	19.4	9.3
Labour Force Status			
Respondent Works	= 1, else 0	60.9	49.7
Spouse Works	= 1, else 0	46.7	49.8
Ethnicity			
Canadian-born	= 1, else 0	83.2	81.0
Francophone	= 1, else 0	24.2	25.5
Age	21 = 21–24	6.8	8.2
	25 = 25–29	7.5	10.7
	30 = 30–34	8.8	14.9
	35 = 35–39	10.4	12.0
	40 = 40–44	12.4	13.5
	45 = 45–49	11.9	10.0
	50 = 50–64	29.2	20.1
	65 = 65 and over	13.0	9.0
Male	= 1, else 0	42.1	46.5
Education: University	= 1, else 0	29.4	6.3
N of cases		35,391	133,866

*Unweighted, since it is a sample-stratification variable, but the other 2005 distributions here are weighted to the 2001 census distributions for the five regions.

model, 13.1 prestige points, would instead be smaller than 12.1 (the actual increase in mean scores over forty years), rather than slightly greater. Socio-demographic change has suppressed about one point of upward shift. Education is a large component of the suppression, with the historical increase in the proportion university-educated combined with a tendency (B = −3.69) to downrate the prestige of occupations. The same pattern of lower prestige ratings by more educated respondents occurs in the year 2000 data too (Goyder 2005b, 16). The aging of population, in contrast, the other main demographic change between the 1960s and the 2000s, has

Table 5.2
Individual-Level Regression of Prestige Score on Social Characteristics of Raters, Both Years

	Predicting Prestige Score, 1965 and 2005 Merged		
	B (Unstandardized)	*Beta* (Standardized)	*Interactions across Year*
Year	13.056***	.191***	
Atlantic	1.234	.015	Higher scores in '05 (*)
Quebec	–2.183	–.035	Higher scores in '05 (*)
Ontario	0.431	.007	
Prairie	1.358	.020	
Works	–0.729	–.013	Lower scores in '05 (*)
Spouse works	–0.843	–0.15	
Can. born	–0.562	–.008	
Age	0.024	.011	
Male sex	–0.976	–.018	Lower scores in '05 (***)
Francophone	3.168**	.050**	Higher scores in '05 (*)
University	–3.690***	–.042***	
Constant	46.738		
R^2		.037	
N	163,801 lines complete on all variables		

Note: British Columbia is reference category for region here and in models in later tables.

* p < .05.   **p < .01.   *** p < .001, with all significance tests using bootstrapped standard errors owing to clustering in the long-file.

minimal implications for the rating of occupations, with beta a mere +.01 in the merged file for 1965 and 2005. The models here in table 5.2 and the series below generate truly minute explained variance, but that does not make them bad models. The computations are showing that only trace effects from socio-demographics happen when a person in the survey rates any particular occupational title. Looking ahead to a later chapter, there is high dissensus, person to person, title to title, but it is unstructured dissensus, not organized around age, sex, etc. City size is not part of this analysis, owing to the difficulty in finding a common code between the 1965 and 2005 samples. From work just with the 2005 data, which had under-representation of people in large cites, increasing the response rate for Montreal-Toronto-Vancouver would have reduced the mean score by about 1/10 of a point.

All two-way interactions with the year of study were tested, and the results are summarized in the text in the right-hand portion of table 5.2 Residents of Atlantic Canada became more generous with prestige scores in 2005. People in the 2005 workforce granted relatively less prestige to all occupations than non-paid workers, contrary to expectations suggested in chapter 2. This downgrading was non-significant among 1965 respondents. A slight prestige premium is given by female respondents in 2005, although as with work status, the blended effect is non-significant. Francophones assigned higher scores than Anglophones, and more so in 2005 than in 1965, although for the French-speaking majority in Quebec the effect was offset (B of 3.17 minus B of 2.18). Pineo and Porter's arguments about industrialization and language community, noted in chapter 2, are not especially supported.

THE BEHAVIOUR OF RESPONDENTS AS THEY RATE DIFFERENT SKILL LEVELS

The socio-demographic story is less about how different kinds of respondent rate *any* occupation than about how their ratings vary across the main skill levels. Table 5.3 takes the 2005 respondents and examines their ratings within the five skills of the NOC (four levels organized around formal education and on-the-job skill acquisition, with managerial skill as a fifth category). Skill "A" refers to occupations usually requiring university level education; "B," college diploma or apprenticeship; "C," school completion or job-specific training; "D," on-the-job training. Managers are set aside as holding a different form of skill, although in the era of the ubiquitous MBA these skills can closely resemble A skills. Coefficients in this table are tested for significance both "down columns" (e.g., the coefficient of 8.144 for Atlantic respondents is significant at p < .001 within the model for rating D skill occupations) and also "across rows." Across rows, the pattern of relatively more prestige granted to low-skill occupations by Atlantic region respondents and less to the high-skill ones is statistically significant at p < .001. The difference across the Atlantic row between managerial skill and the other four is also highly significant, but not differences in size of effect between managerial skill and A skill. Again, the standard errors have been bootstrapped to correct for clustering.

Two sets of respondents exhibit the distinctive pattern of granting a bonus to the lowest skill level occupations, tapering that down as the skill level ascends: Atlantic Canadians, as just noted, and also Francophone respondents. The university-educated reverse the pat-

Table 5.3
Individual-Level Regression of Score on Social Characteristics of Raters, 2005, within NOC Skill Levels

Characteristic	Unstandardized Regression Coefficients					Significance across Rows		
	Skill D (Low)	Skill C (High)	Skill B	Skill A (High)	Managers	Within Skill Levels	Managers vs Others	Managers vs Skill A
Atlantic	8.144***	5.432***	3.293**	0.297	4.029**	***	***	ns
Quebec	−2.030	−0.049	−0.403	−0.985	5.716*	***	**	ns
Ontario	1.288	0.449	0.928	0.671	2.995	***	**	ns
Prairie	2.954	0.779	1.824	−1.544	4.184**	ns	ns	***
Works	−1.296	−2.677**	−1.924*	−1.051	−0.030	*	ns	ns
Spouse works	−1.483	−0.488	−0.692	0.078	−2.244*	*	*	*
Can. born	−2.204	−2.551*	0.084	0.586	−0.120	ns	ns	*
Age	0.105*	0.082*	0.112***	0.008	−0.094*	**	ns	**
Male sex	−3.540**	−3.351***	−3.259***	−5.844***	−3.662***	ns	*	*
Francophone	11.219***	7.064***	3.880*	2.052	3.176	***	***	ns
University	− 8.116***	−6.473***	−4.879***	0.420	−0.996	***	***	*
Constant	43.599	51.697	56.757	72.606	68.299			
R^2	.064	.047	.027	.017	.011			
N	3,556	8,362	12,133	7,681	3,659			

* p < .05.   **p < .01.   *** p < .001.   ns = not significant..

tern, which allows us to specify further the pattern for education discussed earlier of low prestige scores assigned by the highly educated. The tendency for the university-educated to give low prestige scores occurs mostly for low-skill occupations and then tapers off, moving up the skill hierarchy. Hodge and Rossi (1978, B60-B63) noticed the same pattern long ago, and we are congruent with Wegener (1992, 271) here too. Some of these fluctuations are strong enough to severely compress the skill prestige gradient within the already prestige-squeezed 2005 scale. For example, whilst among all respondents the mean ratings are 45.2 for D-level occupations and 50.5 for C, a difference of 5.3 points, for Atlantic Canada respondents, the difference in prestige between levels D and C shrinks to only 2.6 points.

The same tabulations were repeated for 1965, with results appearing in table 5.4, and found some of the main themes from 2005. The pattern of bonus prestige to lower skill levels from 2005, for example, re-appeared among 1965 Francophones, although no longer among Atlantic region Canadians. Once again, a distinctive pattern for education shows the university-educated being harsh judges of occupations lower in formal educational prerequisites.

THE "INSTITUTIONAL REALM OF VALUES AND BELIEFS": VALUE PLACED ON SCIENCE AND TECHNOLOGY

Seen in chapter 1 was the skeptical stance among occupational-prestige researchers toward the role of culture as a determinant of ratings. At one time, articles on occupational prestige would routinely flag the tension between "the structuralists" and "the culturalists" (Villemez 1974, 46). Zhou (2005, 91), noted earlier, challenged the structuralist hegemony in the literature by viewing the approbation placed on science and technology as part of an "institutional realm of values and beliefs" within a societal value system, one that held consequences for occupational prestige. Occupations commanding the highest prestige, he argued, are those that can splice their power and privileges into these values and beliefs. This splice "naturalizes" (i.e., legitimates) prestige differences. Therefore, an occupation having a knowledge base rooted in science should receive a prestige premium.

Table 5.4
Individual-Level Regression of Score on Social Characteristics of Raters, 1965, within NOC Skill Levels

	Unstandardized Regression Coefficients					Significance Across Rows		
	Skill D	Skill C	Skill B	Skill A	Managers	Within Skill Levels	Manages vs Others	Man. vs. Skill A
Atlantic	−1.486	−0.658	0.314	0.177	1.079	ns	ns	ns
Quebec	−4.495*	−4.014*	−3.768	−0.594	−2.206	*	ns	***
Ontario	−2.969	−1.189	0.097	1.318	1.349	***	***	ns
Prairie	1.819	1.828	0.946	−0.370	0.662	*	*	*
Works	−2.398*	−1.929	−1.473	0.209	1.019	ns	ns	*
Spouse works	−0.676	−0.762	−0.552	0.362	0.454	*	*	*
Can. Born	−0.434	−0.052	−0.343	−0.677	−0.144	ns	ns	ns
Age	0.079	0.048	−0.002	−0.050	−0.019	***	***	ns
Male sex	1.258	0.943	1.367	−1.861	−0.275	*	***	*
Francophone	6.150***	5.677***	3.319	−0.748	−1.581	***	***	**
University	−7.087***	−5.450***	−5.234***	3.075**	−1.140	***	***	***
Constant	24.890	33.278	45.803	68.717	62.881			
R^2	.026	.014	.007	.007	.006			
N	14,274	34,892	48,373	30,134	14,274			

* p < .05.   **p < .01.   *** p < .001.   ns = not significant

Table 5.5
Canadian Attitudes towards Science and Technology

	Percentage Agreeing	
	1989	2005
Approval Items		
"Science and technology are making our lives healthier, easier, more comfortable."	80.0	79.9
"On balance, more jobs will be created than lost as a result of computers and factory automation."	51.9	33.6
"The benefits of science are greater than any harmful effects."	*	52.4
Disapproval Items		
"We depend too much on science, not enough on faith."	44.7	53.1
"It is not important for me to know about science in daily life."	21.9	19.2
"Science makes our way of life change too fast."	46.0	63.3

Sources: 1989, Einsiedel (1994, 39), national telephone survey of 2,000 adults; 2005, Occupational Prestige in Canada: 2005 survey (n = 2,053).
*Not asked in 1989.

Zhou (2005, 106–7) worked from the occupation side, rather than from characteristics of raters. Using a data set of occupational traits compiled by England and Kilborne (2002) and based on the Dictionary of Occupations (DOT) data from the U.S. Census Bureau, the key variable was the percentage of workers in an occupation having a preference for scientific or technical activities ("scinpref").

For the Occupational Prestige in Canada: 2005 survey I included among the questions a six-item scale of attitude toward science and technology from a larger set developed for the 1989 Eurobarometer survey (Bauer et al. 1994, 183–4). The question wordings appear in table 5.5. Each item was rated on a five-level scale from "strongly agree" to "strongly disagree," with "neither agree nor disagree" as midpoint. For "comfortable," "automation," and "harmful effects," agreement points to pro-science and technology attitude, while "faith," "daily life," and "too fast" are scaled in the opposite direction. Correspondence analysis coupled with classification analysis was applied, using SPAD software. This procedure allows the classification of each respondent into a discrete "class," based on the similarity of answers to the six questions. Among the seven classes obtained, two were characterized by strong coherent opinions – positive and negative – towards science and technology.[1]

Table 5.6
Individual-Level Regression of Prestige Score on Social Characteristics of Raters

Characteristic	Unstandardized Regression Coefficients	
	Simple Model	Expanded Model
Atlantic	4.261***	3.698***
Quebec	3.718***	−0.123
Ontario	1.122	0.949
Prairie	1.241	1.165
Works		−1.644*
Spouse works		0.643
Can. Born		0.667*
Age		0.057*
Male sex		−3.760***
Francophone		4.363**
University		−12.769***
Skill level		7.239***
Managerial skill		−46.251***
University by skill		3.076***
University by managerial		−15.223***
Respondent has science/technology orientation	−6.354***	−4.715**
Science orientation of occupation ("scinpref")	1.183***	0.716***
Interaction, science orientation of respondent by title	0.260*	0.240*
Constant	43.105	30.707
R^2	.034	.130

Note: Model for 2005 including respondent's attitude toward science and technology and science-technology profile of title being rated.

* p < .05.   **p < .01.   *** p < .001.

By coding Zhou's "scinpref" onto the set of occupation titles rated in the 2005 Canadian survey data, it was possible to specify his hypothesis more pointedly into whether those respondents most allied with valuation of science and technology are the most likely to raise the prestige of occupations having a science-technology profile. Results appear in table 5.6, for the 2005 data only, since 1965 did not have these measures. An increase of 1 percent (in the percentage of workers in an occupation having a preference for scientific or technical activities) corresponds to an increase of 1.18 in the prestige score for that occupation, from the first model in this table. Since titles were distributed randomly to the sub-samples in 2005, the scinpref effect with respondent's science-technology values excluded is hardly different (B = 1.22, not part of table 5.6).

Seemingly a little paradoxically in relation to the scinpref effect for titles, *respondents* holding pro-science-technology values give lower prestige to all occupations (B = −6.35, or B = −3.2 if re-computed to exclude the interaction). Here they are behaving like the highly educated respondents that they often are, since those with university education were twice as likely as others to hold a pro-science-technology attitude. The increment from expanding Zhou's design, and a resolution to the paradox just noted, comes from the statistically significant interaction term (B = .26) between the science-technology profile of the rater and the title rated, showing that, indeed, pro-science-technology respondents grant premium prestige to occupations from the science-technology sector. The finding is congruent with Stehr's (1974) work, noted in chapter 1. Zhou's analysis had a functionalist cast, despite dating from the 2000s, and assumed by implication that the societal value system is held by almost everybody. But values are not diffused as constants throughout a population like Canada's, especially in the pluralistic environment of the twenty-first century. As just seen, it is people who themselves most endorse the scientific-technological society who are most likely to grant a premium to occupations identified with those values. This part of the analysis stands independently from the earlier modeling in this chapter (i.e., table 5.3). That is demonstrated in the right-hand portion of table 5.6, with an expanded model that includes the interaction between skill level and university education. The skill-level A occupations are those having high scinpref scores, but the values analysis holds its effect within the larger model (e.g., B = .24 for interaction between science orientation of respondent by title).[2]

Can we take the above as part of the explanation for the general upward rise in prestige scores in Canada? Occupations have been growing ever more tied up with science and technology, and it might be supposed that the population's acceptance of technological society has been growing over time. The diffusion and increase in computer, Internet, cell telephone, and related technologies would suggest that. *In fact, it seems not.* Several of the valuation of science and technology items were posed to Canadians in a survey collected in 1989 (Einsiedel 1994). Referring back to table 5.5, which compares the 1989 and 2005 results, the public valuation of science and technology eroded, if anything, over the sixteen years. The person in the street, iPod equipped though he or she may be, is not keeping pace with the more official voices of Canada, which exhort a race into the future technological society.

SELF-RATINGS

Breaking ratings for occupations of different skill levels down by education of rater gets close to self-ratings – the ratings that respondents give their own occupation or some cluster of occupations within which theirs fits. For a long time, it has been realized that "[e]ach social stratum is evaluated more favorably by its own members than by others" (Blau 1957, 392). This is the "ethnocentric tendency" that Svalastoga (1959, 103) reported in his Danish data. Pineo and I (Goyder and Pineo 1977) found self-enhancement on self-ratings in the 1965 prestige study to be much greater for a stimulus explicitly named the "occupation of my family's main wage earner" than from the more complicated measure resulting from matching up names of occupation titles rated to names of occupations of respondents and deriving self-ratings from these. For the 1965–2005 comparison, I will begin with the simple "main earner" stimulus and then move into matching. Figure 5.1 shows the frequency distribution for the main earner ratings for 1965 and 2005, using the one-to-nine scale that respondents were working from. Considerable upward movement is clearly visible, but some of this will be part of the general upward drift over the forty years in the scoring of the prestige of occupations.

A more nuanced comparison comes from comparing the main-earner ratings against all other scores in each year, as shown in table 5.7. Since it seemed possible that self-inflation of scores might be greatest for main earners rating themselves, the table separates out those respondents not in the paid labour force from the rest. The "respondent works" group would include both main earners and secondary earners. Since in the demographics of the twenty-first century the notion of the male main earner has little meaning, the 2005 working respondents are probably rating themselves, essentially. For 1965 that was less likely, so in the lower portion of table 5.7, results are reproduced for males only, to strengthen the historical comparison. These details prove to have little consequence. The main finding is the growth in self-enhancement of status over the forty years. Looking at 1965 workforce respondents of both sexes, for example, "occupation of my family's main wage earner"

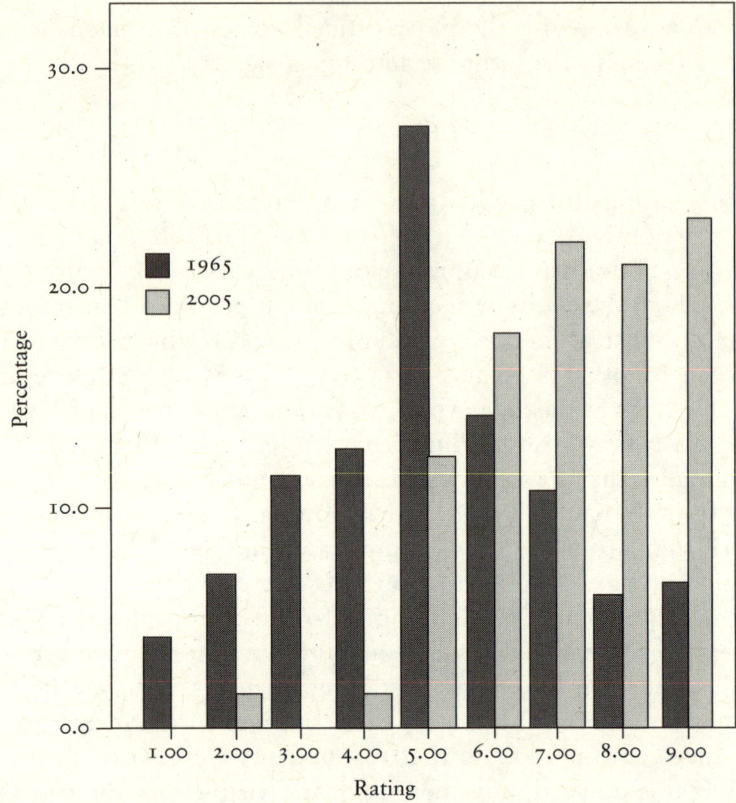

Fig. 5.1   Ratings of "occupation of my family's main wage earner"

received a score of 49.5 over the 366 respondents making the rating. All titles, as scored by working respondents, showed an average of 46.1, meaning that the self-ratings averaged 3.4 more points
than all other ratings. In 2005, the spread was massively more, 19
points of enhancement. In percentile terms, the theoretical expecta-
tion would place the average self-rating at the 50th percentile. The
1965 ratings crept up to the 62nd percentile, not too far above reality, but by 2005 the mean self-rating had closed to no less than the
91st percentile.

Pineo and I matched occupation titles being rated to the 1961
census code for occupations and examined how people whose own
occupation fell into the same code as the rated title scored that
occupation. The scores were several points less inflated than the
ratings of "occupation of my family's main wage earner." We concluded that a hierarchy of degrees of awareness about a self-rating

Table 5.7
Ratings of "Occupation of My Family's Main Wage Earner"

| | Mean Prestige Scores | | | | | |
| | 1965 | | | 2005 | | |
Respondent	OFME	All Titles	Difference	OFME	All Titles	Difference
Both males and females						
Respondent works	49.5	46.1	3.4	76.3	57.3	19.0
Respondent is not in paid lf	52.3	46.8	5.5	79.3	60.9	18.4
Males only						
Respondent works	49.6	46.3	3.3	70.8	55.7	15.1
Respondent is not in paid lf	52.4	47.2	5.2	75.8	57.9	17.9

Key: OFME = "occupation of my family's main wage earner"; lf = labour force.

Table 5.8
Prestige Self-Ratings Using Matching Titles, Working or Formerly Working Respondents Only

| | Mean Prestige Score for | | |
	All Titles	Matching Titles*	"Main Earner" Score Less Match Score
1965	46.1	46.4	3.1
2005	58.7	68.7	7.6

* "All fits" as described in Goyder and Pineo (1977, 238)

being sought lay behind the variations in self-enhancement (Goyder and Pineo 1977, 243). With the sub-sample design of the 2005 survey, matches were much rarer than in 1965, just 145 cases out of the 2,053 respondent base. This little shard of data shows a mean score of 68.7 prestige points, some 8 points less than the rating of main earner's occupation, as documented in table 5.8.

The changes over time just described are so large that the reader may want to see further evidence. Knowing from the 2000 pilot that high amounts of self-enhancement were appearing in the recent data, I built a second self-rating of occupational prestige into the 2005 design, and this one included all 2,053 respondents rather than the sub-sample of 208 who were presented with the main-wage-earner probe. After having completed the main ratings of titles, and embedded within the section of the questionnaire dealing

Table 5.9
Self-enhancement Replications from 2005 and 2000 Surveys

	2005 National Data: Mean Prestige Scores	
Respondents	*"What social standing would you give this occupation you've just described?"*	*Self-enhancement*
Those with a current occupation	67.3	10.0
Reporting on a former occupation	69.0	8.1
Blended mean	67.9	9.2
	2000 KW Data: Mean Prestige Scores:	
For gender combinations of rater and rated	*Matching Titles*	*Self-enhancement*
Male rating male	73.4	18.8
Male rating gender un-specified	75.0	19.1
Female rating female	75.7	6.8
Female rating gender un-specified	59.0	3.5

with own employment status, all respondents were asked to rate the prestige of the current occupation they had just named on the same 1-to-9 scale used earlier. Those not currently working but having once worked were asked to rate that earlier occupation. As shown in the upper portion of table 5.9, respondents' ratings here (again transformed to 0–100 scale) were 67.3 for current occupation, 69.0 if rating an earlier one, with 67.9 as the blended rate across the two. Even though lower than the figures from the main (table 5.7) rating set (77.3, blended across working and non-working respondents), there is still much more status self-inflation than seen in 1965.

More data on self-enhancement can be drawn from the 2000 pilot study from Kitchener-Waterloo. The overt rating of main earner's occupation or the one just described was not used here, but it is possible to perform the match of respondent occupations to occupations rated. An additional wrinkle from the 2000 data is the gender-specification of titles rated (not done in 2005), allowing a view of how male respondents rated the title best corresponding to their own, both when gender-specified (e.g., "male accountant") and when gender-neutral (e.g., "accountant"). Recall that the 2000 respondents (N = 351) were randomly allocated into three groups, two rating the titles with gender-specification and the remainder for the gender-neutrals. Their current occupations were coded into NOC unit (i.e., four-digit) groups The lower portion of table 5.9 shows the mean scores, which reproduce 2005 results quite well. Males rated their own occupation some 19 points above average, and it made little difference whether the comparison was with male-specified or neutral. One might infer that for males rating their own NOC unit group, it is assumed that the incumbent is male. Women self-enhanced much less (6.8 points) for female-specified titles and even less (3.5 points) for neutral titles. The self-enhancement for men and women blended and rating only gender-neutral titles was 11.3 points, which is very close to the corresponding 10.0 (68.7 − 58.7, from table 5.8) from 2005.[3]

In the 1977 article, Pineo and I reported correlations between self-ratings and sample-wide scores for occupations. That is hard to replicate precisely for 2005, given the small proportion of matches between title rated and occupation of rater, but an approximation is made possible by moving to the level of the 26 NOC major groups. There was reason from Gerstl and Cohen (1964, 256) to believe that "egocentric tendency" would hold at this broader level. Respondents in 2005 rated the prestige of groups of occupations, along with the specific titles (details in Goyder and Frank 2006). By re-coding occupations of respondents from 1965 (which were in the 1961 census code) into 2001 NOC major groups, we arrive at a common classification for the 1965 and 2005 surveys. Some of the 1961 codes are hard to reconcile into NOC detailed (unit group) codes, but less error occurs if 1961 unit scores are placed into the broader 2001 NOC groups, and so this is a good application for the scale of major-group prestige.

These results are shown in table 5.10, organized by the five NOC skill levels for occupations. By laying out the skill of the rater against the skill of the title, we produce the mean group prestige score assigned by respondents within and across their own skill level. The design is similar to one reported first by Blau (1957, 393) and later by Alexander (1972, 769), both of them re-analyzing the 1947 NORC study. See also the similar results in Burshytn (1968, 174). Table 5.10 shows the same pattern, holding to an approximately equal extent both for 1965 and 2005. Thus in 2005, A-level (highest-skill) raters gave a mean group prestige score of only 40.5 to D-level (lowest-skill) occupations, against 73.9 for their own high-skill level, for a prestige spread of 33.4 points. Respondents on

Table 5.10
Mean Prestige-of-Group Scores by Skill Level of Title and of Rater

| | Skill Level of Title Rated | | | | |
Skill Level of Rater	D	C	B	A	M
	1965				
D	**28.5**	35.8	45.6	64.5	61.6
C	26.5	**34.7**	45.3	65.5	62.0
B	25.4	34.2	**45.0**	65.0	62.6
A	21.0	30.8	41.6	**69.1**	62.3
M	20.6	28.8	41.6	67.0	**62.9**
	2005				
D	**54.1**	57.2	63.6	70.5	62.1
C	48.4	**53.2**	60.8	71.1	65.8
B	45.9	50.7	**59.8**	69.3	62.9
A	40.5	47.5	56.3	**73.9**	64.9
M	38.3	45.0	55.7	70.3	**63.8**

Note: Ratings within each NOC major group are in bold, with italics if self-enhancement within the group has taken place.

the bottom (D) skill level exhibited the Alexander-squeeze, bunching highest and lowest to 70.5 − 54.1 = 16.4 points, just half the spread that A-skill respondents perceived. As a related and secondary pattern, self-enhancement is occurring at both the A- and the D-skill levels, in both the 1965 and the 2005 samples. The managerial skill level (coded "M" in table 5.10) also self-enhanced (but just a little) in 1965, albeit not at all in 2005. Note the comparatively low managerial scores for 2005, a tendency already seen in an earlier chapter. Prestige scores by managers for skill levels A to D were higher in 2005, and especially at the D level, but changed little between the two samples separated by forty years.

Hodge and Rossi (1978, B63) saw this same pattern and concluded that the squeezing should not be termed "the rubber band of status grading" but, rather, was an epiphenomenon of the higher inter-individual consensus among high, compared with low, SES raters. I report the same pattern around consensus in chapter 7. For me, it is not that the "rubber band" or "squeeze" does not exist, but rather that the reason for the squeeze is tied up with a tendency for some (importantly, not all), low SES raters to grant surprisingly (through labour market economist eyes) high prestige to seemingly humble occupations and low prestige to seemingly important, high authority and cognitive skill occupations.

SUMMARY

Historical upward drift in prestige scores far outweighs variations, either in 1965 or in 2005, in how socio-demographic categories of people rate occupations. The university-educated give noticeably lower scores to occupations, especially lower-skilled occupations and especially so in 2005. These university-educated respondents are severe in rating low-skill occupations, stretching out the scale, while low-skill-level raters squeeze the prestige hierarchy by pushing up from the bottom. Francophones give high prestige, especially at the low-skill end, but that is most noticeable outside Quebec. Most evidence of regional differences comes from Atlantic Canada, with a tendency in 2005 (not seen in 1965) to grant a premium to lower-skill occupations. Respondents who give high value to science and technology respond logically by granting extra prestige to occupations with a clear science-technology profile. This extends conclusions drawn by Zhou, using the 1989 NORC data. Self-ratings have leaped upward over the forty years, more indeed than scores in general. The amount of self-enhancement, the prestige given to self's occupational position beyond what others grant the same position, has moved from some 5 points to between 15 and 20. When assessed unobtrusively, by matching respondents' own occupations or occupation groups to those being rated, the status-inflation is much less, showing that it is not so much the occupational title as the sense of the prestige of self that is being protected so assiduously in the 2005 sample. Crossing the skill level of respondents' occupations with the skill level of titles, the lower SES upwards squeeze is again seen. The lower the skill level of the respondent, the higher the rating of low-skill occupations, and this part of the squeeze was, again, far more pronounced in 2005 than in 1965.

6

The Prestige Distribution

Where chapters 4 and 5 examined what makes a prestige score large or small, this chapter concerns the shape of prestige, that is, how clustered or dispersed scores are. Since the distinction between analysis of prestige at the level of the occupation title versus the individual respondent was explained in the two previous chapters, here both units of analysis are examined and the two analyses integrated into one chapter, beginning with titles, then proceeding to respondents.

TITLE-LEVEL ANALYSIS

From the notion of prestige squeeze we predict an increasingly egalitarian shape of distribution for the scale of occupations. Figure 6.1 shows the compression between 1965 and 2005 in bar graph format, for 10-point intervals on the 0-to-100 scale for occupational prestige. For the 179 labour force titles common to both surveys, no occupation scored below 30 in the 2005 data, since the 22.1 for "someone who lives on social assistance," from table 4.1, is not part of the present comparison. In 1965, scores fell as low as the 10s. With its pronounced right-hand skew, the 1965 prestige distribution resembles a typical distribution for income, in which most people earn modest amounts and only few have incomes of multiples beyond the mean. While the eye can tell that the 2005 prestige distribution is not a smooth bell curve, it is clearly approaching the normal bell curve distribution characteristic of so many human traits such as intelligence quotient. A large mode of scores in the middle-of-scale 50s dominates the 2005 distribution.

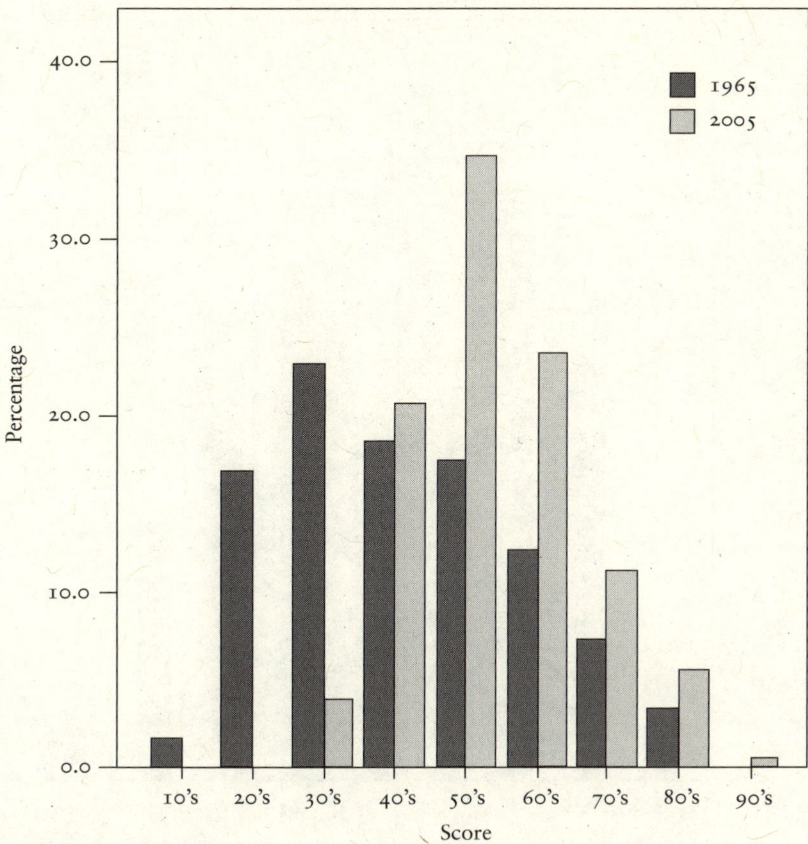

Fig. 6.1 Distribution of prestige scores for 1965 and 2005, for 179 titles common to both surveys

The equivalent comparison from the 1975 to 2000 data for Kitchener-Waterloo, shown in figure 6.2, is broadly concurrent, albeit not quite so clear-cut. There are only 80 titles in this plot, less than half the number in 2005, and of course the historical coverage is twenty-five years against forty for the two national surveys. Nevertheless, the outlines of the 1965–2005 pattern are detectable, with the characteristic upward creep of scores in the more recent period. The 1975 distribution is bimodal, with relatively few title-scores falling in the mid-scale 50s range. While the year 2000 KW scores give only an awkward approximation of a normal distribution, they do have the core feature of an unbroken ascent to

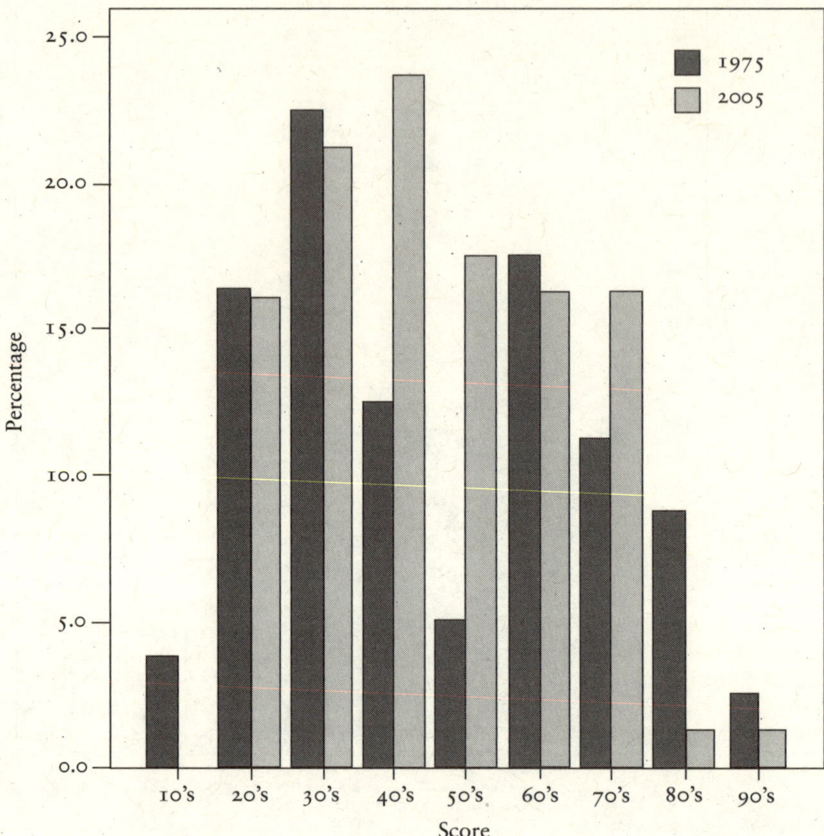

Fig. 6.2   1975–2000 Kitchener-Waterloo distribution of prestige scores for 80 titles common to both surveys

a single mode, followed by monotonic decline until the leveling off in the 80s and 90s.

Table 6.1 gathers together several statistics describing the shape of distribution for the 1965–2005 and 1975–2000 pairs of prestige surveys. While the 3-point increase in mean prestige between 1975 and 2000 Kitchener-Waterloo data was insufficient to pass .05 significance over the 80 titles examined, the 12.1 points nationally between 1965 and 2005 does easily. As expected from the upward squeeze, the standard deviation for prestige scales has shrunk in both the 1965–2005 and 1975–2000 comparisons, shifts significant at the one in a thousand level according to a bootstrap test (Simon 1995).

The Gini coefficient, the next comparison in table 6.1, is not commonly applied to occupational-prestige data. This coefficient

Table 6.1
Summary Indicators for Shape of Prestige Distribution, National and
Kitchener-Waterloo Data

	Grand Mean for Scale	Standard Deviation	Gini Coefficient	Skewness
National Data				
1965	46.46	16.92	.207	.403
2005	58.53	11.70	.113	.362
Change (later less earlier)	12.07	−5.22	−.094	−.041
Significance test for 1965–2005	< .001	< .001	< .001	ns
Kitchener-Waterloo Data				
1975	50.48	21.40	.241	.299
2000	53.65	16.08	.170	.252
Change (later less earlier)	3.17	−5.32	−.071	−.047
Significance test for 1975–2000	ns	< .001	< .001	ns

Note: 179 titles for 1965/2005; 80 for 1975/2000. Significance tests are by the bootstrap method described by Simon (1995) using *Resampling Stats* software.

indexes the area between the diagonal and the actual curve in a Lorenz plot, with increasingly large coefficient values as the observed curve bows away from the theoretical diagonal (for more details, see Marsh 1988, 89–92). The Lorenz curve/Gini coefficient is more familiar in applications to income inequality (e.g., figure 4 from chapter 2), where the question asked is, what percentage of wage earners receive which percentage of the income distribution? A high Gini coefficient for an income distribution could happen when a small number of people hold a large proportion of the collective income. Although the units in the present tabulation are occupations, not individual people, it is part of the research tradition in occupational prestige to speak of the prestige "in the system" (Hodge, Siegel, and Rossi 1966, 325), and one can ask how the ensemble of occupations share in this total quantity of prestige. If a small number of titles in management and the professions, for example, held scores many points differentiated from trades, the Gini would be high. When prestige is spread out with even increments between each occupation, the Gini falls. Between 1975 and 2000, in the KWMAS data, the Gini value declined from .241 to .170, a non-chance amount of .071 points change. Over the longer period spanned by the two national-level samples, the change is greater still, .094 points change in Gini coefficient.

Reference back to the Gini coefficients for income inequality included in chapter 2 shows that "subjective inequality" as reflected by prestige scores is less than the "objective reality" of income distribution. And over the forty years between 1965 and 2005, this disjuncture became increasingly true as income Gini's increased from the mid-thirties to nearly .40 while prestige Gini's fell below .20, as shown in table 6.1. Income Gini coefficients move around a little as one "plays with" the exact definition of income, adjustment for family size, etc. (cf., Dhawal-Biswal 2002 and Heisz 2007, with CANSIM series from figure 2.4), but even forty years ago income Gini's, no matter what the details behind the computation, ran several points above the .207 for occupational prestige just noted.

I commented above on the right-hand skewness of the prestige distribution in 1965. While the 2005 skew statistic in table 6.1 indeed is some 4 points lower, the non-significant (at .05) test result flags a need for caution and a second look at the bar graphs. Although the 2005 titles have a much more normal-curve appearance left of the mean compared with 1965, the twenty-first-century data have some of the mid-twentieth-century right-hand skew resulting from the migration of scores into the 90s for a few occupation titles. The 1975–2000 duo of samples both give lower readings on skewness than the 1965–2005 pair, but revealingly in these Kitchener-Waterloo samples, shift over time is again toward less skew. Again the decline is not large enough to be statistically significant, but there is a generic significance established by the preciseness by which the decline in skew is reproduced in two pairs of samples.

The scale of movement in recent years toward more egalitarian distributions of occupational prestige can be appreciated by looking back to the earlier research in the United States. From information in Siegel (1971, 69–91), scores from the scale used by NORC in their 1947 and 1963 occupational-prestige surveys can be transformed into the 0–100 metric used in most later research. Change in prestige can thereby be examined for 1947 to 1963 and from 1964 to 1989. There is a difficulty of only 60 titles appearing jointly in all four surveys, and so in table 6.2 the means, standard deviations, and Gini coefficients are presented both for those 60 (listwise deletion) and for the larger sets of titles common to one or the other pair of surveys (pairwise). By either method, a clear pattern of stability is present. Over the first period, 1947–1963, change in the distribution of prestige was non-existent. The mean scale score increased by about one

Table 6.2
The Shape of the Distribution of Occupational Prestige over 1947–63 and 1964–89
(NORC Studies)

	Grand Mean for Scale	Standard Deviation	Gini Coefficient
	"PAIRWISE" SELECTION OF TITLES		
1947–1963			
1963	48.65	21.00	.247
1947	47.71	21.17	.254
Change (later less earlier)	0.94	–0.17	–0.003
1964–1989			
1989	44.69	14.33	.174
1964	42.10	15.74	.212
Change (later less earlier)	2.59	–1.41	–.038
	"LISTWISE" SELECTION OF TITLES		
1947–1963			
1963	48.04	18.76	.223
1947	46.66	18.65	.228
Change (later less earlier)	1.38	0.11	–.005
1964–1989			
1989	50.42	17.05	.192
1964	47.60	19.35	.232
Change (later less earlier)	2.82	–2.30	–.040

Note: In "pairwise" comparison (upper portion) 90 titles for 1947–1963; 266 (the labour force set) for 1964–1989; in "listwise" 60 of the 90 titles from 1947–1963 also tested in both 1964 and 1989.

point, the exact figure hinging on the set of titles examined. Reduction in standard deviation could be detected only in the first decimal place, and the Gini coefficient dropped merely in the third decimal place. Considering that these are all sample data, with the largest N being about 2,900 and the rest much smaller, the stability in estimates of the shape of occupational prestige in this earlier U.S. research is astounding, as observers at the time realized. One cannot quarrel with the "no change" reading of these data by Hodge, Siegel, and Rossi (1966). In the 1964–1989 interval, there were stirrings of change, as Nakao and Treas (1994) had reported, but still nothing to compare with the more recent pattern.

Scanning across all the prestige surveys that have been referred to here (NORC 1947, 1963, 1964, 1989; Pineo-Porter 1965; Guppy-Siltanen Kitchener-Waterloo survey of 1975; year 2000 Kitchener-Waterloo replication; 2005 Canadian survey), 29 occupations appear in every one. As a sample of the many hundreds of titles

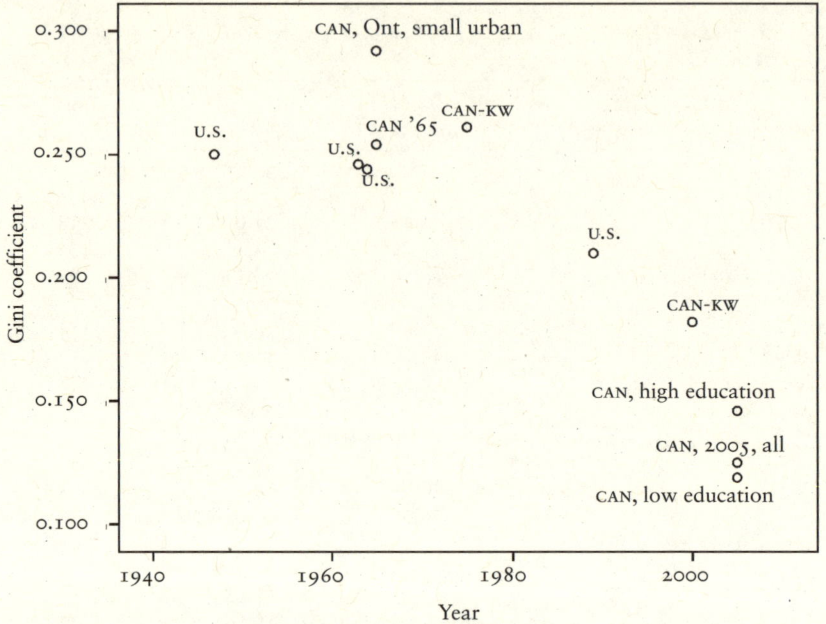

Fig. 6.3   Gini coefficients for u.s. and Canadian prestige studies, 1947–2005, for 29 common titles: accountant, architect, auto repairman, barber, bartender, biologist, bookkeeper, chemist, civil engineer, clerk in a store, college professor, economist, farm hand, filling station attendant, insurance agent, janitor, lawyer, mail carrier, physician, plumber, policeman, psychologist, restaurant cook, restaurant waiter, taxi driver, trained machinist, truck driver, undertaker, welfare worker

appearing in Canadian and u.s. occupational classifications, these make a small slice. Nakao and Treas (1994), after all, looked at 740 occupations. Nevertheless, several of the titles considered to be of interest in previous pages appear in the set of 29 (e.g., lawyer, physician, and the older title of policeman in police officer), and the mix of white collar and blue collar is adequate. I therefore computed Gini coefficients for the 29, over the eight surveys, plotting results against year in figure 6.3. The function is quite an elegant quadratic in which the decline in Gini coefficient over time has an accelerating pace. There is no detectable Canada-u.s. difference, the best reading on that being the Gini coefficient of .254 for Pineo and Porter's 1965 study, which was expressly designed to replicate the NORC 1964 (Hodge and Seigel) work, where Gini = .244. The coefficient for 1975 Kitchener-Waterloo is a slight outlier on the high side, and that can be attributed to the urban Ontario setting for that fieldwork, since the Gini for Ontario cases from 1965 residing in places of 30,000 or more was .292, well above the national result in 1965. Figure 6.3 shows three results for 2005: one for all respondents, one for those with university education, and another for those with less than university. While the 2005 Gini coefficient is remarkably low across both education levels, it is (we see again) the less-educated portion who are most emphatically pushing the recent scores into an egalitarian distribution.

INDIVIDUAL-LEVEL ANALYSIS

The bunching just seen of occupational-prestige scores aggregated over all respondents in 2005 is accompanied by a similar squeeze when the ratings of each individual are examined. That congruence is not inevitable. If, for example, 2005 respondents began assigning scores virtually on a random basis, as exasperated respondents interested only in satisficing (Tourangeau et al. 2000, 17) their way through the survey might, the aggregated scale resulting would show little differentiation from top to bottom, yet this would not be meaningful. On the contrary, the pattern for the aggregated scores is even clearer when examined for individuals. It was easy using SPSS "compute" commands to calculate the standard deviation for the ratings for every one of the 793 respondents from 1965 and the 2,053 from 2005. Just the 179 matching titles across the two studies were used, and 2005 people (it will be recalled from chapter 3) were rating only 25 titles each. The median standard deviation dropped from 10.6 in 1965 to a much reduced 5.8 in 2005. The reduced variance in the typical 2005 respondent's scale is graphed in figure 6.4, based on grouping the standard deviations into seven clusters of five points each.

Now we can complete a circle and contemplate the standard deviations for each title, which were shown in table 1 of chapter 4. This statistic did not change appreciably between 1965 and 2005. The mean standard deviation of 21.1 per title in 1965 floated up just slightly to 22.6 in 2005 (as median standard deviations, 21.0 and 22.6 respectively). In this aspect of the comparison of occupational prestige in 1965 and 2005, two forces are pushing against each other. As just seen above, people in 2005 were squeezing their scales (producing small standard deviations for the scale unique to each individual rater). At the same time, the disagreement between one

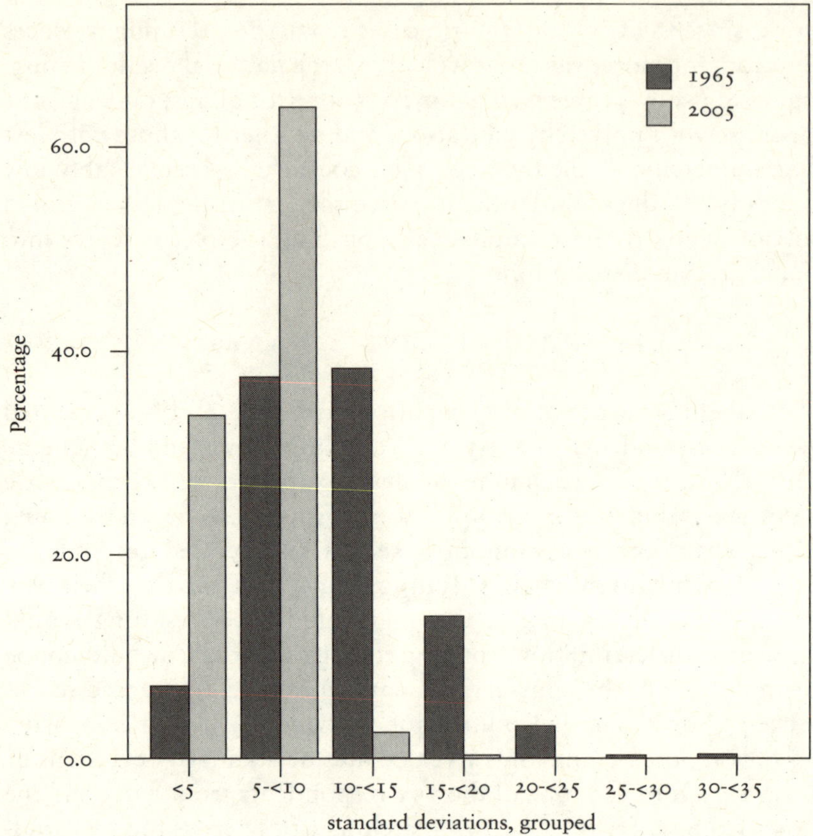

Fig. 6.4   Distribution of standard deviations of ratings by each respondent, 1965 and 2005

person and another was much greater in 2005 than in 1965. This, the topic of chapter 7, offset, and indeed won out over, the individual squeezing in prestige, making for the slight upward float in the standard deviation for a typical occupation title in the 2005 ratings.

CONCLUSION

Looking at the style by which scores have been analyzed in the many surveys on occupational prestige over the years since 1925, we see that little attention has been placed on shape of distribution, the focus of this present chapter. Far more stress by previous researchers has gone into consensus and dissensus, the topic of the chapter to follow. From sociological first principles, however, the shape of the distribution of inequality is just as important as which positions score high or low or whether people are agreed on their ratings. It is easier on the psyche being toward the bottom of a very undifferentiated, level distribution than at the foot of a steep hierarchy. This is a theme to be re-visited in the concluding chapter, but in keeping with the historical approach of the present chapter, with its excursion right back to NORC's 1947 data, I shall conclude here by noting that older studies of inequality usually took careful note of the distribution of inequality. Lloyd Warner's (1949) *Democracy in Jonesville* is typical in a discussion at the beginning of its second chapter. The classes in the Warner studies were intended as discrete social groups with clear demarcations. Occupational-prestige scores, in contrast, are continuous distributions in which there is no cut-off point to separate, say, the "Level of the Common Man" (woman) that Warner (1949, 23) identified.

This issue of discrete vs continuous categories cannot, however, be the main reason for the neglect of the shape of the prestige distribution in research on occupations. Income research takes shape of distribution seriously and yet uses a continuous scale looking much like prestige points. I think the emphasis in analysis of occupational-prestige data was set by the 1960s stress on status attainment. Ideologically, in the 1960s North American social environment, it was not the amount of inequality that counted – the shape of the inequality distribution in other words – it was whether the determinants of high or low attained status were achieved or ascribed. Hope (1981) dissected some of the implications of inequality vs ascription. Sociological theorizing around structural-functionalism, examined in an earlier chapter, concurred with prevailing ideology in positing a need for inequality alongside a meritocratic regime for status attainment. The 1960s emphasis on modeling the process of status attainment, rather than describing inequality distribution, was reflected in the priority status-attainment analysis gained over occupational-mobility research. Admittedly there was always debate back and forth between the two approaches, but for a period following the publication of Blau and Duncan's American *Occupational Structure*, my reading is that status attainment held primacy. Even within the mobility school, effort was directed to statistical techniques for controlling out shape of distribution, articulated as the distinction between structural and net mobility.

Admittedly, the privileging of process of attainment over shape of distribution was a characteristic of American, rather than British, sociology. The British preoccupation with discrete social classes and the proportion of population in each, rather than with status hierarchies whose distribution has less obvious meaning, is easily demonstrated by entering key words such "social class" and "Great Britain" into an electronic database for sociological literature. Discussion on whether social classes still existed in Britain, and the conceptual meaning of class, seemed particularly thick during the 1990s. Morris and Scott (1996, 49), for example, wrote in one of the many scholarly exchanges about class and status in the United Kingdom, "five occupational categories – we hesitate to call them 'social classes.'" Toward the end of the decade, Gerteis and Savage (1996, 252) commented, "[o]ver the past decade sociologists have hotly debated whether the salience of social class for cultural identification and political mobilization is declining ... [m]uch of this debate has a British-centred flavour." In my examination of prestige between 1965 and 2005 I am working thoroughly within the North American frame.

Insofar as occupational prestige was simply an adjunct to the status attainment model, in the style of Duncan and Hodge's (1961) work, one can understand the de-emphasis of distribution. In the present study, however, I have wanted to treat prestige as informative in its own right, and so it was logical to examine the shape of the distribution of prestige.

7

Dissensus in Ratings

The first evidence of declining consensus over the rating of prestige was encountered in chapter 5, showing an inflation in ratings of own occupation since the 1960s. If people do not agree about their own places in the occupational hierarchy, they may disagree about scores generally. In this concluding section of the analysis, attention centers on consensus in ratings. Some would feel this is *the* issue about occupational prestige. Most of the implications drawn about occupational prestige in earlier years were based on an assumed high inter-rater agreement. The familiar Davis and Moore theory, for example, concerning the need to motivate workers for important but difficult occupations, assumes consensus around the legitimacy of differential rewards, including prestige. More broadly, value consensus was an important assumption for Talcott Parsons's (e.g., 1940) image of a viable, integrated social system. Some earlier research about consensus was touched on in chapter 1. Scholarly exchanges such as the one between Guppy (1982) and Balkwell et al. (1982) showed an unwillingness among some researchers to concede that dissensus was either existent to any important extent in the 1960s data or meaningful where non-agreement was found. Guppy and I (Guppy and Goyder 1984) perceived an inclination among researchers to dismiss non-agreement too hastily as "error" on the part of respondents.

With the rise of post-modernist thought between the 1960s and 2000s, it has become less plausible to dismiss as erroneous prestige ratings not closely corresponding to educational prerequisites and income rewards for occupations. Blaikie's (1977, 113) commentary from over thirty years ago about "working-class views of reality" being "likely to be judged as unreliable or 'distorted'" seems prescient today, even though contemporaries saw his article as controversial, with a series of lively exchanges appearing in the February 1978 (13, 3) edition of the *Australian and New Zealand Journal of Sociology*. We are more sociologically inclined nowadays to think that people have reasons for their scores, even when their prestige rating for an occupation appears incongruous. It is not that I utterly dismiss the possibility of respondents "satisficing" their way quickly and unreflectively through the ratings. Surveys respondents may also, it is true, hold inaccurate information about the educational prerequisites and income rewards for an occupation. "Unfamiliarity" with some occupations has been perceived in raters right back to Counts's (1925, 24) time. People may equally, however, be operating from non-upper-strata class ideologies or be deliberately blending non-SES considerations into the score. I would rather err in the direction of supposing that people have reasons for their thoughts and actions. The analysis begins at the aggregate level and then moves behind the aggregation to examine agreement in ratings between one survey respondent and another.

CORRELATING AGGREGATED SCALES

Since the time of Riess's (1961) report on the 1947 NORC survey it has been routine to tally up the occupational-prestige scores for various aggregates within or across surveys and then compute the Pearsonian correlation between the scales. This interest extends well beyond the work of figures such as Treiman, already discussed (e.g., Fossum and Moore 1975). Since individual variation is being averaged away as part of the computation, such correlations tend, as noted in earlier chapters, to be high – often 0.9 or more. The coefficients nevertheless can be informative, partly because so many results to compare against exist within the literature but also because they may pick up incongruities strong enough to show through despite the averaging.

Such correlation-based comparisons supported the notion of an unvarying prestige hierarchy. Blau and Duncan (1967, 120) were among those impressed that "[a] set of ratings obtained as long ago as 1925 correlated to the extent of .93 with the latest set, obtained in 1963." Figure 7.1 maps the correlation between the scale for the Occupational Prestige in Canada: 2005 survey and the 1965

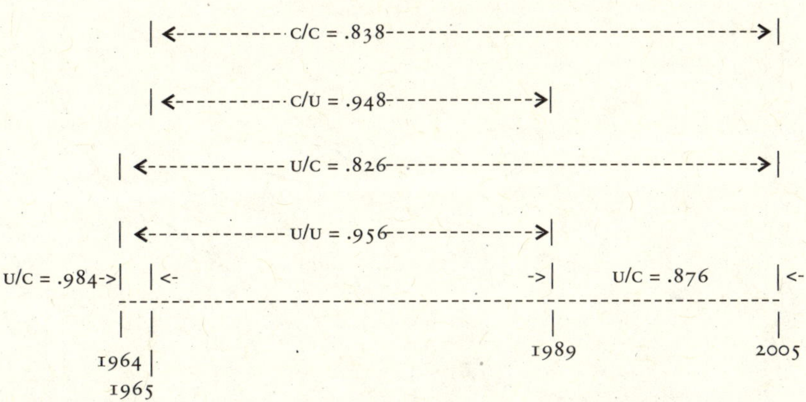

Fig. 7.1 Strength of correlation between four scales, 1964 to 2005, based on 136 titles common across all four surveys. c = Canada; u = United States

Pineo-Porter scale, along with the two most recent NORC scales, from 1964 and 1989.[1] There are 136 names of occupations common across the four surveys. The key result is the Canada 1965 with Canada 2005 fit, which, at r = .838 is noticeably lower than the .90 plus correlations traditionally found between the scales from different years but from the same country.[2] For context, .838 is about midway between the two correlations reported by Haller et al. (1972, 948) in their study of exceptions to the 1960s universal prestige hierarchy in which they compared prestige in the urban centre of São Paulo, Brazil, with the agricultural town Bezerros (r = .89) and the subsistence farming/mining rural outpost Açucena (r = .69). An observation by Pineo and Porter (1967, 30) that 1960s Canadian and u.s. scales were virtually interchangeable is re-expressed in the present tabulations using the set of 136 titles. The fit between the u.s. 1989 and Canada 2005 scales is revealing. At r = .876, that is some 12 correlation points of deterioration from perfect interchangeability over 16 years. The legendary NORC comparison between 1947 and 1963 also, by coincidence, spanned 16 years, but here the correlation between scales was r = .99, giving just one point of change. The prestige hierarchy was shuffling over ten times faster per 16 years between 1989 and 2005 than between 1947 and 1963.

This feature of accelerating dissensus across time since the later 1940s is portrayed graphically in figure 7.2. For the 29 titles common across all the surveys since 1947 (see table 3.1), the correlation

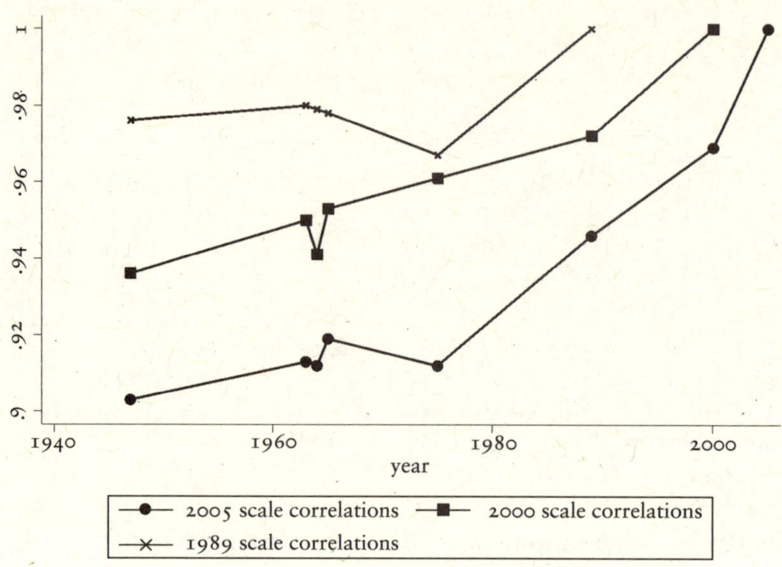

Fig. 7.2   Change in points of Pearsonian correlation between scales for periods since 1947, for 29 common titles

between the three most recent scales, 2005, 2000, and 1989, was computed with those for earlier years. The pattern is quite tidy. Reading along the x-axis from left to right, the 1947 NORC scale (remembering this is just for the 29 common titles) correlated r = .976 with the 1989 scale, slipping to .936 with 2000 and .903 with 2005. One could object that a national boundary is being crossed in this comparison, but all the evidence points toward essentially interchangeable scales for Canada and the United States, at least for the earlier period. For the 1964 NORC and 1965 Canadian (Pineo-Porter) scales, for example, the fit was r = .993 over the 29 titles. Over 174 matching Canada-U.S. titles from these 1960s studies, the cross-country correlation was .98, as reported by Pineo and Porter (1967, 30), prompting their comment: "had the correlation between the rankings produced in our study and that of the recent NORC study been smaller than any previous ones some questioning of the hypothesis of identical rankings in all industrialized nations would be appropriate. In fact, the correlation was higher."

The era of rapidly changing occupational-prestige hierarchies seems, from figure 7.2, to begin in the mid-1970s; the 2005 scale correlations have a "hockey stick" shape, falling off rapidly until just before 1980, then settling into the r = .90–.92 range. Admittedly there is only the Kitchener-Waterloo 1975 scale to represent the 1970s in this graph, but that small and local data set is historically important, since up to the mid-1960s, prestige was hardly changing at all. Over the 29 titles, the 1947-with-1963 correlation was .993, the same near perfect correlation found when comparing all matching titles for those years. Occupational prestige used to be a constant, as observers in the 1960s noticed, but sometime after the mid-1970s a period of accelerating change began giving declines in aggregrate correlations unprecedented against the 1960s norms. A result from Poland, by Sawiński and Domański (1991b), of a .94 correlation between scales from 1975 and 1989 fits with the interpretation of prestige change beginning toward the end of the 1970s. Six points is much deterioration in the correlation between scales over just fourteen years, even for the post-1975 period, but as the authors note in their report, 1975 to 1989 was an especially turbulent period for Poland, which was going through a political transformation away from communism.

CORRELATING DISAGGREGATED SCALES

The typical correlation between the occupational ratings for any two respondents, both within and across samples, has been computed in many studies (e.g., Goldthorpe and Hope 1974, 163; Featherman and Hauser 1976, 404; Broom et al. 1977, 214; Kraus et al. 1978; Balkwell et al. 1980; Guppy and Goyder 1984; Sawiński and Domański 1991a, 256). Such disaggregation gets around the "profile fallacy" of drawing conclusions about what lies within the minds of individuals from data aggregated across groups (Coxon and Jones 1978, 9). Treiman (1977, 60) was aware of dissensus at the level of individuals in his international data base, noting a typical individual with individual correlations of about .6.

Creating correlations for disaggregated scales across the 1965–2005 samples required data manipulation, owing to the 2005 design of regional stratification into groups of 400 crossed with ten sub-samples of approximately 200 each rating different sets of 21 occupations (plus the 4 rated by all respondents). Taking all of the 400 cases from the largest region and the appropriate fraction from 400 cases for each of the other four main regions, a regionally representative sample was formed from the 2005 data, giving 1,212

Table 7.1
Median Correlations, Individual with Individual and Individual with Mean

	Median r	*p, difference*
1965, individual with individual	.554	
2005, individual with individual	.328	< .001
1965, individual with mean	.770	
2005, individual with mean	.644	< .001

Note: Based on 390 pairs of correlations in each individual-with-individual comparison, 780 pairs for individual with mean. See note 2 for details. Significance for differences between 1965 and 2005 computed using Resampling Stats software (Simon 1995).

cases from the full 2,053. Within each of the ten sub-samples within the 1,212, the order of cases was randomized, then the file was transposed row-for-column, so that respondents became columns ("variables") and occupations became rows ("cases"). The first 78 respondent/columns were retained (see below for reason) for each of the 10 sub-samples, giving a sample now having 780 cases. Within each sub-sample, the correlation between the 1st respondent's and the 39th respondent's scale was computed (remembering the order of respondents was randomized earlier), then the 2d with the 40th, and so on, giving 39 correlations. Over ten sub- samples, 390 correlations between pairs of randomly selected respondents, over approximately 21 occupations, resulted.[3] Summary statistics for these within-sample correlations appear in table 7.1. The 1965 data were set up to match. The sample n of 793 was trimmed to 780, which factors evenly by 10 into 39 pairs. The 780 were randomly assigned to ten sub-samples. Each sub-sample retained only the same occupation titles rated by the corresponding sub-sample from 2005. Again, the 1st respondent's scale was correlated with the (random order) 39th, and so on, to produce 390 correlations of respondent scale with respondent scale for 1965. The mean (sample-wide) score for each occupation in each sample was also coded into these two data sets. Here, 780 correlations could be computed for each sample, examining how closely a randomly selected respondent's scale agreed with the aggregate scale.

The results from Table 7.1 are clear. The median inter-respondent correlation dropped from r =.554 in 1965 to .328 in 2005, easily a statistically significant change.[4] The 1965 figure is in line with those from other studies reported above, considering that for present purposes, only 21 or fewer occupation ratings per respondent were used. The 2005 correlation of .3 is well below the historical norm for inter-rater agreement, showing that the level of consensus across individuals has plunged. The same pattern appears when individual scales are correlated with totals, as seen in the lower rows of table 7.1.

Is the new dissensus the result of individuals "bowling alone" when they rate the prestige of occupations, or more one of an identity politics (Calhoun 1994) society of consensus within groups complicated by dissensus across groups? To address this question, I returned to the long file described in chapter 5, in which the title scores for both 1965 and 2005 were gathered in one long column, with respondent data repeated for each title. The independent variables amenable to common codes from the two surveys are, recalling from chapter 5, region, respondent in the workforce, respondent's spouse in the workforce, Canadian vs foreign-born, age group, male vs female, Francophone vs other language, university- educated.

Further file-manipulation was needed to create a data set of randomly assigned pairs of respondents. The steps were (a) randomly select one line for deletion from the file to give an even number of data lines; (b) randomize the resulting long stacked file of 169,256 lines and divide into two sub-samples so that each respondent could be paired with another; (c) merge the pairs on an SPSS "add variables" basis to give a file of 84,628 lines, each line describing the ratings and socio-demographics of two randomly paired respondents.

Thus, sometimes a 2005 respondent was compared with another 2005 respondent, sometimes with a 1965 respondent, and so on. This approach reproduces in another form the design used in Guppy and Goyder (1984). The 2005 data do not have enough cases per rating to support our method from 1984. When just the cases in which the pairs happened to be rating the same occupation title were retained, the catch was only some 400 cases, about 5 per 1,000 lines of data. Eleven more random draws were therefore made, to build up the data base. Since university education was far less common in 1965 than in 2005, the number of pairs sharing this educational level was only about 50 cases. Given the importance of education for the proposed analysis, a second sampling was made, selecting only high-education pairs, sufficient to bring the number of such cases to near 200 for each year (a number that coincides with the size of sub-samples from the 2005 survey design). After all duplicate cases in the data base of pairs were eliminated, the N was 5,076 (4,804 from the first stage draw plus 272 from the draw of high-education pairs). Since a respondent can appear more than once in this data set of pairs (the average was three appearances per respondent), a mixed (i.e., HL) model was applied, in which the intercept for the second member of each pair was entered as a random effect.

Results appear in table 7.2, admittedly a complicated array of figures. The first model (labelled "base model 1") is a deliberately simple beginning in which the score given to an occupation by a respondent is predicted from whether that respondent was in the 2005 sample (coded 1) or the 1965 sample (coded 0). In an echo of earlier analysis presented in simpler form (chapter 5), scores from 2005 average 11.5 points more than those from 1965. It's that same margin of about 12 points that keeps cropping up in various workings of the data. For the next coefficient, it is correct that whether the second rating was from 2005 or 1965 has nearly zero effect (i.e., the coefficient of −0.358). We are not yet predicting one score from a pair score, merely re-establishing as a baseline and validation of approach the main effect that 2005 scores are higher than 1965 scores. Since the second member of the pair has been assigned randomly, the year that second person comes from should have no bearing on the first score (it's not his or her rating score, just the fact of being in one sample or the other).

The next model, however, *does* include the rating made by the paired respondent. To illustrate, the first line in the paired dataset happens to give scores for "Protestant Minister," rated by a 1965 respondent paired with another 1965 respondent. The first respondent gave the title 8 on the 1-to-9 scale, transforming to 87.5. The paired respondent scored Protestant Minister at 7 (75.0 transformed). The dependent-variable score is 87.5, predicted by 75, and so on down the remaining 5,075 lines of data. In the resulting regression model, the term of 12.070 is multiplied by zero to indicate a 1965 rating in the dependent variable for this first line of data. Since the second rater in this pair is also from 1965, the coefficient of −4.343 also is multiplied by zero and disappears. More interesting is the coefficient of 0.339, which indexes congruency from one respondent to the next averaged across both within-sample and cross-sample pairs. It is the regression slope form of the within-sample correlations from table 7.1 averaged for 1965, 2005,

Table 7.2
Mixed-Model Fixed Effects: Prestige Scores Given to Occupations by Pairs of Respondents in the 1965 and 2005 Surveys

	Base Models		Model with Slope	Education Models		Gender Model	Official Languages Models	
	1	2	3	4	5	6	7	8
Main Effects								
Intercept	46.361	30.519	27.912	23.257	27.369	#	26.794	#
Predicting a 2005 score (*vs.* 1965)	11.513	12.070	19.976	19.501	14.450	#	20.881	#
Second rater from 2005 (*vs.* 1965)	−0.358ns	−4.343	0.288ns	1.495ns	−11.660	#	1.759ns	#
Rating of occupation by second rater ("slope")		0.339	0.394	0.490	0.410	#	0.398	#
Both: Low education				5.768	0.638ns			
Male						ns		
Francophone							5.774ms	#
Both: High education				−5.930ns	−10.625			
Female						−3.037ms		
Anglophone							1.209ns	#
Two-Way Interactions								
2005 score by second rating from 2005			1.393ns	2.672ns	18.893	#	1.559ns	#
2005 score by slope			−0.172	−0.203	−0.120ns	#	−0.174	#
2005 score by:								
Both low education				2.841ns	10.720			
Both male						ns		
Both Francophone							4.931ns	#
2005 score by:								
Both high education				−0.635ns	4.055ns			
Both female						ns		

Table 7.2 (continued)

	Base Models		Model with Slope	Education Models		Gender Model	Official Languages Models	
	1	2	3	4	5	6	7	8
Both Anglophone							−1.831ns	#
Second rating from 2005 by slope			−.080	−0.109	0.124ns	#	−.085	#
Second rating from 2005 by:								
Both low education				−0.100ns	19.794			
Both male						ns		
Both Francophone							ns	#
Second rating from 2005 by:								
Both high education				−2.174ns	17.353ns			
Both female						ns		
Anglophone							1.732ms	#
Slope by: Both low education				−0.118	−0.017ns			
Both male						ns		
Francophone							−0.152	#
Slope by: Both high education				0.141	0.218			
Both female						ns		
Anglophone							0.011ns	#
Three-way interactions								
2005 score by second rating from 2005 by slope					−0.239ns			#
2005 score by second rating from 2005 by:								
Both low education					−36.583			
Both male								
Both Francophone								ns

Table 7.2 (continued)

	Base Models		Model with Slope	Education Models		Gender Model	Official Languages Models	
	1	2	3	4	5	6	7	8
2005 score by second rating from 2005 by:								
Both high education					−21.991ns			
Both female								
Both Anglophone								ns
2005 score by slope by:								
Both low education					−0.140ns			
Both male								
Both Francophone								
2005 score by slope by:								
Both high education					−.017ns			
Both male								
Both Francophone								ns
Second rating from 2005 by slope by:								
Both low education					−0.344			
Both Francophone								ns
Second rating from 2005 by slope by:								
Both high education					−.301ns			
Both Anglophone								ns
2005 score by 2005 rater by slope by:								
Both low education					0.572			
Both high education					0.237ns			

ns: Not significant, at p < .05.

ms: Marginally significant, at p >.05 < .1.

#:   Entered into equation, but the size of coefficient is not pertinent.

Table 7.3
Summary Table of Consensus Scores (Regression Coefficients for Paired Respondents)

Respondents	Predicting 1965 Score from 2005 Score	Predicting 2005 Score from 1965 Score	Predicting 1965 Score from 1965 Score	Predicting 2005 Score 2005 Score
All respondents	.314	.222	.394	.142
Low-education pair	.173	.150	.393	.246
High-education pair	.451	.190	.628	.312

Note: These results are derived by substituting the relevant values into equations from table 7.2.

and both cross-year pairs (see note 4). If it were a 1965 score being predicted from a 2005 score, the slope of .339 between raters would lead to an over-estimate without the −4.343 correction factor recognizing that 1965 scores tended to be lower than in 2005. Subsequent models in table 7.2 track this coefficient under various conditions. From model 3, when both ratings are from 2005, the slope decreases from .339, as in model 2, down to .142 (.394 − .172 − .080). That expresses in another form the finding of low consensus in 2005, from table 7.1. If a 2005 score is predicted by one from the set of ratings for 1965, the slope rises to .222 (.394 − .172), and that makes sense given the higher consensus in 1965. Table 7.3 summarizes the four combinations of slope as derived from model 3. It might seem strange that the slope of the 2005 score on the 1965 score is smaller than 1965 on 2005. The explanation lies in the much larger variance in the scores for the earlier year, relative to the prestige-squeezed 2005 ones.

The next set of columns, returning to table 7.2, examines variations in consensus by education, gender, and language. Education, consistently the most important socio-demographic source of variation in prestige ratings (Hodge and Rossi 1978), is entered in model 4 and proves the dominant factor here too. The education code is the same as the one used in chapter 5, university-educated versus others. Model 4 distinguishes pairs in which both are low (i.e., less than university) education or both high against the reference category of mixed. Less-educated respondents give occupations higher prestige scores, the expected result (Alexander 1972, 769; Hodge and Rossi 1978, B61) already confirmed in the 2005 data. The converse, whereby the highly educated mark occupations down, fails the .05 significance test, despite the efforts at enhancing the case base of high-education pairs. Low-education pairs have lower consensus about prestige ratings, as seen from how the baseline slope between ratings, .490 in model 4, moves when adjusted for details about the education of raters (.490 − .118 = .372) when both raters are low education. This too reproduces a previous result (Guppy and Goyder 1984, 715, or even earlier, DeFleur and DeFleur 1967, classifying child-raters by parents' social class). Sawiński and Domański (1991a) did not find the same differentiation in their Polish data and discuss why in their article.

Education is further specified in table 7.2 by year (i.e., 1965/2005), addressed in model 5. Among low-education pairs from 1965, the estimated slope between ratings is (.410 − .017 = .393); among 2005 low-education pairs, the slope drops to .246 (.410 − .120 + .124 − .017 − .239 − .140 − .344 + .572). For high-education pairs, the slopes are .628 for 1965 pairs and .312 for 2005. With consensus higher across the board in 1965 than in 2005 and with consensus in both years higher among the highly educated pairs, the two come together, reinforced by statistically significant interaction effects between the two years, to yield very high consensus among 1965 highly educated pairs (the slope of .628, noted above). Since so many figures are being processed through a complex model, I again summarize the consensus-measuring slopes in table 7.3.

By far the strongest lines of cleavage in consensus about occupational prestige revolve around education. The gender alignment of pairs makes no difference either to the magnitude of the rating given occupations or to the level of consensus between randomly selected respondents (model 6, table 7.2). (Note that we do not have the complication here of variation in gender-specified occupation titles, as in chapter 6). For official language (French, English), the only effect is less consensus among pairs of Francophones than Anglophones (− .152 subtraction from main effect slope). Findings for region, country of birth, work status, and age are too uneventful to be worth mentioning; the 2005 dissensus in rating occupational prestige is widely diffused among socio-demographic sets.

CONSENSUS AND CRITERIA

As seen already (chapter 3), people vary in the weight they place on different criteria for rating occupational prestige. Indeed, recall that about 250 respondents in the 2005 sample of 2,053 confided, in response to an early question in the survey, that they could not attribute meaning to the term social standing.

The next analysis explores the relationship between criteria-preference and consensus in ratings. There are only 2005 data here, so the longfile initially described in chapter 5 was re-created for all the labour force titles used in the 2005 fieldwork. Again, the file was repeatedly randomized for case order, then divided into pairs to be matched up. After 20 passes, there were 1,677 unique combinations of two respondents rating the same title, and 134 duplicates to be set aside.

I was interested here in whether any pockets of higher consensus were detectable within the 2005 data. Three questions about the ratings asked of respondents bore on the issue, beginning with whether the term "social standing" held meaning. After completing the ratings, respondents were questioned about the criteria they had used, and after scoring several of the common factors described in the literature as "important" or "not important" in their own ratings, they were asked, "Are there any other factors that, for you, determine the social standing of occupations?" and "[d]o you think most other people would give our list of occupations the same ratings you just did?" It seemed that those understanding social standing, those content with standard criteria for occupational prestige, and those perceiving their own ratings to be in line with those of others would exhibit the greatest consensus. The logic would be that some people are "post-moderns," while others, possibly over-selected from the older age-brackets, would carry more of the 1960s industrial-society consensus about prestige.

Working within one year enabled simpler calculations than the ones above. In table 7.4, the regression (un-standardized, owing to the comparisons across sub-groups) of first pair member's score on second pair member's score is reported. This gives an index of consensus between randomly selected respondents and, owing to the importance of education for consensus and linkages between education and the questions about criteria (to be detailed below), results are broken down between pairs where both had less than university education and pairs where one or both did have university education. This delving into respondents' reports on their criteria for occupational prestige ratings does not discover any important centres of consensus. The range of coefficients extends only from a low

Table 7.4
Zero-Order Unstandardized Regression Coefficients, Regression of First Pair Member's
2005 Score on Pair Member's 2005 Score

Respondents	Unstandardized Regression Coefficients	N
All pairs of respondents	.215	1,677
Do the words "social standing" have meaning to you?		
Both *do* give meaning to social standing, and		
One or both have university education	.246	630
Neither pair member has university education	.211	669
One or both *do not* give meaning to social standing, and		
One or both have university education	.095	166
Neither pair member has university education	.219	212
Are there other criteria for prestige? (not part of possibilities suggested)		
No, for both members of pair, and		
One or both have university education	.176	413
Neither pair member has university education	.185	564
Yes, for one or both members of pair, and		
One or both have university education	.249	383
Neither pair member has university education	.269	317
Would others give the same ratings?		
Both members of pair *agree*, and		
One or both have university education	.179	178
Neither pair member has university education	.153	166
One or both *do not agree*, and		
One or both have university education	.229	618
Neither pair member has university education	.227	715

Source: Pairs file for 2005 survey only.

of .095 to a high of .269, around the mean of .215 for this version
of the pair data. Recall that the lowest consensus in the 1965 sample was the .39 between low-education pairs. None of these 2005
estimates from table 7.4 come near that. There are two main anomalies arising from the questions about criteria; (i) the way that those
perceiving non-standard criteria for prestige hold higher consensus
between themselves than those content with standard criteria, and
(ii) that those who think others would disagree with their ratings
in fact have the greatest agreement among themselves. Perhaps
these questions are picking up the more reflective respondents
who, despite their self-doubts or perceptions of complexities in the

Table 7.5
Polychoric Correlation Matrix for Rating Criteria

Prestige Criterion	C3	C4	C5	C6	C7
c2. Standard of living	.266	.316	.117	.355	.293
c3. Power and influence		.249	.101	.221	.171
c4. Qualifications			.300	.257	.311
c5. Value to society				.192	.248
c6. General desirability					.309
c7. Difficulty of finding a replacement					

Note: Run using PRELIS, 2,053 cases (with series mean replacement of missing values), from Occupational Prestige in Canada: 2005 data.

occupational-prestige hierarchy, in fact gave the ratings more thought and came closer to the societal consensus, such that there is any consensus in 2005.

A clue to the low consensus in 2005 ratings may reside within the structure of the statistical relationship among the six prestige criteria presented to respondents. Recalling from chapter 3, which gives exact wordings and frequency distributions, the six were standard of living, power, qualifications, value to society, general desirability, and replaceability. The correlation matrix for this set appears in table 7.5. These are polychoric, or adjusted, correlations, given the non-normal-distribution ordinal variables being examined. Each is coded into just four categories and responses tend to cluster within the two agreement alternatives. Even pumped up with the polychoric adjustment, the pattern of relationships is weak. Five correlations fall into the 0.3 range, six in the 0.2s, and four under 0.2. A factor analysis, which I shall not actually perform, given the hypothetical nature of polychoric correlations, clearly would single out "value to society" as the most separated from the other five criteria. See Goldthorpe and Hope (1974, 157) and Adler and Kraus (1985, 32) for a complementary result. The "general desirability" criterion, which was stressed in British literature on occupational prestige as the common denominator, has no more prominence than any other criterion, in this correlation matrix. Selecting just those pairs who both gave the maximum importance to the value-to-society rating criterion does not produce a distinctive prestige scale. The regression between pairs for that sub-set of 515 cases (from the file of 1,677 pairs rating the same title) is just B = .145, less than the sample-wide figure. Even within these pairs, respondents perhaps had their distinctive views about other determinants of prestige, and these would not be agreed upon between respondents just because they agreed about the value-to-society criterion.

CONCLUSION

[T]he Treiman constant [stands] first among the achievements of RC28 ... The slight variations in occupational ranking are trivial compared to the regular patterns established by dozens of RC members and codified by Treiman.   M. Hout (2002, 3)

To my knowledge, the only important empirical discovery of empirical sociology is the remarkable robustness of occupational prestige ratings.
                                                J. Davis (2001, 100)

[I]t does not matter much who does the ratings. This is one of the most well established findings in all of sociology. Occupations are rated about the same by all, at all times, and wherever these occupations are found.
                                                A.B. Soørensen (2001, 290)

That occupational-prestige ratings are invariant across societies and time is one of the most cherished beliefs held by the social-inequality research community, as the above quotations articulate. In hindsight, an early warning sign of stirring in the hierarchy can be spotted in the 1989 replication of 1964–65 NORC data (Nakao and Treas 1994, 15). With the 2005 data for Canada, Marsh's (1971, 214) "great empirical invariant" becomes still harder to retain. This chapter has shown that the prestige scores aggregated across samples of raters no longer correspond in the close way they used to forty years ago. And at the micro-level, agreement from rater to rater is far lower in 2005 than it was in 1965. The multiple realities of the twenty-first century are very multiple indeed, to the extent that not even pockets of consensus could be located. I see the consensus results as more suggestive of the individualized society than the identity politics society, and in the final chapter I will attempt further placement of the occupational prestige findings within cultural commentaries on twenty-first century.

8

The "Guns and Butter" of Occupational Prestige

Theories about occupational prestige two generations ago were, as mentioned now several times, closely tied to social-structural arguments about an imperative resulting from the division of labour, namely the variant functional importance of occupations. And yet viewed retrospectively, from the vantage point of the early twentieth century, it is the cultural embeddedness of those prestige ratings that leaps off the pages of reports from the 1960s and 1970s. For example, compared with the 2000s, people forty years ago did not fuss too much about bruised feelings. "Someone who lives on relief" scored a brutal 7.3 on the 100-point scale in Pineo and Porter's 1965 study. Eighty-seven percent of the sample consigned that title to the lowest or second-lowest rung on the nine-level ladder. By 2005, the title had been gentrified to "someone who lives on social assistance," owing to anxiety that "relief" would offend the twenty-first-century respondent. The score was still low, at 22 points, but now only a bare majority – 52 percent – relegated the title to the lowest two categories. Ten percent in 2005 placed social assistance at the fifth level, the midpoint on the rating scale, the choice of only 3 percent of the 1965 raters evaluating people on relief. Compared with today, the occupational-prestige scale of the past was like an accordion pulled out, ready to make a chord. The scale today has squeezed back together. Even if the rank order of prestige had not changed between 1965 and 2005 (and in fact it has, as shown in the preceding chapter), the altered shape of the occupational-prestige hierarchy would require explanation, and structural sociology alone is ill-equipped to handle the task.

Two cultural aspects of 1960s society contrast especially starkly with today's less "deferential" (Nevitte 1996) culture. First, the occupational-prestige scores two generations ago suggested conformity by nearly all citizens to a central value system, and any evidence to the contrary required careful explanation. Hodge and Rossi (1978) give a clear statement in their article about dissensus in ratings. They took for granted "the *true* prestige of an occupation" (their emphasis), which reflected a "core value system to which" people "are commonly exposed in the school system" (1978, B63, B68). Some, especially lower socio-economic-status raters, committed "random errors in their estimates" of this true prestige, but it was a particular kind of randomness. Hodge and Rossi (1978) were detecting no consistent ideological clustering of ideas about prestige among groups at the bottom of the social stratification, and that lack of structure to the dissensus was one argument for the randomness interpretation. Guppy and I (1984) contended that the lower social stratum in a society is subject to mixed ideologies, lowering consensus within their group. The mixed ideologies could create deviation from the establishment hierarchy both within the minds of individual respondents seeking to balance off competing criteria and within the working class as a whole if it were subdivided in the way envisioned by Young and Willmott (1956, 337).

Another of Hodge and Rossi's arguments concerned incomplete knowledge of occupations. Prestige ratings were based on "knowledge of who occupies which posts ... Some respondents – in particular higher status ones – are better at playing this game than others" (Hodge and Rossi 1978, B69). It is true that evidence exists of class differences in occupational knowledge, extending back even into childhood (DeFleur and DeFleur 1967, 784), but non-knowledge could lead to highly consensual stereotypical readings of occupational prestige as much as to chaotic, non-consensual ones. Svalastoga (1959, 104–7) felt that ignorance simply had a "leveling effect," analogous to plugging the mean for item nonresponse. The weakness I see in the random-error argument is that, if the "random" errors occurred more often among the lower than the upper stratum, that would be a form of non-randomness. The scholars in the 1960s who were expecting all members of the public to behave like well-trained labour market economists did not realize how well off they were with the error rate of the time. From chapter 7, in one of the central conclusions of the present study, the consensus is much lower now than in 1965. Even those children of the middle class who paid close attention in school, thus picking up the core value system as Hodge and Rossi (1978) suggest and even those who have the social capital to know their way around different parts of the occupational structure now show greatly reduced agreement compared with earlier times. Perhaps people two generations ago had fuller knowledge of the labour market, but raters today are not merely proceeding in ignorance. We saw earlier how they are articulate in their awareness of making ratings others might not agree with, taking us a long way from the random-error interpretation. The survey respondents in 2000 and 2005 took the trouble in replies volunteered in open-ended questions to explain their non-socio-economic criteria for occupational prestige. The satisficing survey behaviour described in sources such as Tourangeau et al. (2000, 17) would have been to move quickly along in the interview, skipping open-end response invitations.

I confess to finding strange the whole sub-literature around error in occupational prestige. The chosen method of validation of scaling methods (prestige vs SES indexes based on census data on education-income) was to pick a clearly socio-economic sociological problem, the transmission of status across generations (Featherman and Hauser 1976). Education and income are two of the most transferable pieces of capital, human-cultural and economic respectively, so it had to be that a scaling of occupations based on mean education and income, the components in a scale such as the Duncan SEI (Duncan 1961), would show a strong correlation across two generations. The prestige ratings for occupations, which certainly carry education and income considerations, but other ones such as value to society as well, did not give as strong a father-to-son correlation. "The pattern of occupational inheritance is not one of conserving honor," Rytina (1992, 1680) observes. That was the basis for perceiving something erroneous about prestige ratings, but other validity claims for prestige were ignored. From Stewart et al. (1980) for example, or from Laumann (1966), for an American example, prestige predicts the patterns of social interaction – who is friends with whom, social-distance scores, etc.

– that constitute much of the meaning of the term "social structure." There was a wish within the social-inequality researching community to downplay prestige, and the dismissal of prestige as a pretentious-name-for-good argument from Great Britain played into that and was enthusiastically picked up by u.s. researchers. Occupational-prestige data are messy, to be sure; the methodological explorations surveyed in chapter 1 show that, but so are all probes into the consciousness of people, using the survey method. Reports of facts, such as census questions about a person's education, income, and job are more reliable than reports of opinions and attitudes. Occupational prestige ratings have an affective component along with their cognitive component, MacKinnon and Langford (1994) remind us, and are thus predestined to have lower reliability than reports of demographic facts. We can code that fuzziness with the "goodness"or "desirability" label, but those who do must contend with the wide usage of the term "prestige" in public discourse. This was touched on in chapter 3, and further examples appear every day. From the closing days of writing this book, I clipped a page from the *Globe and Mail* business section reading, "Mr. Carney clearly had his eye on more prestigious jobs" (26 January 2008, B4). Not good jobs or desirable jobs, prestigious jobs. Harvard University's website refers to "prestige," not to "goodness" or "desirabilty.[1] Prestige does not mean goodness, it means prestige. "Occupational prestige scores measure prestige, " Hauser and Logan (1992, 1691) have rightly stated.

A second part of the cultural context of prestige in the 1960s and 1970s is how socio-economically saturated the scales were. Socio-economic status, or SES, referred in this research literature specifically to the average education and income pertaining to occupations. As Featherman and Hauser (1976, 404–5) stated in a well-known passage that echoed at the aggregate level what Hodge and Rossi (1978) had said about the ratings by individual respondents, "over three-quarters of the linear variance in prestige scores is a reflection of the educational and economic properties of the ranked occupations." The remaining 25 percent of variance meant that "prestige scores are 'error-prone' estimates of the socio-economic attributes of occupations." The Davis and Moore (1945) functional theory of social stratification had of course several years earlier stressed that same focus on the socio-economic realm. One of the curious aspects of Davis-Moore when read in the twenty-first century is their inattention to intrinsic interest in a job. That lacuna was realized at the time too (e.g., Tumin 1953, 391) but stood out even more clearly in the postmaterialist era. The functionalist theory of inequality and the 1960s occupational-prestige research that interacted so symbiotically with the theory were deeply rooted indeed in the value type Inglehart (1990) described as materialist.

The 2005 occupational-prestige ratings are not just culturally postmodern in their individuality from person to person but post-materialist in their attention to the non-socio-economic, non-education-income criteria for evaluation. Evidence of drift away from education-income-based ratings appeared in chapter 4. The dignity of simple tasks properly performed counts for 2005 prestige scores. Witness the spectacular rise for titles such as "garbage collector." Respondents also give a premium to public-interest sectors of worklife such as the health occupations. Any occupation perceived as serving the public good, "firefighter" and "police officer" being the lead examples, is rewarded in twenty-first-century ratings.

Is the above cultural description of conformist, SES-obsessed mid-twentieth-century society that I have derived from 1960s and 1970s research on occupational prestige accurate? Admittedly, by the time of the 1965 Pineo-Porter study, the reference point for most of the comparisons herein, social and political changes in the post-materialist direction were in the air. Inglehart was detecting the Silent Revolution as far back as 1971. By 1965, in the United States, the presidency of not just Eisenhower but Kennedy too had come and gone. The civil rights movement had gained momentum and had begun to splinter away from Martin Luther King's Gandhian tactics. Canada got involved with protest, Lester Pearson making a speech at Temple University in 1965 criticizing American bombing of North Vietnam. But still there was much in the culture to cite in support of the core value system centered on socio-economic status. A small library of books commented on over-conformity, ranging from fictional works such as *The Man in the Grey Flannel Suit* to sociological commentaries such as *The Organization Man*, *The Lonely Crowd*, or *Culture against Man*. In the latter, Henry (1965, 5) wrote of a "lopsided preoccupation with amassing wealth." John Porter's defining sociological work outlining the elitist complacency of the St Laurent-Diefenbaker-Pearson era in Canada appeared in the same year, 1965, that he and Pineo had their prestige study in the field. Pierre Berton's *The Smug Minority* dates from shortly after: 1968. Reinforcing the SES-saturated themes of the *Vertical Mosaic*, Porter's 1966 MacIver Award Lecture was all about the need for even more socio-economic aspirations. "[T]he occupational structure which is emerging demands more positive values about education and stronger mobility aspirations than appear to have been current in what we have been calling the modern industrial stage" he wrote (1968, 5). John Porter was not the only one preoccupied with mobility aspirations. Think of the Joe Lampton character in John Braine's early postwar British novel *Room at the Top*. Or the title of Vance Packard's (1961) popular sociology work *The Status Seekers,* corroborating the SES-striving image a dozen years following the end of the world war. As Merton's (1957, 132) work on anomie explained, not everybody in the 1950s or 1960s was a status seeker who accepted "culturally defined goals, purposes and interests, held out as legitimate objectives for all or for diversely located members of the society." Still, accepting the goal of seeking money, so "peculiarly well adapted to become a symbol of prestige," together with the legitimate means such as advanced education, was the normal mode, and others were deviant (Merton 1957, 136–7).

In noting these cultural themes, I am of course a long way from how occupational-prestige ratings were interpreted when the 1940s, 1950s, and 1960s scales were being constructed. A 1976 article by Donald Treiman gives an especially clear summary of the structuralist arguments, because it addressed a predominately non-sociological audience reading the *Journal of Interdisciplinary History*. Obviously influenced by Robert Marsh's (1971) piece exploring the linkage between the division of labour and power differentials by occupation, Treiman (1976, 288) explained: "Specialization of functions into distinct occupational roles necessarily results in inequalities among occupations with respect to skill, authority, and control over capital ... [H]igh prestige is allocated to those occupations which require a high degree of skill or which entail authority over other individuals or control over capital." It was this concentration on objectively verifiable factors such as "specialization of functions," "skill," "authority," and "control over capital" in the structural-functionalist interpretation that made it plausible for Hodge and Rossi (1978) to insist that there is a "true prestige" score for every occupation. Respondents as conceived in the 1976 article do not "allocate" prestige, but rather, "prestige is allocated," the passive societal un-seen hand rather than the active personal voice. Since the "nature of occupational specialization" is part of the social structure of industrial societies and is "relatively invariant" in skill "across time and space," then naturally "the prestige of specific occupations is relatively invariant as well." In fact, the passage continues, "it is so uniform that a single occupational prestige scale will capture the basic features of the occupational hierarchy of any society" (Treiman 1976, 288). This article is exceptionally clear for the way it expresses Davis and Moore (1945) reasoning about how prestige serves a further need of helping motivate the most-skilled people to perform the most-important occupational functions. "For example, if a garbage collector does his job poorly, little is lost; but if a surgeon is incompetent, a life can be lost" (Treiman 1976, 288). We recall from chapter 4 that "garbage collector" jumped from 15 points in 1965 to 48 in 2005, a full 33 points; "physician" crept up as part of the general inflation of scores by just three points, from 87 to 90. Has the skill requirement for refuse collection risen so much over forty years? No, our conception of what occupational-prestige ratings are all about needs to be broadened. Functionalist theory is elegant and satisfying to the scientific mind, but it is only one way of viewing the world.

Even though occupational-prestige researchers in the 1960s used structural rather than cultural concepts in their interpretations, a culturalist retrofitting is plausible. The cultural climate of the times, with its high level of inter-rated consensus, elitist view of such lower strata dissensus as did exist, and materialist and SES-centered priorities, was necessary to make the structural-functionalist interpretation of occupational prestige believable. The two were synchronized. The logical structural unfolding of specialization leading to inequality in skill-authority-capital, leading to differential rewards, rested on cultural prerequisites such as the assumption about the dominance of one value system. An integrated value system is of course not unique to industrial society or automatically part of it. Durkheim's (1964 [1893]) famous work *The Division of Labour* expressed wonderment that such integration had survived from pre-industrial to industrial times. It was a cultural belief as well as a structural fact that one occupation required higher skill than another. The very definition of which types of occupational skill are most valued is an item of culture. "In our society ... we have put linguistic and logical-mathematical intelligences, figuratively speaking, on a pedestal" (Gardner 1993, 8). A prestige rating for an occupation is a cultural datum embedded in structure. It is a product of the human mind, mediated by various external facts. Hyper-structuralists in the 1960s wanted these cultural beliefs about prestige to look like structural data (e.g., average income) and were disappointed when the cultural data looked like ... cultural data.

Why do I feel entitled to thus reinterpret past research on occupational prestige? In answer, researchers forty years ago did not have sufficient cultural variation among industrialized societies on display for the cultural aspects of occupational prestige to show themselves clearly. Contrary evidence from names such as Penn (see chapter 1) remained buried within the dominant research literature. By 2005 in the Canadian nation state, a fairly typical postindustrial middle power (see, for example, Glatzer and Hauser 2002), a verifiable transition had occurred, from the culture of 1965 to the culture of 2005. As seen, the cultural shifts taken together with changing patterns in occupational-prestige ratings cast doubt on the strength of a strictly structuralist interpretation.

This conviction was arrived at by accident with my having no idea late in the 1990s that, owing to such emerging cultural themes as postmodernism, postmaterialism, and Canadian multiculturalism, occupational-prestige data were about to deviate sharply from the mid-twentieth-century norm. Textbooks still taught students that occupational prestige derived from a fixed structural base rather than a shifting cultural one. Beeghley (1989, 39), for example, invoked Marsh's (1971) formula that prestige derived from the skill and the responsibility involved in an occupation. My involvement with new research on occupational prestige came from an interest in revisiting the gender-specification aspect a quarter century after the Guppy and Siltanen (1977) study of 1975. I wanted to promote a local-area survey of Kitchener-Waterloo and viewed the gender replication as a good vehicle for funding. The need for a larger study became apparent only once the results from the 2000 Kitchener-Waterloo work were in hand, showing a sharply increased mean score, a surprisingly low correlation of mean scores with the 1975 scale, and evidence of low consensus among raters. It would thus be misleading to say that theory predicted changes in

| | SHAPE OF PRESTIGE DISTRIBUTION | |
	Elongated	Squeezed
LEVEL OF CONCENSUS — *High*	1965	
Low		2005

Fig. 8.1   Typology of prestige changes

the prestige regime; the structural-functionalist theory conventionally invoked in occupational prestige predicted non-change. I knew that structural-functionalism had lost its hold on sociologists, moving to "neo-functionalist" form (Alexander and Colomy 1990), but was too imprinted with the writings of Hodge, Siegel, Rossi, Treiman, Duncan, and the other giants of the 1960s to independently re-theorize the causes of occupational prestige.

In this section I have wanted to summarize the main drift in empirical patterns in occupational prestige from 1965 and 2005 and to set up for further re-interpretation. A simple two-by-two figure, appearing as figure 8.1, summarizes the shifts. My point here is that the pattern has moved down a diagonal from the elongated/ high-consensus form of occupational prestige to a squeezed, low- consensus form in 2005. As seen in earlier chapters, different subsets of population have moved toward the off-diagonal cells. Chapter 7, for example, revealed how the university-educated respondents from 2005 elongated their scale somewhat and also had enhanced consensus (within the very low general consensus). The main drift, however, is clearly the one shown.

RE-THEORIZING OCCUPATIONAL PRESTIGE

The structuralist arguments will not be abandoned but instead augmented. Figure 8.2 lays out some of the concepts next to be discussed. The diagram depicts cultural structure as an environment

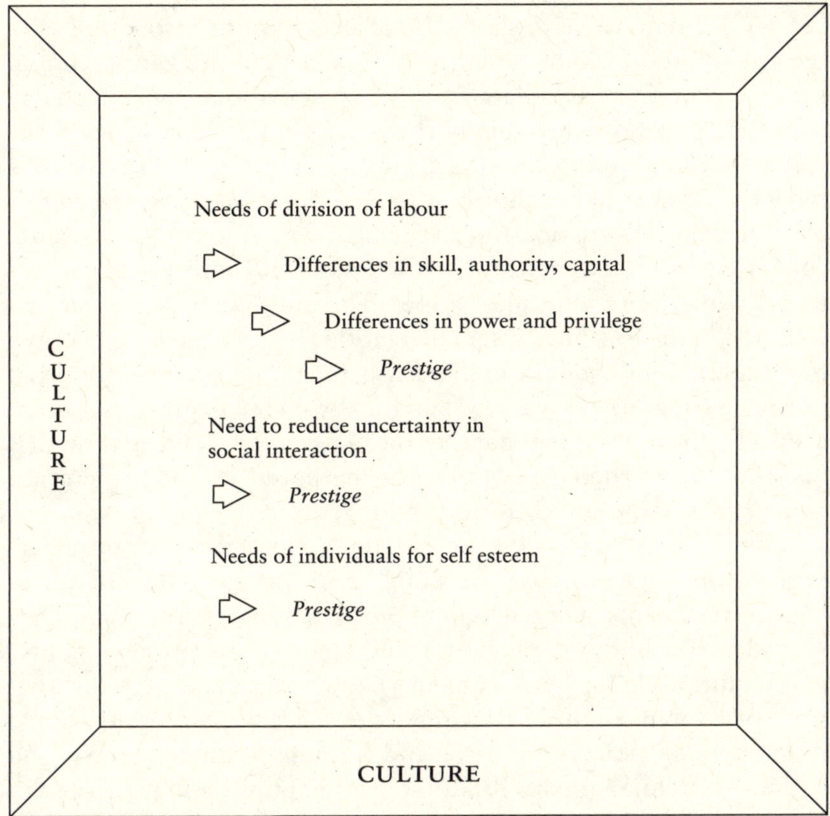

Fig. 8.2   Levels of functionalist analysis of prestige changes

within which to think about social structural factors. It is hard to diagram these grand sociological themes precisely, but the notion intended is that social culture and structure are intertwined, rather than opposites. I like the way that the shape imported from Word Perfect produces an optical illusion. According to how the eye focuses, culture is either the foreground or the background to the structural themes.

The cultural themes have already been mentioned and need just a little more filling in. The cultural context important for occupational prestige ratings involves, of course, the relative importance of materialist versus postmaterialist values, the strictly socio-economic view of occupations, on the one hand, against aspects of intrinsic satisfaction, service to humankind, etc., on the other. Zhou

(2005), I'll remind here, showed that occupations resonating with the science and technology ethos of modern culture gain premium prestige. The Canadian data from 2005 added that this effect also depends upon how thoroughly the individual rater adheres to the value of science and technology. This specification brings to focus the whole issue of one culture or many. I have been arguing in this chapter that the situation forty years ago was closer to one culture, compared to the twenty-first-century time of more fractured cultures giving rise to multiple realities. The multiple realities seem, as reflected in the low inter-rater correlations in 2005, to extend down to the level of individuals. In this sense, the argument by Hodge that prestige ratings do not vary systematically by ideologies is not questioned by the more recent data, to the extent they could bear on that question. Class ideologies were not measured in 2005, there not being room in the survey for everything.

Within this cultural environment, the upper portion of the structural component of figure 8.2 simply reproduces the macro-sociological arguments worked out by writers such as Treiman. They were described both in chapter 1 and again in the present chapter and require little further comment. The social structure of the division of labour in industrial societies necessitates occupational differences in skill, authority, and capital, both monetary and social. As Treiman theorized, differences in power and privilege can be observed and are recognized within people's consciousness as prestige. The high prestige for occupations deemed most important motivates people to hold mobility aspirations, the Davis and Moore argument.

The middle section of figure 8.2 introduces the meso-macro level of analysis lying between the society and the individual. Groups form their own prestige communities, and the purposes served by such prestige can be analyzed structurally, parallel to the macro-sociological analysis of societal prestige systems. William Foote Whyte's (1943) classic study *Street Corner Society* is still a wonderful exposition of a prestige community. Whyte detected the anomaly that in activities such as bowling, baseball, even flirting with girls, performances depended on whether the setting was within the street gang or outside. "Frank," for example, was a semi-professional baseball-level member of the gang who said: "I can't seem to play ball when I'm playing with fellows I know" (i.e., fellow members of the Nortons [Whyte 1943, 19]). For Frank, a low-ranking gang member, to have outplayed the leaders would have upset the prestige hierarchy, therefore the "highly organized and integrated social system" (xvi) that was Cornerville. As Whyte (1943, 35) wrote: "It was essential to the smooth functioning of the group that the prestige gradations be informally recognized and maintained." Similar reasoning has been applied at the diametrically opposite end of the social structure from youth gangs in a Boston slum. Podolony's (2005) *Status Signals* describes market places such as investment banking, a timely topic as I make a final fall 2008 review of these pages, to understand the way prestige reduces risks. "Status flows through deference relations," Podolony (2005, 15) says, in a passage reminding that not only does prestige lead to deference, as noted in chapter 1, drawing from Shils, but acts of deference create prestige. Research at this meso-macro level of prestige communities captures the way in which "status," meaning here prestige, "leaks" (Podolony (2005, 15). That is the principle behind the "Cambridge" scales for occupations, in which prestige is inferred from who is friends with whom, an approach described in chapter 1. Prestige served a need for the investment bankers studied by Podolony, reducing uncertainty and fear of risks as large financial deals were put together.

I noted in an earlier chapter the intensity of prestige communities within academe. For university professors, tightly bunched in terms of pay in comparison to the corporate world, prestige is paramount. Rhode (2006, 143) wryly suggests that "those practicing the crudest elitism are often the most politically egalitarian." For academics as for bankers and gang members, prestige serves as a market signal that simplifies and reduces risks in decisions. Without academic-prestige distinctions, academic novels would lose much of their humour. It is the accuracy of caricatures of fictional institutions such as Benedict Arnold University (Bradbury 1965) that makes the books amusing. For academics, prestige reduces uncertainty by predicting which young faculty members will be future research stars. This reduction-of-uncertainty function of prestige inequality seems likely to generalize to many settings. Indeed, it was a theme for Edward Wilson's (1975) synthesis of research, *Sociobiology*. Wilson (1975, 280) notes that dominance systems among animal communities do not produce chaos but, on the contrary, stability and predictability. "[A]fter the issue has been settled, each individual gives way to its superiors with a minimum of hostile exchange. The life of the group may eventually become so pacific as to hide the existence of such ranking from the observer."

Another example of prestige serving needs within groups brings up a further point: Blau's (1963 [1955]) study of an office work setting led to the importance of social exchange. Agents within the U.S. government regulatory agency he observed were not, within the formal social structure, allowed to consult with each other. Within the informal structure they did, expediting the work of the agency. Less-skilled agents sought consultations with the more-skilled for advice on difficult cases. Why did the skilled agents agree to both break a rule and siphon off time from their own duties? Because, Blau argued (138), they gained recognition of their prestige within the organization. Prestige served the larger goals of the organization by facilitating social exchange. In all these meso-macro level examples, differentiation by prestige adds to the whole, unlike a facetious functionalist analysis such as Gans's (1972, 281) deliberate caricature, in which poverty has the positive function of helping "guarantee the status of those who are not poor."

At the micro-level of the psychology of the individual person, too, prestige seems to serve needs, and this is primarily where I look to account for differences between 1965 and 2005. The fragility of the twenty-first-century psyche was noted earlier. It is a matter of broad cultural assessment and interpretation to say why today's ego is so vulnerable and hooked on prestige, and I am not qualified to be definitive here. As one possibility, baby boomers would have been getting deep into parenthood by the mid-1980s, and it may be the ascent up the Maslow hierarchy of needs, away from the material and toward self-actualization, brought about by the affluence enjoyed by the children of baby boom parents, that leads to issues of self-esteem. It was during the 1980s that Nevitte (1996, 1–7) perceived sea changes in Canadian society. By the late 1990s the term self-esteem was in wide general usage in Canada (recall table 3.4). Prestige seems to be a crucial food for the psychological needs of the individual today.

Why so, all of a sudden in the twenty-first century? I will argue that society today is perceived as more meritocratic than two generations ago. When a widely read newspaper correspondent concludes, from reviewing Rhodes Scholarship applications, that "Canada is a high-functioning meritocracy where people with ability from any background can get ahead" (*Globe and Mail*, 18

December 2007, A27), the imagery begins to seep into the culture. Canada is not alone in embracing this image, for reference in the mass media to "the rise of the American meritocracy" (*New York Times*, 30 December 2007, "Week in Review," 5) and "the rise of the global meritocracy" (*Globe*, 15 December 2007, F3) is frequent. The imagery permeating into the culture may be more important here than the realities of social-mobility tables. The combination of fragile egos with a culture of meritocracy seems likely to create stress, especially in a culture that, as Seligman (1989, 89) notes, has become so individualistic. If this is "a kind of inherited meritoc- racy," if "[g]rades and test scores, rather than privilege, determine success today, but that success is largely being passed down from one generation to the next" (Leonhardt 2005, 90), that only compounds the stresses of the twenty-first century.

Nowhere is the tension between the merit principle and self- concept seen more clearly than in the university admissions process in the United States, where Robbins (2006, 73, 186, 359), describ- ing "the secret lives of driven kids," found "an obsession with pres- tige" by admission counseling services and a conviction among parents that admission of their children to any but the very most elite institution means "a student is doomed to failure." The conse- quence: soaring rates of adolescent depression. At least until the time to apply to Harvard arrives, the twenty-first-century culture resolves much of the tension between aspiration and self-esteem by a grade inflation much derided by the older generation (Côté and Allahar 2007), and a proliferation of career awards and prizes warmly accepted by the selfsame oldsters (Best 2007)! As part of the "feel-good" culture (Côté and Allahar 2007, 35), the popula- tion who are not part of the 5 percent strongest, quickest, and most intelligent scramble for the prestige that helps rescue the threatened self-esteem.[2] The more the dimensions of evaluation, the better the chance of maintaining self-esteem. For example, adolescents seek the prestige "leaks" Podolony described by taking up minor sports favoured by prestigious universities ("And for Sports, Kid, Put Down 'Squash,'" *New York Times*, 9 December 2007, "Sunday Styles," 1). That is part of the middle-class advantage; they hold more role identities, hence enhanced chances of scoring high self- esteem-preserving prestige in at least one (Thoits 1991, 101).

The quest for self-esteem is not unique to spoiled children of affluent baby boomers, although they make a good social laboratory for seeing how the stresses of meritocracy are handled. Lamont's (2000) *The Dignity of Working Men* contains many quotations from workers struggling to reach terms with the semi-inherited meritocracy. Self-respect needs to be maintained somehow, whether by minimizing hierarchy, removing oneself from it, making minute distinctions within a narrow status band, or taking options such as cheering for successful professional sports teams and leeching prestige by social-identity nurturing (Tajfel 1974; Dunning et al. 1988, 206).

In this twenty-first-century context, it would not be surprising if the culture of meritocracy has affected how people rate the prestige of occupations. We saw in earlier chapters the massively inflated self-ratings in 2005, compared with 1965, and a heightened tendency to raise the prestige of all occupations bearing similarities to one's own. Perhaps it is as a result of so many people struggling to reconcile their own self-respect with prestige inequality that consensus on ratings has dropped so precipitously and the scale squeezed together so much. Burshytn's (1968, 174–7) small Ottawa survey measured anomie (Srole scale) and detected the more anomic respondents granting higher prestige to the "lower-class" occupations detected by his factor analysis. I wish in retrospect that I had measured anomie in the 2005 survey, for this might have moved me closer to having firm evidence for the speculations being advanced in this chapter.

The best statement of this theme was, for me, written some fifty years ago, in Michael Young's (1958) satire, *The Rise of the Meritocracy*. From his vantage point shortly following "The Hitler War," Young looked at British policies such as the 1944 education act, designed to reduce hereditary social-class inequality. Projecting forward to 2033, he imagined that equality of opportunity developed so completely that inequality of condition became greater than ever before. In the new class system, everyone in the upper class had a high IQ and a strong work ethic; everyone in the lower class was "stupid" and lazy (77). The seeming utopia proved to be anti-utopia, owing to the way meritocracy is stressful for all but the most meritorious: "For the first time in human history the inferior man has no real buttress for his self-regard," said Young (87), as futurist/historian writing in 2033. *The Rise of the Meritocracy* may be the single most important work of the dozens cited already for making sense of changes in occupational prestige between 1965 and

2005. The world has moved closer to the form Young imagined than reviewers at the time would have guessed (e.g., Acland 1959), albeit perhaps more so in North America than in Young's native England. Meritocracy taken to advanced form would, he argued, create "inescapable strains" (1958, 131) for those with less merit than others; "consciousness of a just inferiority" would prove unmanageable (115). "Sulkily discontented" (89), people in 2033 groped for solutions. "One of the symptoms of rampant ambition was the upgrading by name alone of occupations which could not be upgraded in any other way" (112). For the "technicians" (i.e., lower class, of limited ability), "the cult of the child became the drug of the people" (111). In the most extreme reaction of all to the stresses of meritocratic society, "the dissidents then turned back to an old idea much in vogue in the century before 1944 – the idea that manual work was as valuable as mental" (133). When I entitled this book *The Prestige Squeeze*, it was this squeeze between meritocracy and self-respect I wanted to refer to, along with the more statistical aspects of the squeeze.

Interpreting twenty-first-century ratings of occupational prestige as reactions in part to the stresses of meritocratic society handles the central puzzle of squeezing prestige scores in a time of expanding inequality in the distribution of income. The growth of income inequality, described in chapter 2, has entered the realm of taken-for-granted knowledge as the twenty-first century proceeds (e.g., "now that economic inequality is greater than it has been since the 1920s," *New York Times*, 23 December 2007, first section, 26). As Young (1958, 85–6) argued, the greater the meritocracy, the greater the inequality of condition. And as he further suggested, playing the social historian of the 2030s, the prestige system of the information society as defined by the elite rested on a "narrowness in the paramount values, or criteria" (134) not necessarily shared by the majority of population, such as those represented in my 2005 random selection-sample of Canadians.[3]

I have intended with the comments in this section to retain the 1960s notion that inequality, and inequality in occupational prestige as a case in point, serves needs, has "functions." The argument has been that the functional analysis holds not only at the macro, societal, level but also at the middle level of organizations/institutions and, as well, down to the micro-level of the individual. Viewing occupational stratification from the twenty-first century, following a period of profound cultural change, it is natural to allow the cultural, socially constructed, aspects of prestige increased prominence.

From viewing inequality from the societal level, sociologists are familiar with the notion that if occupational inequality is functional or "good" in some aspects, a reciprocal lesson is how dysfunctional or "bad" inequality is too, and this even if no-one were in actual poverty. This indeed is probably more clearly realized in the 2000s than it was in the 1960s. The problems of inequality are not just moral, but operational, holding implications not only for a working class but for whole societies. Thus, a vibrant line of research in the 1990s documented the link between inequality and society-wide health (see Kawachi et al. 1999). Inequality does not simply have an adverse material impact on those of low income, for the health and well-being of a whole society is affected. A "culture of inequality" (Wilkinson 1999, 492) holds society-wide implications for stress levels, impairing good health and compromising the national stock of social capital. Awareness of the implications of inequality for crime and deviance is, all sociologists know, a long-standing part of the sociological research tradition (e.g., Merton 1957).

The next section develops that notion of seeking a balance between inequality and equality to include the intermediate and micro levels.

THE PRESTIGE TRADE-OFF

If prestige differences become too weak and non-consensusal, the problems central to the mid-twentieth century may reoccur in the twenty-first. People could become unmotivated to strive and mediocracy could replace meritocracy. Economists are alert to this argument and take it for granted, perhaps more than most sociologists do (see, for example, Sharpe 2003). But as suggested above, a society can become too prestige-laden when the level of meritocracy, or perception of meritocracy, becomes too great. Staying with the economics mindset and drawing on an "Econ–101" distinction, the trade-off between more and less inequality could be seen as a "guns and butter" problem whereby it is inefficient for a country to spend all its gross national product on defense (guns) and none on consumption (butter). Neither all guns nor all butter is optimal, and countries finding a middle position get more benefit out of the same

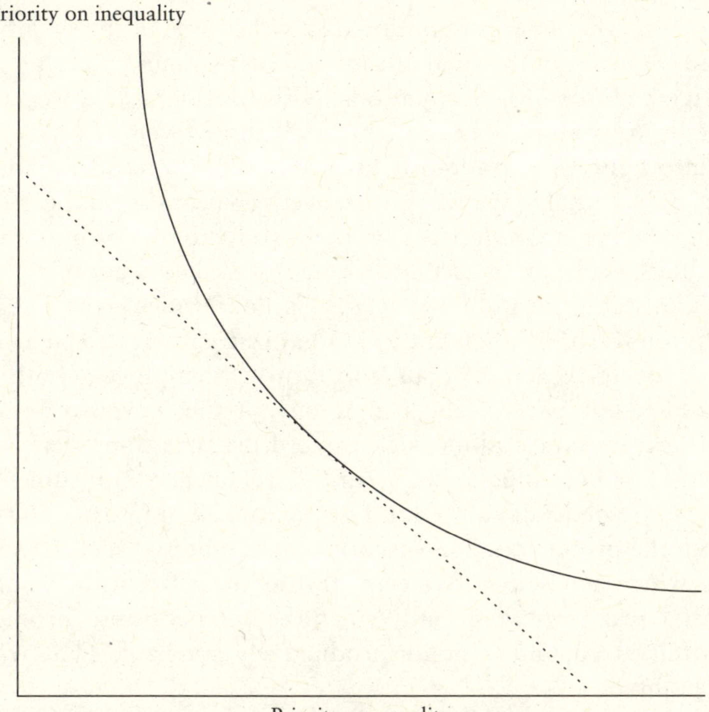

Fig. 8.3   Occupational prestige as guns and butter

economy than from either extreme. Figure 8.3 sketches this out, imagining in place of a national economy the proportionate weighting of a national value system on fostering a high-consensus inegalitarian versus a low-consensus egalitarian value system. The dotted line gives percentage combinations summing to 100. The point where the curved line meets the straight dotted line imagines an optimal combination, wherein the society's value system motivates people but does not crush them.

The guns and butter graph is commonsensical enough. The purpose in mentioning it is to surmise that forty years after the 1965 Pineo and Porter survey of occupational prestige, people were replacing some of their societal guns with butter, if guns stand here for inequality and butter for equality. If the structural-functionalists between the 1940s and the 1960s believed that the valuation placed on inequality, as represented by the prestige regime, was "an unconsciously evolved device" (Davis and Moore 1945, 243), evolved by public opinion, that is, it is tempting to say the same of the twenty-first-century public. In the current times, perhaps some squeezing in the prestige hierarchy for occupations, with considerable dissensus from person to person, is necessary. At all three levels of analysis defined into figure 8.2, trade-offs between inequality and equality can be seen. Nationally, the workforce needs to be motived, but not to the point where stress impedes worker productivity nor in a way creating bottlenecks such as the shortage of skilled tradespeople, the issue constantly in the news (e.g., "Skilled Trades – the Great Canadian Job Rush" [Cohen 2007]). Organizations need to be hierarchical in order to retain focus and motivate employees with a career ladder, but part of the technology of the New Economy seems to have been a pulling back toward organizations that are more level. For individuals, competition creates accomplishment, but in the extreme leads to the kind of cheating seen in drug abuse cases from the professional sports world or to phony "special me" prestige, which feeds a self-esteem devoid of self-efficacy (Côté and Allahar 2007, 70). Especially when the competition is, ironically, too fair, it becomes counterproductively stressful. That was Young's point.

Admittedly, to perceive the 2005 survey respondents as seeking a middle ground between the excesses of inequality and equality assumes that most of them took seriously the task of rating occupational prestige. Based especially on the extent of replies on open-ended probes, material noted in earlier chapters, I retain confidence that such is largely the case and see much of the existing literature on occupational prestige as mechanistic in its conception of human societies and dismissive of the reasoning power of the individual. If this view is correct, there is an implication for future research on occupational inequality.

THE FUTURE OF OCCUPATIONAL PRESTIGE

When sociologists began long ago to study social inequality, what was verifiably correct independently of the consciousness of one person and what was believed within the minds of individuals – the objective and subjective realms – received about equal weight. That was true of the Lynds's investigation of 1929, some of the early British studies (e.g., Rowntree and Kendall 1917), and Lloyd Warner's work on American communities in the 1930s (Warner and Lunt

1941). Richard Centers (1961[1949]), in one of the first applications of the national survey method to issues of inequality, paid close attention to the relationship between self-ratings of social class and corroborating objective indicators such as occupation and education. Most of these earlier sources mentioned Marx at some point, for the great nineteenth-century radical theorist, although entered into history as a philosophical materialist, drew distinctions such as structure versus superstructure that suggested objective versus subjective. He may have believed that material circumstances of history had causal priority, but he remained aware of the importance of class consciousness for influencing the history of social-class relations.

Somewhere around mid-twentieth century, the tradition of duality between objective and subjective approaches to social inequality became lost. The subjective aspects of inequality, especially ratings of people in a community by their fellow townspeople, are most richly revealed at the level of small-scale, local research. Thus Warner claimed that "all America lives in Jonesville," but could not turn to national survey data to authenticate that claim. This was the heart of Duncan and Artis's (1951) critique, and with colleagues such as Blau, Featherman, Hauser, and Sewell the national survey method was honed to produce precise estimates of factual indicators of inequality, including education, occupation, and income. Relations among the indicators were meticulously mapped and the transmission of status across generations modeled. The full details of the consciousness of individuals could never be exhaustively captured within a brief structured survey. Attention to the subjective components of social inequality remained alive, but proceeded largely within its own literature, un-integrated with the more demographic approach led by the Wisconsin school. When the subjective realm was introduced into the Wisconsin modeling, in the form of variables defining aspirations, the results seemed to point back toward models based on objective indicators (e.g., Sewell et al. 1970).

In other areas of research, the objective-subjective complementarity has remained more vibrant. Research on quality of life illustrates this, with Andrews (1974, 281) making the wise comment that "[w]hile there is undoubtedly a real distinction, worth preserving, between these two types of indicators, the terms 'subjective' and 'objective' carry unfortunate connotations. Given that science values objectivity and eschews subjectivity, it is easy to suppose that the 'subjective' indicators are not as valid or useful as the 'objective' ones. However, to believe this would be to pre-judge the situation."

Occupational prestige helps keep research into social inequality from becoming unbalanced with a demographic bias. The prestige ratings allow one tap into inequality as it is lived and experienced by people, and maintain this connection within the realm of national-level surveys representative of whole populations. One can quibble about the design of the rating question on "social standing," but the advantage of continuous application of this wording over many decades overwhelms the objection. The style prevailing now is to advocate the measurement of inequality using objective indicators, conceptually empty though they may be (Hodge 1981), so that if researchers want to scale occupational status, they are best off simply taking the average education level of incumbents of each occupation. Although believing that occupational prestige ratings are important, I would agree that the results of the 2005 research do little to establish the priority of prestige scales for occupations over socio-economic scales based on average education or the combination of average education and income among occupational incumbents. As the two approaches diverge – occupational prestige, the perceived, subjective aspect, and occupational SES derived from census figures on education and income for holders of occupations – the practice of making scales that try to predict prestige scores from the SES scores seems less and less advisable.

I believe that studies of occupational prestige will continue to ground researchers in reality as it exists in people's minds. Researchers can scale occupations by mean education-income all they like, but the legitimacy of these scales is no longer as fulsomely conceded by the public as it used to be. When the explanatory power of models using occupational SES as predictor falls below expectations, here will be one possible explanation. Changes in prestige ratings for occupations such as those in protective service may indeed be the early-warning indicators of coming transformations in incomes and other benefits. Prestige ratings may thus have their own predictive value, cautioning sociologists that even socioeconomic scorings for occupations are impermanent.

Appendix

Table A
Comparison of OLS and Ordinal Regression

	Predicting 1965 Prestige Score	
	Ordinal Logistic Regression Coefficients	*OLS Unstandardized Regression Coefficients*
Atlantic	−.019	−.010
Quebec	−.203***	−.243***
Ontario	−.015	−.011
Prairie	.059**	.076**
Works	−.062***	−.081***
Spouse works	−.018	−.024
Canadian born	−.019	−.029
Age	<.001	.001
Male sex	.026	.026
Francophone	.187***	.227***
University	−.214***	−.263***
Constant	4.776	
Cut 1	−2.596	
Cut 2	−1.580	
Cut 3	−0.830	
Cut 4	−0.183	
Cut 5	0.539	
Cut 6	1.193	
Cut 7	1.955	
Cut 8	2.940	
Pseudo R² / OLS R²	.001	.003
N = 131,553 lines complete on all variables		

Note: See the final section of chapter 3 for a discussion.

British Columbia is reference category for region. Computed in STATA.

* p < .05 (all p's from conventional test, for this comparison). ** p < .01. *** p < .001.

Notes

CHAPTER ONE

1 Freeman says: "The material world we cohabit is infinitely rich in details,
far beyond the capacity of even the most powerful mind to grasp except
in small but sufficient fragments. We shape ourselves in coming to terms
with those portions, not by imbibing them, but by assimilating to them
through hypothesis testing."
2 For a nice summary of some of the other very early studies, see
Svalastoga (1959, 62–7).
3 Wegener (1992, 264) gives sources for some of the other prestige studies
taking place around the same time as the Coxon-Jones research and also
using multi-dimensional scaling of data in sorted or paired rank form.
The approach worked well for non-Westernized populations (e.g.,
Seligson 1977). Yet another source of methodological work on occupation rating comes from psychology, in research seldom noted by main-
stream sociological studies of prestige. Kuennapas and Wikstroem (1963)
applied the magnitude scaling method by Stevens to occupational data.
Dawson and Brinker (1971), psychologists from the United States,
extended the magnitude-scaling approach, which concerns validating attitudinal judgements against external physical criteria. Dawson and
Brinker had their university student subjects rate occupations by "desirability," using handgrips and a sound scale, and reported high agreement
between the two methods.

CHAPTER TWO

1 As early as 1922, Schlesinger was noting "a tendency for the American
people to live on the latest sensations and exhaust themselves with

superficial emotions" (1922, 261), and warning that "[o]ne of the most alarming tendencies of contemporary times in the United States has been the steady decline in the proportion of citizens who perform their periodical functions at the polls" (267).

2 See statistics published by Environment Canada, on the website www.ec.gc.ca/Ind/english/Energy/Tech Sup/ecsup1e.cfm.

3 Maybe the correct position is that the main consequence of industrialization was skill-churning, some occupations gaining skill, some losing, many undergoing lateral shifts. I argued for this in Goyder (2005a, 137–48).

4 By 2001, Canadians were describing themselves as "world-class energy gobblers" (*Canadian Geographic*, May/June, 2001, 11).

5 From the Statistics Canada website, as accessed on 27 July 2007: "The objective of the Initiative on the New Economy (INE) is to help Canada and Canadians adapt successfully to and benefit from the new economy. In 2001, after in-depth consultations with researchers and practitioners, SSHRC launched this five-year initiative as an integrated suite of programs to provide funding for researchers to explore the social, cultural and economic dimensions of the global, knowledge-driven new economy." http://www.sshrc.ca/web/apply/background/ine_about_e.asp.

CHAPTER THREE

1 The key historical data, the 1965 Pineo-Porter data, came to me thanks to Peter Pineo, who had kept a personal copy.

2 Computed following AAPOR Standard Definition number RR3 (AAPOR 2000).

3 Peter Pineo recalls that "social standing" was not part of the general vocabulary in 1965 when he and Porter were designing their Canadian study. Conversation in Lanzville, BC, 22 December 2000.

CHAPTER FOUR

1 http://www.ctv.ca/servlet/ArticleNews/story/CTVNews/20060319/ profession_jobs060319/20060319?hub=Canada (accessed 23 August 2007). Harris Poll from www.harrisinteractive.com (accessed 8 September 2005).

2 In a project for an honours thesis in sociology, Thacker (2005) sampled two issues a week from the *Globe and Mail*, for 1964 and 2004. In the first week she selected the Monday and Tuesday editions, in week two

Wednesday and Thursday, in week three Friday and Saturday, and so on, using this rotating sampling scheme. This gave 104 papers sampled from each year. Each article was examined for mention of an occupation, and when such references did occur, all adjectives to do with the occupation were coded. Thacker (2005, 22) notes that "as often no specific adjective was used surrounding the occupation, the way the occupation was depicted in the article was also recorded and given a favourable, unfavourable or neutral rating." When adjectives were present, they would help inform the coding of general favourability/unfavourability. It is this general evaluation that is used in the present analysis. Thacker weighted articles directly about an occupation as two and passing references within articles on other topics as one.

3 The 17 percent comes from using prestige change as the dependent variable in table 4.8, rather than the 2005 score as the dependent variable, with the 1965 score as an independent variable. The two are different ways of expressing the same findings.

CHAPTER FIVE

1 Thanks and acknowledgment to Claire Durand for suggesting this method. See Goyder and Durand (2008).
2 The 1965 data has a question about what kind of knowledge respondents think is most likely to be true. Selecting the "science" category, the analysis just shown using the more extensive science-technology measures in 2005 in fact reproduces quite precisely for 1965.
3 The coding for this was done by Mike Civak, as part of an honours thesis at the University of Waterloo.

CHAPTER SEVEN

1 My data set for "1964" has the occasional score from the 1965 NORC survey plugged in, for titles common across the other samples, not present in 1964 but rated in 1965.
2 For the 179 titles matching between just the 1965 and 2005 Canadian surveys, r = 0.817.
3 "Approximately," because the set of 179 matching 1965–2005 titles were used here, not the full 210.
4 Naturally, correlations in this form of the individual level are far smaller than the aggregate scale ones shown in figure 7.1. Thus, while the correlation between the 1965 and 2005 scales as aggregates is, as just shown,

r = .838, the equivalent disaggregated cross-scale correlation, 1965 to 2005, is about half that, at .389. The latter figure was derived by randomly pairing each of the 780 respondents for 1965 described above with one of the 780 respondents for 2005 computing the correlation between their set of ratings of occupations, and taking the average.

CHAPTER EIGHT

1 "Harvard began in colonial days with a handful of students, little property and limited power and prestige, but a determined mission." Harvard University website, President's Office, accessed 8 February 2008.
2 Côté and Allahar (2007) was a helpful guide to the literature on the feel-good culture, and points the reader to further sources that I do not need to duplicate here.
3 In the style of Young (note 4, chapter 5), see Goyder's article in the February 2047 *Canadian Review of Sociology*, reporting on his 2045 replication of the 2005 survey of occupational prestige in Canada, showing how the revolution in ratings of occupational prestige had intensified by mid-twenty-first century.

Bibliography

Acland, Richard. 1959. Review of *The Rise of the Meritocracy*. *Sociological Review*. New Series 7:269–71.

Adler, Israel, and Vered Kraus. 1985. Components of occupational prestige valuations. *Work and Occupations* 12:23–39.

Alexander, C. Norman. 1972. Status perceptions. *American Sociological Review* 37:767–73.

Alexander, Jeffrey C., and Paul Colomy. 1990. Neofunctionalism today: Reconstructing a theoretical tradition. In *Frontiers of Social Theory: The New Synthesis*, ed. George Ritzer. New York: Columbia University Press, 33–67.

American Association for Public Opinion Research (AAPOR). 2000. *Standard Definitions: Final Dispositions of Case Codes and Outcome Rates for Surveys*. Ann Arbor, MI: AAPOR.

Andrews, Frank M. 1974. Social indicators of perceived life quality. *Social Indicators Research* 1:279–99.

Anonymous. 2008. Review of the Prestige Squeeze manuscript for McGill-Queen's University Press. Six-page document.

Armer, J. Michael. 1968. Intersociety and intrasociety correlations of occupational prestige. *American Journal of Sociology* 74:28–36.

Aron, Raymond. 1967. *The Industrial Society: Three Essays on Ideology and Development*. New York: Praeger.

Aronowitz, Stanley. 1992. *The Politics of Identity: Class, Culture, Social Movements*. New York: Routledge.

Babbitt, Charles E., and Harold J. Burbach. 1990. A comparison of self-orientation among college students across the 1960s, 1970s and 1980s. *Youth and Society* 21:472–82.

Balkwell, James W., Frederick L. Bates, and Albeno P. Garbin. 1980. On the intersubjectivity of occupational status evaluations: A test of a key assumption underlying the "Wisconsin Model" of status attainment. *Social Forces* 58:865–81.

– 1982. Does the degree of consensus on occupational status evaluations differ by socioeconomic stratum? Response to Guppy. *Social Forces* 60:1183–9.

Bates, Frederick L., Albeno P. Garbin, and James W. Balkwell. 1986. Occupational prestige hierarchy: Methodological artifact or cultural category system? *Sociological Spectrum* 6:321–43.

Bauer, Martin., J. Durant, and G. Evans. 1994. European public perceptions of science. *International Journal of Public Opinion Research* 6:163–86.

Beeghley, Leonard. 1989. *The Structure of Social Stratification in the United States*. Boston: Allyn and Bacon.

Bell, Daniel. 1973. *The Coming of Post-Industrial Society: A Venture in Social Forecasting*. New York: Basic Books.

Bendix, Reinhard, and Seymour Martin Lipset. 1953. *Class, Status and Power: Social Stratification in Comparative Perspective*. Glencoe: Free Press.

– 1966. *Class, Status, and Power: Social Stratification in Comparative Perspective*. 2d ed. New York : Free Press.

Berton, Pierre. 1968. *The Smug Minority*. Toronto: McClelland and Stewart.

Best, Joel. 2007. Prize proliferation. Talk given at the Department of Sociology, University of Waterloo, 14 November.

Blackburn, Robert M., Jennifer Jarman, and Bradley Brooks. 2000. The puzzle of gender segregation and inequality: A cross-national analysis. *European Journal of Sociology* 16:119–35.

Blaikie, Norman W.H. 1977. The meaning and measurement of occupational prestige. *Australian and New Zealand Journal of Sociology* 13:102–15.

Blau, Peter. 1957. Occupational bias and mobility. *American Sociological Review* 22:392–9.

– 1963 [1955]. *The Dynamics of Bureaucracy: A Study of Interpersonal Relations in Two Government Agencies*. Revised edition. Chicago: University of Chicago Press.

Blau, Peter M., and Otis Dudley Duncan. 1967. *The American Occupational Structure*. New York: Wiley.

Blishen, Bernard R. 1958. The construction and use of an occupational class scale. *Canadian Journal of Economics and Political Science* 24:519–31.

– 1967. A socio-economic index for occupations in Canada. *Canadian Review of Sociology and Anthropology* 4:41–53.

Blishen, Bernard R., William K. Carroll, and Catherine Moore. 1987. The 1981 socioeconomic index for occupations in Canada. *Canadian Review of Sociology and Anthropology* 24:465–88.

Blishen, Bernard R., and Hugh McRoberts. 1976. A revised socio-economic index for occupations in Canada. *Canadian Review of Sociology and Anthropology* 13:71–9.

Bolter, J. David. 1984. *Turing's Man: Western Culture in the Computer Age*. Chapel Hill: University of North Carolina Press.

Bose, Christine E., and Peter H. Rossi. 1983. Gender and jobs: Prestige standings of occupations as affected by gender. *American Sociological Review* 48: 316–30.

Boyd, Monica. 1982. Sex differences in the Canadian occupational attainment process. *Canadian Review of Sociology and Anthropology* 19:1–28.

– 2008. A socioeconomic scale for Canada: Measuring occupational status from the census. *Canadian Review of Sociology* 45:51–91.

Boyd, Monica, John Goyder, Frank E. Jones, Hugh A. McRoberts, Peter C. Pineo and John Porter. 1985. *Ascription and Achievement: Studies in Mobility and Status Attainment in Canada*. Ottawa: Carleton University Press.

Bradbury, Malcolm. 1965. *Stepping Westward*. London: Secker and Warburg.

Braverman, Harry. 1974. *Labor and Monopoly Capital: The Degradation of Work in the Twentieth Century*. New York: Monthly Review Press.

Breakwell, Glynis M. 1986. *Coping with Threatened Identities*. London: Methuen.

Broom, Leonard, and Betty J. Maynard. 1969. Prestige and socio-economic ranking of occupations. *Social Science Quarterly* 50:369–73.

Broom, Leonard, Paul Duncan-Jones, F. Lancaster Jones, and Patrick McDonnell. 1977. The social standing of jobs: Scores for all Australian occupations. *Social Science Research* 6:211–24.

Brzezinski, Zbigniew. 1970. *Between Two Ages: America's Role in the Technetronic Era*. New York: Viking.

Brzezinski, Zbigniew, and Samuel P. Huntington 1965. *Political Power: USA/USSR*. New York: Viking.

Burke, Peter J. 1991. Identity processes and social stress. *American Sociological Review* 56:836–49.

Burke, Peter J., and Judy C. Tully. 1977. The measurement of role identity. *Social Forces* 55:881–97.

Burnham, James. 1941. *The Managerial Revolution: What Is Happening in the World*. New York: The John Day Company.

Burshtyn, H. 1968. A factor-analytic study of occupational prestige ratings. *Canadian Review of Sociology and Anthropology* 5:156–80.

Calhoun, Craig, 1994. *Social Theory and the Politics of Identity*. Oxford: Blackwell.

Caplow, Theodore. 1991. *American Social Trends*. Fort Worth: Harcourt Brace Jovanovich.

Caplow, Theodore, Howard M. Bahr, Bruce A. Chadwick, Reuben Hill, and Margaret Holmes Williamson. 1982. *Middletown Families: Fifty Years of Change and Continuity*. Minneapolis: University of Minnesota Press.

Caplow, Theodore, and Reece Jerome McGee. 1958. *The Academic Marketplace*. New York. Basic Books.

Caplow, Theodore, and Henri Mendras. 1994. Introduction. Convergence or divergence? In *Convergence or Divergence? Comparing Recent Social Trends in Industrial Societies*. Ed. Simon Langlois. Frankfurt: Campus Verlag, 1–21.

Carnoy, Martin. 2000. *Sustaining the New Economy: Work, Family, and Community in the Information Age*. New York: Sage.

Celente, Gerald. 1997. *Trends 2000: How to Prepare for and Profit from the Changes of the Twenty-first Century*. New York: Time Warner.

Centers, Richard. 1961 [1949]. *The Psychology of Social Classes*. Princeton: Princeton University Press.

Clark, S.D. 1966. *The Suburban Society*. Toronto: University of Toronto Press.

Cohen, David. 2007. Skilled trades – the great Canadian job rush. *CIC News* (*Canadian Immigration Newsletter*) October issue. On-line at website =http://www.cicnews.com/ (accessed 12 February 2008).

Cohen, Jacob, and Patricia Cohen. 1975. *Applied Multiple Regression/Correlation Analysis for the Behavioral Sciences*. New York: Wiley.

Collins, Randall. 2000. Situational stratification: A micro-macro theory of inequality. *Sociological Theory* 18:17–43.

Côté, James E., and Anton L. Allahar. 2007. *Ivory Tower Blues: A University System in Crisis*. Toronto: University of Toronto Press.

Cotter, David A., JoAnn M. DeFiore, Joan M. Hermsen, Brenda Marsteller Kowalewski, and Reeve Vanneman. 1995. Occupational gender desegregation in the 1980s. *Work and Occupations* 22:3–21.

Counts, George S. 1925. The social status of occupations: A problem in vocational guidance. *The School Review* 33:16–27.

Coxon, Anthony P.M., and P.M. Davies. 1986. *Images of Social Stratification: Occupational Structures and Class*. London: Sage.

Coxon, Anthony P.M., and Charles L. Jones. 1978. *The Images of Occupational Prestige*. London: Macmillan.

– 1979a. *Class and Hierarchy: The Social Meaning of Occupations*. London: Macmillan.

– 1979b. *Measurement and Meanings: Techniques and Methods of Studying Occupational Cognition*. London: Macmillan.

Crysdale, Stewart, Alan J.C. King, and Nancy Mandell. 1999. *On Their Own? Making the Transition from School to Work in the Information Age*. Montreal and Kingston: McGill-Queen's University Press.

Darmstadter, Joel. 1971. *Energy in the World Economy*. Baltimore: Johns Hopkins Press.

Davis, James A. 2001. What's wrong with sociology? In *What's Wrong with Sociology*. Ed. Stephen Cole. New Brunswick, NJ: Transaction Publishers, 99–119.

Davis, James A., and Tom W. Smith. 1992. *The NORC General Social Survey: A User's Guide*. Newbury Park: Sage.

Davis, Jerome. 1927. Testing the social attitudes of children in the government schools in Russia. *American Journal of Sociology* 32:947–52.

Davis, Kingsley. 1942. A conceptual analysis of stratification. *American Sociological Review* 7:309–21.

Davis, Kingsley, and Wilbert E. Moore. 1945. Some principles of stratification. *American Sociological Review* 10:242–9.

Davies, A.F. 1952. Prestige of occupations. *British Journal of Sociology* 3:134–47.

Dawson, William E., and Richard P. Brinker. 1971. Validation of ratio scales of opinion by multimodality matching. *Perception and Psychophysics* 9:413–17.

de Botton, Alain. 2004. *Status Anxiety*. Toronto: Viking Canada.

DeFleur, Melvin L., and Lois B. DeFleur. 1967. The relative contribution of television as a learning source for children's occupational knowledge. *American Sociological Review* 32:777–89.

Department of Manpower and Labour (Canada). 1971. *Canadian Classification and Dictionary of Occupations, 1971*, Volume 2, *Occupational Qualification Requirements*. Ottawa: Information Canada.

Dewett, Todd, and Gareth R. Jones. 2001. The role of information technology in the organization: A review, model, and assessment. *Journal of Management* 27: 313–46.

Dhawan-Biswal, Urvashi. 2002. Consumption and income inequality: The case of Atlantic Canada from 1969–1996. *Canadian Public Policy* 28:513–37.

Dominion Bureau of Statistics. 1969. *Canada Year Book 1969*. Ottawa: Queen's Printer.

Duncan, Otis Dudley. 1961. A socioeconomic index for all occupations. In *Occupations and Social Status*. Ed. Albert J. Reiss, Jr. Glencoe, IL: Free Press, 109–38.

Duncan, Otis Dudley, and J.W. Artis. 1951. Some problems of stratification research. *Rural Sociology* 16:17–29.

Duncan, Otis Dudley, and Robert W. Hodge. 1963. Education and social mobility: A regression analysis. *American Journal of Sociology* 68:629–44.

Dunning, Eric, Patrick Murphy, and John Williams. 1988. *The Roots of Football Hooliganism: An Historical and Sociological Study*. London: Routledge.

Durkheim, Emile. 1964 [1893]. *The Division of Labor in Society*. Translated by George Simpson. New York: Free Press.

Edwards, Alba M. 1938. *A Socio-Economic Grouping of the Gainful Workers of the United States*. Washington, DC: U.S. Department of Labor.

Einsiedel, Edna F. 1994. Mental maps of science: Knowledge and attitudes among Canadian adults. *International Journal of Public Opinion Research* 6:35–44.

Ellul, Jacques. 1967. *The Technological Society*. New York: Vintage Books.

England, Paula. 1979. Women and occupational prestige: A case of vacuous sex equality. *Signs* 5: 252–65.

England, Paula, and Barbara Kilborne. 2002. *Occupational Measures from the Dictionary of Occupational Titles for 1980 Census Detailed Occupations*. Document in electronic form identified as ICPSR 8942.

Featherman, David L., and Robert M. Hauser. 1976. Prestige or socioeconomic scales in the study of occupational achievement? *Sociological Methods and Research* 4: 403–23.

– 1978. *Opportunity and Change*. New York: Academic Press.

Feldman, Arnold S., and Wilbert E. Moore. 1962. Industrialization and industrialism convergence and differentiation. *Transactions of the Fifth World Congress of Sociology*, 151–69.

Feldman, Saul D., and Gerald W. Thielbar. 1972. Power, privilege and prestige of occupations. In *Issues in Social Inequality*. Ed. Gerald W. Thielbar and Saul D. Feldman. Boston: Little, Brown.

Fossum, John A., and Michael L. Moore. 1975. The stability of longitudinal and cross-sectional prestige rankings. *Journal of Vocational Behavior* 7:305–11.

Fox, Bonnie J., and John Fox. 1987. Occupational gender segregation of the Canadian labour force, 1931–1981. *Canadian Review of Sociology and Anthropology* 24: 80–97.

Fox, John, and Carole Suschnigg. 1989. A note on gender and the prestige of occupations. *Canadian Journal of Sociology* 14:353–60.

Fredrickson, Ronald H., Jun-chih Gisela Lin, and Shaomin Xing. 1992. Social status ranking of occupations in the People's Republic of China, Taiwan, and the United States. *Career Development Quarterly* 40:351–60.

Freeman, Richard B. 1975. Overinvestment in college training? *Journal of Human Resources* 10:287–311.

Freeman, Walter J. 1999. *How Brains Make Up Their Minds*. London: Phoenix.

Frenette, Marc, and Simon Coulombe. 2007. *Has High Education among Young Women Substantially Reduced the Gender Gap in Employment and Earnings?* Statistics Canada, Analytical Studies Branch, Research Paper Series. Cat. no. 11F0019MIE–No. 301.

Friedman, Thomas L. 2005. *The World Is Flat: A Brief History of the Twenty-First Century*. New York: Farrar, Strauss and Giroux.

Furedi, Frank. 2004. *Therapy Culture: Cultivating Vulnerability in an Uncertain Age*. London: Routledge.

Galbraith, John Kenneth. 1967. *The New Industrial State*. Houghton Mifflin.

Gans, Herbert J. 1972. The positive functions of poverty. *American Journal of Sociology* 78:275–89.

Gardner, Howard. 1993. *Multiple Intelligences: The Theory in Practice*. New York: Basic Books.

Gergen, Kenneth J. 1991. *The Saturated Self: Dilemmas of Identity in Contemporary Life*. New York: Basic Books.

Gerstl, Joel E., and Lois K. Cohen. 1964. Dissensus, situs, and egocentrism in occupational ranking. *British Journal of Sociology* 15:254–61.

Gerteis, Joseph, and Mike Savage. 1996. The salience of class in Britain and America: A comparative analysis. *British Journal of Sociology* 49:252–74.

Giddens, Anthony. 1991. *Modernity and Self-Identity: Self and Society in the Late Modern Age*. Stanford: Stanford University Press.

Giedion, Sigfried. 1948. *Mechanization Takes Command: A Contribution to Anonymous History*. New York: Oxford University Press.

Glatzer, Wolfgang, and Richard Hauser. 2002. The distribution of income and wealth in European and North American societies. In *Changing Structures of Inequality: A Comparative Perspective*. Ed. Yannick Lemel and Heinz-Herbert Noll. Montreal and Kingston: McGill-Queen's University Press.

Glick, Peter, K. Wilk, and M. Perreault. 1995. Images of occupations: Components of gender and status in occupational stereotypes. *Sex Roles* 32:565–82.

Goldthorpe, John H., and Keith Hope. 1974. *The Social Grading of Occupations: A New Approach and Scale*. Oxford: Clarendon Press.

Goyder, John. 1975. A note on the declining relation between subjective and objective class measures. *British Journal of Sociology* 26:102–9.

– 1984. Social mobility or status attainment *or* social mobility *and* status attainment? *Canadian Review of Sociology and Anthropology* 21:331–43.

– 2005a. *Technology and Society: A Canadian Perspective*. Second edition. Peterborough: Broadview.

– 2005b. The dynamics of occupational prestige: 1975–2000. *Canadian Review of Sociology and Anthropology* 42:1–23.

Goyder, John, and Claire Durand. 2008. The prestige of survey research. *Canadian Journal of Marketing Research* 24:22–31.

Goyder, John, and Kristyn Frank. 2007. A scale of occupational prestige in Canada, based on NOC major groups. *Canadian Journal of Sociology* 32: 63–83.

Goyder, John, Neil Guppy, and Mary Thompson. 2003. The allocation of male and female occupational prestige in an Ontario urban area: A quarter-century replication. *Canadian Review of Sociology and Anthropology* 40:417–39.

Goyder, John, and Peter C. Pineo. 1977. The accuracy of self-assessments of social status. *Canadian Review of Sociology and Anthropology* 14:235–46.

Grant, George. 1965. *Lament for a Nation: The Defeat of Canadian Nationalism*. Princeton, NJ: Van Nostrand.

Grasmick, Harold G. 1976. The occupational prestige structure: A multidimensional scaling approach. *Sociological Quarterly* 17: 90–108.

Groves, Robert M. 1989. *Survey Errors and Survey Costs*. Hoboken, NJ: Wiley.

Groves, Robert M., and Robert L. Kahn. 1979. *Surveys by Telephone: A National Comparison with Personal Interviews*. New York: Academic Press.

Grusky, David B., and Stephen E. Van Rompaey. 1992. The vertical scaling of occupations: some cautionary comments and reflections. *American Journal of Sociology* 97:1712–28.

Guppy, L. Neil. 1982. On intersubjectivity and collective conscience in occupational prestige research: A comment on Balkwell-Bates-Garbin and Kraus-Schild-Hodge. *Social Forces* 60:1178–82.

– 1984. Dissensus or consensus: A cross-national comparison of occupational prestige scales. *Canadian Journal of Sociology* 9: 69–83.

Guppy, Neil, and John C. Goyder. 1984. Consensus on occupational prestige: A reassessment of the evidence. *Social Forces* 62:709–25.

Guppy, L.N., and J.L. Siltanen. 1977. A comparison of the allocation of male and female occupational prestige. *Canadian Review of Sociology and Anthropology* 14:320–30.

Gusfield, Joseph R., and Michael Schwartz. 1963. The meaning of occupational prestige: A reconsideration of the NORC scale. *American Sociological Review* 28:265–71.

Hall, John, and D. Caradog Jones. 1950. Social grading of occupations. *British Journal of Sociology* 1:31–55.

Haller, Archibald O., D.B. Holsinger, and H.U. Saraiva. 1972. Variations in occupational prestige hierarchies: Brazilian data. *American Journal of Sociology* 77:941–56.

Haller, Archibald O., and David M. Lewis. 1966. The hypothesis of intersocietal similarity in occupational prestige hierarchies. *American Journal of Sociology* 72:210–16.

Harden, Jeni. 2001. "Mother Russia" at Work: Gender Divisions in the Medical Profession. *European Journal of Women's Studies* 8: 181–99.

Hatt, Paul K. 1950. Occupation and social stratification. *American Journal of Sociology* 55:533–43.

Haug, Marie R. 1973. Social class measurement and women's occupational roles. *Social Forces* 52:85–98.

Hauser, Robert M., and John Allen Logan. 1992. How not to measure intergenerational occupational persistence. *American Journal of Sociology* 97:1689–1711.

Hauser, Robert M., and John Robert Warren. 1997. Socioeconomic indexes for occupations: A review, update and critique. In *Sociological Methodology 1997*. Ed. Adrian Raftery. Oxford: Blackwell, 177–298.

Hayes, Vivienne. 1970. Institutionalization and the self-concepts of deviants and nondeviants: A comparative study. Master's thesis, Memorial University of Newfoundland.

Hazelrigg, Lawrence E., and Maurice A. Garnier. 1976. Occupational mobility in industrial societies: A comparative analysis of differential access to occupational ranks in seventeen countries. *American Sociological Review* 41:498–511.

Heise, David R. 1979. *Understanding Events: Affect and the Construction of Social Action*. New York: Cambridge University Press.

Heisz, Andrew. 2007. *Income Inequality and Redistribution in Canada: 1976–2004*. Statistics Canada publication number 11f0019mie2007298, Analytical Studies Branch Research Paper Series.

Henry, Jules. 1965. *Culture against Man*. New York: Random House Vintage.

Herzenberg, Stephen A., John A. Alic, and Howard Wial. 1998. *New Rules for a New Economy*. Ithaca: Cornell University Press.

Hewitt, John P. 1998. *The Myth of Self-Esteem: Finding Happiness and Solving Problems in America*. New York: St Martin's Press.

Hodge, Robert W. 1981. The measurement of occupational status. *Social Science Research* 10:396–415.

Hodge, Robert W., Vered Kraus, and E.O. Schild. 1982. Consensus in occupational prestige ratings: Response to Guppy. *Social Forces* 60:1190–6.

Hodge, Robert W., and P.H. Rossi. 1978. Intergroup consensus in occupational prestige ratings: A case of serendipity lost and regained. *Sozialwissenschaftliche Annen* 2:B59–B73.

Hodge, Robert W., Paul M. Siegel, and Peter H. Rossi. 1966. Occupational prestige in the United States: 1925–1963. In *Class, Status, and Power: Social Stratification in Comparative Perspective*.

2d ed. Reinhard Bendix and Seymour Martin Lipset. New York: Free Press, 322–34.

Hodge, Robert W., Donald J. Treiman, and Peter H. Rossi. 1966. A comparative study of occupational prestige. In *Class, Status, and Power: Social Stratification in Comparative Perspective*. 2d ed. Reinhard Bendix and Seymour Martin Lipset. New York: Free Press, 309–21.

Hope, Keith. 1981. Developments in a populist paradigm. *Contemporary Sociology* 9:8–12.

– 1982. A liberal theory of prestige. *American Journal of Sociology* 87:1011–31.

Hout, Michael. 2002. *What We Have Learned: RC28's Contributions to Knowledge*. Document at website: iss.u-tokyo.ac.jp/~rc28/Hout.doc.

Hughes, Everett Cherrington. 1958. *Men and Their Work*. Glencoe, IL: Free Press.

Human Resources and Social Development Canada. 2001. *Career Handbook*. On the web at http://www23.hrdc-drhc.gc.ca/ch/e/docs/intro_page06.asp.

Inglehart, Ronald. 1971. The silent revolution in Europe: Intergenerational change in post-industrial societies. *American Political Science Review* 65:991–1017.

– 1990. *Culture Shift in Advanced Industrial Society*. Princeton, NJ: Princeton University Press.

Inkeles, Alex, and Peter H. Rossi. 1956. National comparisons of occupational prestige. *American Journal of Sociology* 61:329–39.

Jackman, Mary R., and Robert W. Jackman. 1983. *Class Awareness in the United States*. Berkeley: University of California Press.

Jacobs, Jerry A. 1989. Long-term trends in occupational segregation by sex. *American Journal of Sociology* 95:160–73.

Jacobs, Jerry A., and Brian Powell. 1985. Occupational prestige: A sex-neutral concept? *Sex Roles* 12:1061–71.

Jary, David, and Julia Jary. 1991. *Collins Dictionary of Sociology*. Glasgow: Harper Collins.

Johnson, Susan, and Peter Kuhn. 2004. Increasing male earnings inequality in Canada and the United States, 1981–1997: The role of hours changes versus wage changes. *Canadian Public Policy* 30:155–75.

Kanzaki, George A. 1976. Fifty years (1925–1975) of stability in the social status of occupations. *Vocational Guidance Quarterly* 25: 101–5.

Kawachi, Ichiro, Bruce P. Kennedy, and Richard G. Wilkinson. 1999. *The Society and Population Health Reader*. Volume 1, Income Inequality and Health. New York: The New Press.

Keen, Andrew. 2007. *The Cult of the Amateur: How Today's Internet Is Killing Our Culture*. New York: Doubleday/Currency.

Kendall, Diana, Jane Lothian Murray, and Rick Linden. 2000. *Sociology in Our Times*. Second Canadian edition. Scarborough, ON: Nelson Thompson.

Kerr, Clark, John T. Dunlop, Frederick H. Harbison, and Charles A. Myers. 1964. *Industrialism and Industrial Man: The Problems of Labor and Management in Economic Growth*. New York: Oxford University Press.

Kerr, Michael E. 1988. Chronic anxiety and defining a self. *The Atlantic* 262: 35–58.

Klapp, Orrin E. 1969. *Collective Search for Identity*. New York: Holt, Rinehart and Winston.

Kraus, Vered, E.O. Schild, and Robert W. Hodge. 1978. Occupational prestige in the collective conscience. *Social Forces* 56:900–18.

Kubat, Daniel, and David Thornton. 1974. *A Statistical Profile of Canadian Society*. Toronto: McGraw-Hill Ryerson.

Kuennapas, R., and Inger Wikstroem. 1963. Measurement of occupational preferences: A comparison of scaling methods. *Perceptual and Motor Skills* 17:611–24.

Kuhn, Manford H., and Thomas S. McPartland. 1954. An empirical investigation of self-attitudes. *American Sociological Review* 19:68–76.

Kumar, Krishan. 1995. *From Post-Industrial to Post-Modern Society: New Theories of the Contemporary World*. Oxford: Blackwell.

Lamont, Michèle. 2000. *The Dignity of Working Men: Morality and the Boundaries of Race, Class, and Immigration*. Cambridge, MA: Harvard University Press.

Langlois, Simon. 2006. Canada and Québec: An update. *ASA Footnotes* 34 (March).

Laumann, Edward O. 1966. *Prestige and Association in an Urban Community: An Analysis of an Urban Stratification System*. Indianapolis: Bobbs-Merrill.

Le Bon, Gustave. 1960 [1895]. *The Crowd*. Harmondsworth, Middlesex: Penguin.

Lenski, Gerhard. 1954. Status crystallization: A non-vertical dimension of social status. *American Sociological Review* 19:405–13.

– 1956. Social Participation and Status Crystallization. *American Sociological Review* 21:458–64.

Leonhardt, David. 2005. The college dropout boom. In *Class Matters*. Ed. correspondents of the New York Times. New York: Times Books, Holt and Company.

Lewis, David M., and A.O. Haller. 1964. Rural-urban differences in pre-industrial and industrial evaluations of occupations by Japanese adolescent boys. *Rural Sociology* 29:324–9.

Linton, E. Lynn. 1885. *The Autobiography of Christopher Kirkland*. Machine-readable transcript by W. Charles Morrow, as part of the Victorian Women Writers Project. Bloomington, IN: Indiana University.

Lipset, Seymour Martin, and Reinhard Bendix. 1959. *Social Mobility in Industrial Society*. Berkeley: University of California Press.

Lodge, Milton. 1981. *Magnitude Scaling: Quantitative Measurement of Opinions*. Beverly Hills: Sage.

Lowe, Graham S. 2000. *The Quality of Work: A People-Centred Agenda*. Don Mills, ON: Oxford University Press.

Lowe, Graham S., and Harvey Krahn. 2000. Work aspirations and attitudes in an era of labour market re-structuring: A comparison of two Canadian youth cohorts. *Work, Employment & Society* 14:1–22.

Lynd, Robert S., and Helen Merrell Lynd. 1929. *Middletown: A Study in Modern American Culture*. New York: Harcourt, Brace & World.

Lyon, David. 1986. From 'post-industrialism' to 'information society': A new social transformation? *Sociology* 29: 577–88.

MacKinnon, Neil J., and Tom Langford. 1994. The meaning of occupational prestige scores: A social psychological analysis and interpretation. *Sociological Quarterly* 35:215–45.

Marsh, Catherine. 1988. *Exploring Data: An Introduction to Data Analysis for Social Scientists*. Cambridge: Polity Press.

Marsh, Robert M. 1971. The explanation of occupational prestige hierarchies. *Social Forces* 50:214–22.

Marshall, Kimball B., and Benjamin L. Gorman. 1975. Occupational prestige from preference orientations via the Markov Chain: An alternative to respondent ranking techniques. *Social Science Research* 4: 41–64.

McAdams, Dan P. 1997. A conceptual history of personality psychology. In *Handbook of Personality Psychology*. Ed. Robert Hogan, John Johnson, and Stephen Briggs. San Diego: Academic Press, 3–39.

McCall, George J., and J.L. Simmons. 1982. *Social Psychology: A Sociological Approach.* New York: Free Press.

McKenzie Leiper, Jean. 2006. *Bar Codes: Women in the Legal Profession.* Vancouver: UBC Press.

McLaughlin, Neil. 2005. Canada's impossible science: Historical and institutional origins of the coming crisis in Anglo-Canadian sociology. *Canadian Journal of Sociology* 30:1–40.

McPartland, Thomas S., John H. Cumming, and Wynona S. Garretson. 1961. Self-conception and ward behavior in two psychiatric hospitals. *Sociometry* 24:111–24.

Meijer, Albert Jacob. 2008. E-mail in government: Not post-bureaucratic but late-bureaucratic organizations. *Government Information Quarterly* 25:429–47.

Mensch, Gerhard. 1979. *Stalemate in Technology: Innovations Overcome the Depression.* Cambridge, MA: Ballinger.

Menzies, Heather. 1996. *Whose Brave New World: The Information Highway and the New Economy.* Toronto: Between the Lines.

Merton, Robert. 1957. *Social Theory and Social Structure.* Revised edition. New York: Free Press.

Meyers, Stephen, and Lee Schipper. 1992. World energy use in the 1970s and 1980s: Exploring the changes. *Annual Review of Energy and the Environment* 17: 463–505.

Mills, C. Wright. 1956 [1951]. *White Collar: The American Middle Classes.* New York : Oxford University Press, Galaxy edition.

Moore, Eric G., and Michael A. Pacey. 2003. Changing income inequality and immigration in Canada, 1980–1995. *Canadian Public Policy* 29: 33–52.

Moore, Wilbert E. 1963. *Social Change.* Englewood Cliffs, NJ: Prentice-Hall.

More, Douglas M., and Robert W. Suchner. 1976. Occupational situs, prestige, and stereotypes. *Sociology of Work and Occupations* 3:169–86.

Morris, Lydia, and John Scott. 1996. The attenuation of class analysis: Some comments on G. Marshall, S. Roberts and C. Burgoyne, "Social class and the underclass in Britain and the USA." *British Journal of Sociology* 47:45–55.

Morris, Richard T., and Raymond J. Murphy. 1966. A paradigm for the study of class consciousness. *Sociology and Social Research* 50: 297–313.

Naisbitt, John. 1982. *Megatrends: The New Directions Transforming Our Lives*. New York: Warner.

Nakao, Keiko, and Judith Treas. 1994. Updating occupational prestige and socioeconomic scores: How the new measures measure up. In *Sociological Methodology*. Vol. 24. Ed. Peter V. Marsden. Oxford: Blackwell, 1–72.

National Opinion Research Centre (NORC). 1953 [1947]. Jobs and occupations: A popular evaluation. In *Class, Status and Power: Social Stratification in Comparative Perspective*. 1st ed. Ed. Reinhard Bendix and Seymour Martin Lipset. Glencoe, IL: Free Press, 411–26.

Nevitte, Neil. 1996. *The Decline of Deference: Canadian Value Change in Cross-National Perspective*. Peterborough: Broadview Press.

Nietz, John A. 1935. The depression and the social status of occupations. *Elementary School Journal* 35:454–61.

Nisbet, Robert A. 1959. The decline and fall of social class. *Pacific Sociological Review* 2:11–17.

Nosanchuk, Terrance A. 1972. A note on the use of the correlation coefficient for assessing the similarity of occupational rankings. *Canadian Review of Sociology and Anthropology* 9:357–65.

Ogburn, William Fielding. 1966 [1922]. *Social Change with Respect to Culture and Original Nature*. New York: B.W. Huebsch.

Ollivier, Michèle. 2000. Too much money off other people's backs: Status in late modern societies. *Canadian Journal of Sociology* 25:441–70.

Packard, Vance Oakley. 1961. *The Status Seekers: An Exploration of Class Behavior in America and the Hidden Barriers That Affect You, Your Community, Your Future*. New York: D. McKay.

Parsons, Talcott. 1940. An analytical approach to the theory of social stratification. *American Journal of Sociology* 45:841–62.

Penn, Roger. 1975. Occupational prestige hierarchies: A great empirical invariant? *Social Forces* 54:352–64.

Perman, Lauri. 1991. *The Other Side of the Coin: The Nonmonetary Characteristics of Jobs*. New York: Garland.

Pineo, Peter C. 1967. Public evaluation of occupations: Fieldwork procedures, weightings. Mimeograph, dated May 1967, Carleton University.

– 1981. Prestige and mobility: The two national surveys. *Canadian Review of Sociology and Anthropology* 18:615–26.

Pineo, Peter C., and John Porter. 1967. Occupational prestige in Canada. *Canadian Review of Sociology and Anthropology* 4:24–40.

Pineo, Peter C., John Porter, and Hugh A. McRoberts. 1977. The 1971 census and a socioeconomic classification of occupations. *Canadian Review of Sociology and Anthropology* 14:91–102.

Plata, Maximino. 1975. Stability and change in the prestige rankings of occupations over 49 years. *Journal of Vocational Behavior* 6: 95–9.

Podolny, Joel M. 2005. *Status Signals: A Sociological Study of Market Competition*. Princeton: Princeton University Press.

Porter, John. 1965. *The Vertical Mosaic*. Toronto: University of Toronto Press.

– 1968. The future of upward mobility. *American Sociological Review* 33:5–19.

– 1987 [1979]. *The Measure of Canadian Society: Education, Equality and Opportunity*. Ottawa: Carleton University Press.

Porter, Marion. 1981. John Porter and education: Technical functionalist or conflict theorist. *Canadian Review of Sociology and Anthropology* 18:627–38.

Powell, Brian, and Jerry Jacobs. 1984. Gender differences in the evaluation of prestige. *Sociological Quarterly* 25:173–90.

Prandy, Ken. 1990. The revised Cambridge scale of occupations. *Sociology* 24: 629–55.

President's Research Committee on Social Trends. 1933. *Recent Social Trends in the United States: Report of the President's Research Committee on Social Trends*. New York: McGraw-Hill.

Putnam, Robert. 2000. *Bowling Alone: The Collapse and Revival of American Community*. New York: Simon and Schuster.

Rainwater, Lee. 1974. *What Money Buys: Inequality and the Social Meaning of Income*. New York: Basic Books.

Reich, Robert B. 1991. *The Work of Nations: Preparing Ourselves for Twenty-first-Century Capitalism*. New York: Knopf.

Reiss, Albert J., Jr. 1961. *Occupations and Social Status*. New York: Free Press.

Rhode, Deborah L. 2006. *In Pursuit of Knowledge: Scholars, Status, and Academic Culture*. Stanford: Stanford University Press.

Riesman, David. 1953 [1950]. *The Lonely Crowd : A Study of the Changing American Character*. Garden City, NY: Doubleday Anchor.

Rifkin, Jeremy. 1995. *The End of Work: The Decline of the Global Labor Force and the Dawn of the Post-Market Era*. New York: Putnam.

Riska, Elianne. 2001. Towards gender balance: But will women physicians have an impact on medicine? *Social Science and Medicine* 52:179–87.

Robbins, Alexandra. 2006. *The Overachievers: The Secret Lives of Driven* Kids. New York: Hyperion.

Roscoe, Bruce, and Karen L. Peterson. 1983. The TST for assessing the self-concepts of college students: Comparisons with earlier years. *College Student Journal* 17:134–6.

Rosenau, Pauline Marie. 1992. *Post-Modernism and the Social Sciences: Insights, Inroads, and Intrusions.* Princeton: Princeton University Press.

Rossi, Peter H., and Alex Inkeles. 1957. Multidimensional ratings of occupations. *Sociometry* 20:234–51.

Rowntree, B. Seebohm, and May Kendall. 1917. *How the Labourer Lives, A Study of the Rural Labour Problem.* London, Thomas Nelson.

Rytina, Steve. 1992. Scaling the intergenerational continuity of occupation: Is occupational inheritance ascriptive after all? *American Journal of Sociology* 97:1658–88.

Saltiel, John. 1990. Occupational prestige and sex typing in the collective conscience. *Quality and Quantity* 24: 283–96.

Sandefur, Rebecca L. 2001. Work and honor in the law: Prestige and the division of lawyers' labor. *American Sociological Review* 66:382–403.

Sarapata, Adam, and Wlodzimierz Wesolowski. 1961. The evaluation of occupations by Warsaw inhabitants. *American Journal of Sociology* 66: 581–91.

Sawiński, Zbigniew, and Henryk Domański. 1991a. Stability of prestige hierarchies in the face of social changes: Poland, 1958–1987. *International Sociology* 6: 227–41.

– 1991b. Dissensus in assessments of occupational prestige: The case of Poland. *European Sociological Review*: 253–65.

Schlesinger, Arthur Meier. 1922. *New Viewpoints in American History.* New York: Macmillan.

Schlesinger, Arthur M., Jr. 1950. *The Age of Jackson.* Boston: Little, Brown.

Schwirian, Kent P. 1964. Variation in structure of the Kuhn-McPartland twenty statements test and related response differences. *Sociological Quarterly* 5:47–59.

Scott, Sir Walter. 1819. *A Legend of Montrose.* London: Nelson (Nelson Classics edition).

Schumacher, E.F. 1973. *Small is Beautiful: A Study of Economics as if People Mattered.* London: Penguin Abacus.

Schurr, Sam, and Bruce C. Netschert. 1960. *Energy in the American Economy, 1850–1975.* Baltimore: Johns Hopkins Press.

Seligman, Martin E.P. 1989. Research in clinical psychology: Why is there so much depression today? Volume 9, the G. Stanley Hall Lecture Series. Washington, DC: American Psychological Association, 79–96.

Seligson, Mitchell A. 1977. Prestige among peasants: A multidimensional analysis of preference data. *American Journal of Sociology* 83:632–52.

Sennett, Richard. 2003. *Respect in a World of Inequality*. New York: Norton.

– 2008. *The Craftsman*. New Haven: Yale University Press.

Sewell, William H., Archibald O. Haller, and George W. Ohlendorf. 1970. The educational and early occupational status attainment process: Replication and revision. *American Sociological Review* 35:1014–27.

Sharpe, Andrew. 2003. Linkages between economic growth and inequality: introduction and overview. *Canadian Public Policy* 29 (supplemental issue): S1–S14.

Shils, Edward. 1968. Deference. In *Social Stratification*. Ed. J.A. Jackson. Cambridge: Cambridge University Press, 104–32.

Siegel, Paul M. 1971. Prestige in the American occupational structure. PhD diss., University of Chicago.

Simpson, Richard L., and Ida H. Simpson. 1960. Correlates and estimation of occupational prestige. *American Journal of Sociology* 66:135–40.

Simon, Julian L. 1995. *Resampling Stats User's Guide*. Arlington, VA: Resampling Stats Inc.

Smith, Mapheus. 1943. An empirical scale of prestige status of occupations. *American Sociological Review* 8:185–92.

Snow, David A., and Cynthia L. Phillips. 1982. The changing self-orientations of college students: From institution to impulse. *Social Science Quarterly* 63:462–76.

Sørensen, Aage B. 2001. The basic concepts of stratification research: Class, status, and power. In *Social Stratification: Class, Race, and Gender in Sociological Perspective*. Ed. David B. Grusky. Boulder, CO: Westview Press, 287–300.

Sorokin, Pitirim A. 1927. *Social Mobility*. New York: Harper.

Spitzer, Stephan P., and Jerry Parker. 1976. Perceived validity and assessment of the self: A decade later. *Sociological Quarterly* 17:236–46.

Statistics Canada. 1985. *Canada Year Book 1985*. Ottawa: Minister of Supply and Services.

Stehr, Nico. 1974. Consensus and dissensus in occupational prestige. *British Journal of Sociology* 25: 410–27.

Stewart, Andrew, K. Prandy, and R.M. Blackburn. 1980. *Social Stratification and Occupations*. London: Macmillan.

Stone, Louis. 1911. *Jonah*. London: Methuen.

Svalastoga, Kaare. 1959. *Prestige, Class and Mobility*. Copenhagen: Gyldendal.

Tajfel, Henri. 1974. Social identity and intergroup behaviour. *Social Science Information* 13 :65–93.

Thacker, Kristy. 2005. *Occupational Prestige in the Media*. Honours thesis, Department of Sociology, University of Waterloo.

Thielbar, Gerald, and Saul D. Feldman. 1969. Occupational stereotypes and prestige. *Social Forces* 48:64–72.

Thoits, Peggy A. 1991. On merging identity theory and stress research. *Social Psychology Quarterly* 54:101–12.

Thomas, R. Murray. 1962. Reinspecting a structural position on occupational prestige. *American Journal of Sociology* 67: 561–5.

Tiryakian, Edward A. 1958. The prestige evaluation of occupations in an underdeveloped country: The Philippines. *American Journal of Sociology* 63:390–9.

Toffler, Alvin. 1970. *Future Shock*. New York: Random House.

– 1981. *The Third Wave*. New York: Bantam.

– 1990. *Powershift : Knowledge, Wealth, and Violence at the Edge of the Twenty-first Century*. New York: Bantam Books.

Touraine, Alain. 1971. *The Post-Industrial Society, Tomorrow's Social History: Classes, Conflicts and Culture in the Programmed Society*. New York: Random House.

Tourangeau, Roger, Lance J. Rips, and Kenneth Rasinski. 2000. *The Psychology of Survey Response*. Cambridge: Cambridge University Press.

Treiman, Donald J. 1976. A standard occupational prestige scale for use with historical data. *Journal of Interdisciplinary History* 7:283–304.

– 1977. *Occupational Prestige in Comparative Perspective*. New York: Academic.

Triplett, Jack E. 1999. The Solow productivity paradox: What do computers do to productivity? *Canadian Journal of Economics* 32: 309–34.

Tuckman, Jacob. 1947. Social status of occupations in Canada. *Canadian Journal of Psychology* 1:71–4.

Tumin, Melvin M. 1953. Some principles of stratification: A critical analysis. *American Sociological Review* 18:387–94.

Turner, Ralph H. 1976. The real self: From institution to impulse. *American Journal of Sociology.* 81:989–1016.

Urmetzer, Peter, and Neil Guppy. 1999. Changing income inequality in Canada. In *Social Inequality in Canada: Patterns, Problems, and Polities.* 3d ed. Ed. James Curtis, Edward Grabb, and Neil Guppy. Scarborough, ON: Prentice-Hall Allyn and Bacon Canada, 56–65.

Veblen, Thorstein. 1965 [1899]. *The Theory of the Leisure Class.* New York: A.M. Kelley.

Villemez, Wayne J. 1974. Ability vs. effort: Ideological correlates of occupational grading. *Social Forces* 53:45–52.

Wanner, Richard A. 2005. Twentieth-century trends in occupational attainment in Canada. *Canadian Journal of Sociology* 30:441–69.

Warner, W. Lloyd. 1949. *Democracy in Jonesville: A Study of Quality and Inequality.* New York: Harper and Brothers.

Warner, W. Lloyd, and Paul S. Lunt. 1941. *The Social Life of a Modern Community.* New Haven: Yale University Press.

Weber, Max. 1958 [1904]. *The Protestant Ethic and the Spirit of Capitalism.* Translated by Talcott Parsons. New York: Scribner.

Wegener, Bernd. 1992. Concepts and measurement of prestige. In *Annual Review of Sociology.* Volume 18, ed. Judith Blake. Palo Alto, CA: Annual Reviews Inc., 253–80.

Wylie, Ruth C. 1974. *The Self-Concept: A Review of Methodological Considerations and Measuring Instruments.* Lincoln: University of Nebraska Press.

Whyte, William Foote. 1943. *Street Corner Society: The Social Structure of an Italian Slum.* Chicago: University of Chicago Press.

Whyte, William H., Jr. 1957[1956]. *The Organization Man.* Garden City, NY: Doubleday Anchor.

Wilkinson, Richard G. 1999. The culture of inequality. In *The Society and Population Health Reader.* Volume 1, *Income Inequality and Health.* Ed. Ichiro Kawachi, Bruce P. Kennedy, and Richard G. Wilkinson. New York: The New Press, 492–8.

Willimack, Diane K., Howard Schuman, Beth-Ellen Pennell, and James M. Lepkowski. 1995. Effects of a prepaid nonmonetary incentive on response rates and response quality in a face-to-face survey. *Public Opinion Quarterly* 59:78–92.

Wilson, Edward O. 1975. *Sociobiology: The New Synthesis.* Cambridge, MA: Belknap.

Woolf, Virginia. 1919. *Night and day.* London: Hogarth Press.

Yarbrough, Jean M. 1998. *American Virtues: Thomas Jefferson on the Character of a Free People*. Lawrence Kansas: University Press of Kansas.

Young, Michael. 1958. *The Rise of the Meritocracy, 1870–2033: An Essay on Education and Equality*. London: Thames and Hudson.

Young, Michael, and Peter Willmott. 1956. Social grading by manual workers. *British Journal of Sociology* 7:337–45.

Zhou, Xueguang. 2005. The institutional logic of occupational prestige rankings: Reconceptualization and reanalyses. *American Journal of Sociology* 111:90–140.

Zurcher, Louis A. 1972. The mutable self: An adaptation to accelerated socio-cultural change. *et al.* 3: 3–15.

– 1977. *Mutable Self: A Self-Concept for Social Change*. Beverly Hills: Sage.

Index